Becoming a mother

Manchester University Press

GENDER IN HISTORY

Series editors: Lynn Abrams, Cordelia Beattie,
Julie Hardwick and Penny Summerfield

The expansion of research into the history of women and gender since the 1970s has changed the face of history. Using the insights of feminist theory and of historians of women, gender historians have explored the configuration in the past of gender identities and relations between the sexes. They have also investigated the history of sexuality and family relations, and analysed ideas and ideals of masculinity and femininity. Yet gender history has not abandoned the original, inspirational project of women's history: to recover and reveal the lived experience of women in the past and the present.

The series Gender in History provides a forum for these developments. Its historical coverage extends from the medieval to the modern periods, and its geographical scope encompasses not only Europe and North America but all corners of the globe. The series aims to investigate the social and cultural constructions of gender in historical sources, as well as the gendering of historical discourse itself. It embraces both detailed case studies of specific regions or periods, and broader treatments of major themes. Gender in History titles are designed to meet the needs of both scholars and students working in this dynamic area of historical research.

OTHER RECENT BOOKS IN THE SERIES

*The state as master: Gender, state formation and commercialisation in urban Sweden, 1650–1780*   Maria Ågren

*Love, intimacy and power: Marriage and patriarchy in Scotland, 1650–1850*   Katie Barclay (Winner of the 2012 Women's History Network Book Prize)

*Men on trial: Performing emotion, embodiment and identity in Ireland, 1800–45*   Katie Barclay

*Modern women on trial: Sexual transgression in the age of the flapper*   Lucy Bland

*The Women's Liberation Movement in Scotland*   Sarah Browne

*Modern motherhood: Women and family in England, c. 1945–2000*   Angela Davis

*Women against cruelty: Protection of animals in nineteenth-century Britain*   Diana Donald

*Gender, rhetoric and regulation: Women's work in the civil service and the London County Council, 1900–55*   Helen Glew

*Jewish women in Europe in the Middle Ages: A quiet revolution*
Simha Goldin

*Women of letters: Gender, writing and the life of the mind in early modern England*   Leonie Hannan

*Home economics: Domestic service and gender in urban southern Africa*
Sacha Hepburn

*Women and museums 1850–1914: Modernity and the gendering of knowledge*   Kate Hill

*The shadow of marriage: Singleness in England, 1914–60*
Katherine Holden

*Women, dowries and agency: Marriage in fifteenth-century Valencia*
Dana Wessell Lightfoot

*Catholic nuns and sisters in a secular age: Britain 1945–90*
Carmen Mangion

*A woman's place? Challenging values in 1960s Irish women's magazines*
Ciara Meehan

*Out of his mind: Masculinity and mental illness in Victorian Britain*
Amy Milne-Smith

*Medieval women and urban justice: Commerce, crime and community in England, 1300–1500*   Teresa Phipps

*Women, travel and identity: Journeys by rail and sea, 1870–1940*
Emma Robinson-Tomsett

*Imagining Caribbean womanhood: Race, nation and beauty contests, 1929–70*   Rochelle Rowe

*Infidel feminism: Secularism, religion and women's emancipation, England 1830–1914*   Laura Schwartz

*Women, credit and debt in early modern Scotland*   Cathryn Spence

*Being boys: Youth, leisure and identity in the inter-war years*
Melanie Tebbutt

*Women art workers and the Arts and Crafts movement*   Zoë Thomas

*Queen and country: Same-sex desire in the British Armed Forces, 1939–45*   Emma Vickers

*The 'perpetual fair': Gender, disorder and urban amusement in eighteenth-century London*   Anne Wohlcke

*Taking travel home: The souvenir culture of British women tourists, 1750–1830*   Emma Gleadhill

# Becoming a mother

## An Australian history

Carla Pascoe Leahy

MANCHESTER UNIVERSITY PRESS

Copyright © Carla Pascoe Leahy 2023

The right of Carla Pascoe Leahy to be identified as the author of this work has been asserted in accordance with the Copyright, Designs and Patents Act 1988.

Published by Manchester University Press
Oxford Road, Manchester M13 9PL

www.manchesteruniversitypress.co.uk

British Library Cataloguing-in-Publication Data
A catalogue record for this book is available from the British Library

ISBN 978 1 5261 6120 8 hardback
ISBN 978 1 5261 9082 6 paperback

First published 2023
Paperback published 2025

The publisher has no responsibility for the persistence or accuracy of URLs for any external or third- party internet websites referred to in this book, and does not guarantee that any content on such websites is, or will remain, accurate or appropriate.

EU authorised representative for GPSR:
Easy Access System Europe – Mustamäe tee 50, 10621 Tallinn, Estonia
gpsr.requests@easproject.com

Typeset by Newgen Publishing UK

*This book is dedicated to Sofia, whose arrival into the world sparked my own birth as a mother. I never imagined I had such capacity to care until you beckoned it forth.*

# Contents

List of figures   x
Acknowledgements   xi
Prologue   xiii

1 Approaching matrescence: theory, context, methodology   1
2 Mother-in-waiting: pregnancy   40
3 The birth of a mother: labour and childbirth   77
4 Mother love: mothers and their children   116
5 Mothering the mother: maternal relationships and support   147
6 Motherload: maternal work   182
7 The maternalisation of the self: mothering and identity   216
Epilogue   247

Appendix: Narrator biographies   254
Bibliography   261
Index   271

# List of figures

1 Postwar mother with first child, rural Victoria, 1950 (private collection) — 23
2 Pregnant second-wave mother in maternity clothes, 1978 (private collection) — 64
3 Millennial mother with co-mother and newborn twins immediately after caesarean birth, 2015 (private collection) — 104
4 Mothers and babies at the Drouin Infant Welfare Centre, Victoria, circa 1944 (photo by Jim Fitzpatrick, National Library of Australia U-429–122) — 131
5 Millennial mother with first child, inner Melbourne, 2013 (private collection) — 222

# Acknowledgements

This book is a produce of the places in which it has grown. I was born on the lands of the Whadjuk Noongar people and I have lived most of my remembered years on the lands of the Kulin nation, residing on Wurundjeri country for much of my youth before coming to Waddawurrung lands a decade ago. These coastal borderlands, where earth meets sea, have fundamentally shaped my beliefs and my scholarship, sustaining me across more than four decades. I pay my respects to the Elders of these lands and offer my deep gratitude for their custodianship over thousands of years.

There are many other people and places who have offered nourishment to me throughout my intellectual development. I thank the Australian Research Council for funding the Discovery Early Career Research Award (DECRA) which produced this book (and for the anonymous reviewers of my funding application who believed in me and my research). I thank the University of Melbourne, and my colleagues and students there, for offering my DECRA project a home and supporting me across six years of part-time work. And I thank the University of Tasmania for supporting this book project during its final period of gestation.

The Maternal Scholars Reading Group in Melbourne inspired much of my thinking about motherhood and gave me the courage and intellectual foundations to theorise mothering differently to prevailing popular and scholarly directions. The participants in the Australian Mothering symposium in 2018 and the subsequent volume stimulated and broadened my thinking about mothering in interdisciplinary directions.

Alistair Thomson, an unfailingly generous mentor, has supported my intellectual development across the last seven years, including reading an entire draft of this manuscript. Sarah Green provided vital research assistance during the final stages of this project, identifying primary sources we could access online during pandemic lockdowns. Museums Victoria has supported my career through my role as Honorary Associate and through providing a home for these research interviews (where narrators agreed), that they may be preserved for future generations.

I am forever indebted to the sixty women whose lives sparkle throughout these pages. You have shown extraordinary generosity and trust in sharing your personal memories with me. We often spoke together of our hope that mothering could be more honestly and openly discussed in contemporary Australian society. I hope that you feel this book contributes to our shared ambition. You will see that I have shared some of my own intimate maternal memories – that we may be vulnerable together.

Most of all, I am grateful for the friends, family and community who have sustained me across the last decade since I first became pregnant. My own parents and my parents-in-law have helped to care for my children to allow me to pursue my scholarship, mothering the mother that I was becoming. Having inspired this research in the first place, my daughters provide constant encouragement and love, continuing to push me to grow in my maternal identity. They have taught me more about motherhood than anyone else. Finally, it's difficult to adequately capture how much this book has been made possible by my partner, Greg. He nourishes my heart, stimulates my mind and patiently helps to create the physical conditions that make it possible for me to do my work. Thank you for *everything*.

# Prologue

This research was born of my own matrescence. When I became a mother for the first time, I was shocked by how little my expectations prepared me for the reality of maternality. Mothering was both much, much more difficult than I had anticipated, but also one thousand times more enriching than I had suspected.

There was a strange ineffability to many of my maternal experiences. From the moment of conception, so many of the things I experienced on my journey to becoming a mother were unprecedented, and this unprecedence lent them an almost unutterable quality. How to make sense of something that is unlike anything that has come before in one's life?

I found that speaking with other mothers helped me to attach metaphors and descriptors to these novel sensations. Through snatches of anecdote, simile and poetry, we built a language, a mother tongue, together. One friend told me that the first time she felt the quickening – when a foetus moves inside the mother's body – it felt like a little fish turning over. Yes! I thought. Or perhaps a butterfly fluttering gentle wings inside my uterus. Another woman told me that keeping the fact of her pregnancy unannounced during the first trimester felt like holding a 'precious jewel'. My own felt like a sacred secret, an everyday miracle of unparalleled value.

After my child was born, the emotions I felt were wholly novel and of astonishing enormity and ferocity. 'I never knew it was possible to love this deeply,' one new mother confessed to me. Another told me that becoming a mother felt like opening up a new cavern in her heart. My baby similarly carved entirely new spaces inside me, spaces which filled to overflowing with a warm, gushing, liquid love.

I wondered if becoming a mother had always been thus. Had my mother and grandmothers relished and suffered similar maternal experiences? So I looked around me for histories of mothering, histories written from the visceral, passionate, desperate perspectives of maternality. And I found very little. Those that did exist were often histories of mother*hood*, prioritising the expert discourses of doctors, nurses, parenting advice experts, bureaucrats or journalists. Much less concerned mothers' own memories and reflections of raising children.

So during those twelve months of maternity leave that I savoured with my first child, I conducted a piecemeal, happenstance, serendipitous study of maternal experience. A study of mothering using a maternal epistemology, if you will. Reaching out to women I knew, and women they knew, I began interviewing generations of Australian mothers about how they remembered and made sense of their experiences of growing with and caring for children. My young daughter was usually present with me – playing, rolling and gurgling on the floor – and her pterodactyl-like shrieks regularly punctuate the interview recordings.

Among those early interviewees were my grandmothers, my mother, my mother-in-law and many of the friends I made through my first mothers' group. Later, I asked another oral historian to interview me as well. So some of the stories related through this book are not only meaningful to me as an historian – they are also deeply personal to me as a mother, daughter, granddaughter and friend. I have chosen not to reveal these personal connections within the text to preserve the privacy of the women who shared some of their most intimate emotions and experiences with me. Yet I have decided to introduce each chapter with a quote from my own maternography to share the vulnerable position of being a narrator within a piece of research, and to be intellectually honest about how my personal experiences shape my research assumptions.

I formulated a grandiose research project – to examine seventy-five years of Australian mothering – and was fortunate to receive Australian Research Council funding to devote myself to this research. I chose three case study areas with which I am intimately familiar: Malvern, the place of my middle childhood and adolescence;

Fitzroy, the place of my young adulthood and matrescence; and Ocean Grove, the place of my early motherhood. These powerful place connections to Wurundjeri and later Waddawurrung country have given me a detailed understanding of the streets, parks, shops and houses that my narrators recalled during their interviews. Over the next six years, I conducted the research part-time, alongside mothering my first child and then my second. I felt there would be an exquisite, and regrettable, irony if I sacrificed the mothering of my own children in order to study the mothering of others. And so they came first, and the work had to fit around them.

As my daughters grew, so did my maternality. My skills and expertise and emotional abilities had to shift and develop as my children grew in size and capacity. And as my maternal identity developed, so too did my understanding of my research topic deepen and broaden. I am a different mother now to the ecstatic yet tentative woman who first saw two blue strips forming on a strip of plastic held shakily in her hand. I am firmly and fiercely positioned in my maternal identity. And my research has had to adapt and grow with me.

A different person would write a different history of mothering. That is as it should be. Our research is always a product of our subject position in the world. And so I offer up a little of myself in opening every chapter, so that it is clearer to the reader how I am always and forever implicated in my work. This is *my* history of mothering. I hope it resonates and intersects with yours.

# 1

# Approaching matrescence: theory, context, methodology

I remember when I was first becoming a mother, this metaphor that was in my mind. I felt like my heart had kind of burst the confines of my chest ... When I became a mother, it was like my heart just expanded so rapidly and so dramatically that my capacity for all kinds of feelings was enhanced, particularly my capacity for love. I think the experience of loving someone so enormously and overwhelmingly that it sort of fills every tiny part of your being, that changes you forever; it has to. Just to even know that it's possible to love someone that much ...

I felt like it expanded my capacity for all levels of emotional register. Lots of mums talk about feeling really, really sensitive, but that thing of like, when you feel sad about something, you feel really, really sad about it, but particularly if it relates to your children, like if it's seeing children that are hurt or harmed or something. If you feel angry about something, it's like intense, enormous, mother lioness rage, and the protectiveness you know, that you feel towards your children. So, you know, the really big thing ... is that sense of gigantic emotions. The idea, for me, that you could be enriched that much and expanded that much, when you're already almost middle-aged, is amazing. I did not think that it would be possible at this point in my life to be so transformed by anything.

When we're young, we have all these new experiences and so time seems to pass really slowly ... oh, I lost my first tooth and I did my first snorkel ... We're growing and changing and developing. Then, we get to some point where we're still changing, but development is pretty slow. We feel fairly stagnant, like it's a fairly even keel. To me, the fact that motherhood could explode into my life like an atom bomb, just like that, and change the way I felt about everything, was amazing. Like, changed the way I felt about my living surroundings, changed the way I felt about my work, changed the way I felt about

> my family, my partner ... I mean, the fact that G is the father of my children connects us in a way that can never be broken. Even if something broke between us, we would always be connected on this fundamental, cellular level and bonded by that. The way that it changes your relationship to your parents and your sort of visceral appreciation of what they've done for you is amazing. It changes everything.[1]
>
> Carla Pascoe Leahy

This book began with my simple observation that contemporary women in Australia, as in other industrialised societies, find that becoming a mother transforms almost every aspect of their lives. In a physiological sense, women becoming birthgiving mothers find that their bodies expand and change dramatically during pregnancy, birth and breastfeeding. Aside from a long list of physical symptoms that begin with gestation, the hormonal changes of biological motherhood influence a woman's emotional state. Motherhood changes the very brain chemistry and neural pathways of a woman.

Compounding these physiological changes, a majority of women change their lifestyles when they are pregnant and mothering. Health advice recommends that pregnant women avoid alcohol, tobacco and other drugs, moderate exercise regimes and eliminate a diverse range of foods from soft cheeses to alfalfa sprouts. Once a baby is born, many mothers perform the role of primary carer, resulting in reduced time and energy for activities they once enjoyed including exercise, socialising, relaxation and work. Relationships stretch and shift with motherhood, particularly relationships with a woman's partner (where one exists), family (especially her own mother) and friends. The meaning of work in a woman's life often changes, with many women in Australia, as across the industrialised societies of North America, Oceania and Europe, taking some form of maternity leave and/or working part-time while their children are young.

If we consider that all of these changes occur within a period of twelve to twenty-four months, it is little wonder that many contemporary women report feeling that they have been fundamentally transformed by motherhood. Most describe feeling that the core of who they are – their sense of self – has shifted permanently. While I have described a series of physical and social changes above, they are mediated through and in many ways superseded by a dramatic emotional transition in the woman as she experiences unprecedented extremes of feeling: ecstasy and grief, joy and frustration, and the most all-consuming, limitless love she has ever known. I call this psychic transformation *the maternalisation of the self*.

As I experienced these changes myself, I began to wonder: did previous maternal generations experience similar transformations when they became mothers? To what extent does the transition to maternality change over time? Are there elements which are core and unchanging? Physiological changes would appear to act outside history. Yet as the average age of primigravida (or first pregnancy) has increased, the physical shifts of motherhood are experienced differently by ageing female bodies. Physiological characteristics also have different cultural meanings attached to them. As the pregnant body has become commodified, the bump is now flaunted in specialised maternity clothing rather than hidden under voluminous layers. Since the 1970s, a discourse that 'breast is best' has created a sacralisation of breastfeeding which lends the physical experience heightened moral satisfaction for mothers able to breastfeed.

Other changes accompanying motherhood are clearly specific to this cultural and historic moment we occupy now, such as the balance between paid work and care work. An increasing expectation that a career is central to female identity and life course means that any reduction or alteration to a woman's involvement in paid employment is experienced as a significant identity shift. A core conflict occurs for many twenty-first-century women who have based their identity around their profession yet discover an unexpected yearning for motherhood.

When I became a mother, I was stunned by the enormity and profundity of what I was experiencing. It felt like our cultural scripts had not prepared me for what I encountered. So I began to look around me for other descriptions of becoming a mother, to ascertain whether my experience was unusual. Yet I found a deafening cultural silence. Contemporary media discourses discuss motherhood chiefly in terms of policy challenges to be rectified, such as whether parental leave should be expanded or how to improve the affordability and availability of childcare. I discovered very little on emotional experiences of mothering. Those that do explore this angle frame motherhood as a 'problem' by focusing on experiences of perinatal depression and anxiety. I found very limited public discussion of the enormous rewards of mothering or the love that mothers bear for their children, a love that my initial interviews described as transformational, redemptive and unparalleled. My historian's curiosity was piqued: how *had* the experience of first-time motherhood changed since my grandmothers' days? And so I began pilot research when my first-born was around six months old, searching for historical research while she was napping, or interviewing other mothers while she gurgled in the background.

I made two surprising discoveries. Firstly, while interviewees described becoming a mother as a major transformation in their lives, historical research internationally has not often benefited from the interdisciplinary literature of maternal studies which describes matrescence as a shift in psychological identity and social relations for the new mother. Secondly, the Australian historiography of mothers is surprisingly sparse and has focused upon cultural discourses of mother*hood* rather than personal experiences of mother*ing*. We lack an overarching history of mothers in Australia, particularly one that focuses upon maternal experiences and emotions.

## Constraints and opportunities: the shifting social context of motherhood

The major innovation of this book is to focus specifically on becoming a mother for the first time, and the way this is both a cultural transition point and a psychological transformation. This focus is a distinctively original contribution to the historiography of motherhood and mothering. For this reason, while this book is based upon research conducted in Australia, it has much wider resonance and relevance across Anglophone, industrialised societies. The transformation of matrescence has been experienced and has shifted in broadly similar ways in Australia, Canada, New Zealand, the United Kingdom and the United States since the mid-twentieth century. They have shared and exchanged cultural ideals of motherhood and childrearing through advice texts, popular culture and media, witnessing the locus of child-raising expertise shift from informal advice of friends and family to a privileging of 'expert' discourses. Across the Anglosphere, psychological discourses have been popularised, accompanying the rise of an expressive and therapeutic culture which has transformed the way motherhood is discussed and influenced the medical identification of perinatal depression and anxiety. Perinatal health regimes have expanded as new motherhood has become an increasingly medicalised experience, including the rise of antenatal care, maternity care and postnatal care. Across the industrialised world, rising maternal workforce participation has been supported by a growth in early childhood education and care as well as parental leave, though the extent to which governments subsidise childcare, leave and other family supports varies. All of these countries have experienced mass women's movements which participated in a transnational circulation of feminist debates and activism. This 'second wave' of feminism fought for women to have more control of reproduction through access to birth control, abortion and sex education, changes which have underpinned a rising age of first motherhood. For all these reasons, experiences of matrescence have shared commonalities across the Global North since the end of World War Two, and have shifted in broadly similar ways and at similar times.[2]

Yet the Australian context is also distinctive, and this study pays attention to the specificities of place, culture and history. The country now known as Australia was inhabited by diverse Indigenous groups for more than 50,000 years. Since British invasion in 1788, Australia has developed into a settler colonial nation founded upon violent dispossession of Aboriginal and Torres Strait Islander peoples. The various Australian colonies remained far-flung outposts of the British Empire until Federation unified them into a commonwealth of states in 1901, though Britain continued to be referred to as the 'mother country' for many decades subsequently. One of the first acts of the new nation was the White Australia policy, which privileged British migration to Australia, thus making a powerful early statement that this was to be a nation founded upon whiteness and racial discrimination. Australia's distinctive version of a liberal welfare state was also established early, with the introduction of a maternity allowance in 1912 setting the scene for a series of government supports for mothers and families across the twentieth century.[3] A well-funded public health system developed, with antenatal clinics proliferating from the interwar years, foreshadowing an expansion of hospital-based maternity care and infant welfare clinics after World War Two.[4] In the twentieth century, Indigenous Australians continued to be displaced from ancestral lands and were also subject to cultural dispossession through a set of practices which removed Aboriginal children (later referred to as the Stolen Generations) from their families, sparking profound intergenerational ruptures and trauma for Aboriginal mothers.[5] After World War Two, Australia slowly became more multicultural, as migration brought people from across the globe, adding cultural, linguistic and religious diversity to experiences of mothering.

Australia had been an urbanised, and especially a suburbanised, country from the late nineteenth century, but this trend accelerated in the postwar decades, as an economic boom and rising birth rate led more and more families to aspire to a family home on a quarter-acre block in the suburbs.[6] Although the Australian women's liberation movement took up Betty Friedan's critique of the lonely housewife confined to her suburban home, and more Australians embraced higher density living as inner-city areas deindustrialised and gentrified, this spatial ideal has remained compelling for many when choosing where to raise children.[7]

The shifting social context in which Australian women come to mothering has changed substantially since 1945, and broad social trends are further complicated by a mother's background and identity. As in other industrialised societies, women's ability to understand and control their bodies has shifted immensely. Most postwar mothers were like German-Australian, Catholic interviewee June (who experienced matrescence in 1947), who told me, 'We never talked in my family about sex'. From the 1970s, it was increasingly customary for Australian girls to be educated about their reproductive systems.[8] Family planning was done covertly if at all in the 1950s, whereas the introduction of the birth control pill in 1961 slowly severed the taken-for-granted connection between sex and reproduction.[9] While secret abortions had long been carried out, the slow decriminalisation and legalisation of abortion has allowed women to terminate unwanted pregnancies without having to risk their health or carry to term a baby who would need to be adopted.

Across this period, cultural understandings of gender, sexuality and family, as well as a shifting legal and medical landscape, have influenced a diversification of family types, as has been witnessed across the Global North. In 1950s and 1960s Australia, the assumed family ideal was heterosexual, once-married, dual-parent and nuclear. Any women who strayed outside these borders were penalised, such as working-class, Anglo-Australian interviewee Patsy. When she became pregnant in 1967 while an unmarried teenager, Patsy was sent to an interstate mother and baby home by her family with the intention of adopting out her child. Women who could not have a biological child in the postwar decades often chose to adopt. Middle-class, Anglo-Australian Grace adopted her two sons in the early 1960s. The maternal love she described for her sons was indistinguishable from that of birthgiving mothers – and her struggles just as severe, when she suffered from perinatal (or post-adoptive) depression during her children's infancies. Single mothers also struggled in the postwar decades, within an economy that assumed a male breadwinner and a culture that ostracised them. Anglo-Australian, working-class Adriana had three children with her husband in the early 1950s, but battled financially to support the family on her own after her husband's desertion.

Over the last seventy-five years, understandings and experiences of family life have multiplied. An increasingly multicultural Australia has meant that kinship norms and intergenerational transmission of family values has diversified. Chen was born into a wealthy Chinese family in 1935 and came to Australia as an adult. Her matrescence in 1966 was made more difficult by having to navigate unfamiliar cultural values and health supports in her adopted country. Working-class, Macedonian-Australian Miroslava found her matrescence in 1975 was supported – but also sometimes suffocated – by living with her parents throughout her adult life. Although the Australian Government has apologised for historical practices separating Aboriginal mothers from their children, Indigenous practices of birthing and raising children remain marginalised and inadequately supported within wider Australian society.[10] In relating her experience of being raised by adoptive parents in the 1950s and later meeting her birth mother and wider family, Aboriginal mother Kay described a pattern of intergenerational disconnection from culture, family and country which has been experienced by many Indigenous families. Born into a middle-class family in northern Australia in 1983, Torres Strait Islander woman Somi told me of her difficulties remaining connected to land and family when she decided to raise her children in southern Australia far from her cultural homeland. The introduction of the single parent's allowance in 1973 and no-fault divorce in 1975 allowed many women to leave unhappy relationships and to financially raise children on their own without the support of a male breadwinner. But the story of middle-class, Welsh-Australian Sybil, who had her first child in 1979, reveals the enormous strains of single mothering and the ways in which the pain of these decisions can echo down the years. Sometimes single mothers would re-partner, creating blended families of stepparents and stepchildren. Middle-class, Anglo-Australian Rowena first experienced motherhood when she became a stepmother, before later birthing the first of two biological children in 2010.

Changing cultural norms and growing medical possibilities have also expanded who can have children, and at what age. Since the first Australian baby was born to in vitro fertilisation (IVF) in 1981, Australians have increasingly utilised assisted reproductive technology (ART) to have children. ART has extended the possibilities of who can become a birthgiving mother. While lesbian motherhood was rare in the postwar era, it became more common in the late twentieth century.[11] ART has become legally available to lesbian women and single women, making it easier for women without a male partner to become mothers.[12] Now lesbian mothers like middle-class, Anglo-Australian Kira (who became a mother in 2015) are consciously renegotiating what 'family' means, as well as what it means to be a mother.

While laws once restricted ART to married, heterosexual women in a clear state enforcement of cultural norms, access has broadened in the twenty-first century. In addition to lesbians, single women like working-class, Greek-Australian Connie (who became a mother in 2014) can now choose to have a child without a partner, and increasingly at an older age. But while Connie carefully planned to financially support a child on her own, she was not prepared for the emotional and physical cost of doing so. It is also important to recognise that accessing ART takes a high financial, emotional and physical toll. Access is restricted to those who can afford it, and many women like middle-class, American-Australian Katerina (who became a mother in 2013) find the experience very difficult, from the physiological side effects of the treatment to the pain of losing an embryo that doesn't 'take'.

In Australia, 205 trans men gave birth between 2013 and 2018, complicating our previous understanding that only women can biologically bear children.[13] It is still relatively difficult for gay men in Australia to have a child as laws ban commercial surrogacy although altruistic surrogacy is available in some jurisdictions, or accessed overseas. Surrogacy remains contested among feminists, particularly because global power dynamics of inequality complicate issues of consent when these transactions are between wealthy would-be parents in the Global North and impoverished birthgiving mothers in the Global South.[14]

All these factors have allowed an expansion of understandings of motherhood. Experiences of mothering have also shifted, particularly as the average age of first motherhood, or primigravida, has occurred later. In the 1950s, most women had children in their twenties, whereas by the twenty-first century most women had children in their thirties.[15] The women profiled here range across these ages, with Patsy the youngest first-time mother at 19 (in 1967) and Connie one of the eldest at 43 (in 2014). Age of first motherhood has consequences for a woman's psychological adjustment, physical recovery, financial independence and life options, as will become evident. What is perhaps equally important is the extent to which a woman's age of first motherhood aligns with contemporaneous cultural expectations. Whereas having children at twenty might have been considered appropriate in the immediate postwar decades, it may be seen as premature or problematic in 2020. While first-time mothers were considered 'over the hill' at thirty for the postwar cohort, by the twenty-first century, this judgement was more likely to be levelled at a forty-year-old woman.

Alongside a rising age of first motherhood, average family sizes in Australia have shrunk, meaning that a woman spends less of her reproductive years bearing and raising children. The total fertility rate has fallen from 3.6 babies per woman in 1961 to 1.74 in 2018.[16] While middle-class, Anglo-Australian Jane was unusual in having eleven children between 1954 and 1969, large families were not frowned upon. Popular culture romanticised the joys of big broods, as is evident in films like *The Sound of Music* or television shows like *The Brady Bunch*. Middle-class, British-born Joanna remembers feeling ashamed of being an only child in the 1950s – that people assumed she would be spoilt and selfish – and the loneliness she felt growing up without siblings influenced her decision to have six children herself in the 1970s. But by the twenty-first century, having one child was increasingly common. In 2016, 14 per cent of women had one child (and 16 per cent had no children).[17] For some women, fertility restricted the number of children they could have. For others, personal choices limited their family size due to birth trauma, perinatal depression or anxiety, financial circumstances, environmental concerns or other factors. These kinds of cultural, technological and medical changes have also been underpinned by the growth in women choosing not to have children at all, with around a quarter of Australian women of childbearing age in the early twenty-first century expected to never become mothers.[18]

Mothering is also impacted by the health and/or ability of the mother and her child, and changing cultural attitudes and medical supports. Women who cared for seriously ill or disabled children found their care burden much greater. Anglo-Australian, working-class Pamela described the agony of having her first child in 1967 and being told her daughter would not live to adulthood. Working-class, British-born Valerie moved to Australia in 1961 at the age of twelve. As a new mother in the 1980s, she struggled with a baby who had a hip displacement and consequently had to wear hip casts for the first months of her life. Anglo-Australian, working-class Susan has been deaf since she caught meningitis at two years of age in 1953. While Susan found strategies as she grew up to competently negotiate a hearing-prejudiced world, her matrescence in 1976 threw up new challenges, such as how to know if her baby was crying when she could not hear her. Mothers of premature babies or babies who nearly lost their lives at birth, like Anglo-Australian, working-class Tessa (who had her child in 2013), struggled to deal with the challenging emotions these traumatic experiences provoked, and to let go of their hypervigilance about their child's safety.

Perspectives on children and their needs have shifted significantly in Australia and internationally over the past seventy years. The popularisation of psychology and child development from the mid-twentieth century has influenced childrearing advice, prompting a slow shift from disciplinary and detached parenting to demonstrative and relational styles.[19] From the 1970s, a global children's rights discourse has decried corporal punishment and insisted upon rights to a safe home environment, education and play, among other things.[20] Children's assumed competency has decreased if measured by indicators such as independent mobility (when they are allowed to travel by themselves), assumption of responsibility for others (for example when children are asked to take care of younger siblings) and age of employment (when children are asked or allowed to perform similar tasks to adults). And yet in other ways, children are expected to be more robust and independent, as they are increasingly left in the care of non-family members at younger ages. With the rise of paid childcare across industrialised societies, children once thought to emotionally require their mother's complete attention until school age are increasingly expected to be resilient and flexible enough to be cared for by other adults in settings outside the home. Mothers at the forefront of this childcare transition in the 1970s, like Lebanese-Australian, middle-class Sally, felt conflicting emotions about whether returning to work and utilising paid childcare was in the best interests of their children. This shift in who cares for children, for how long and at what ages has been accompanied by changing cultural attitudes to the relationship between mothers and children. Sociologist Sharon Hays has identified the rise of an ideology of intensive mothering from the late twentieth century, at the same time as mothers have been engaging in paid work in greater numbers. This has led to ever greater guilt for the working mother who can never meet expectations in the home or the workforce.[21]

While mothers have worked across the seventy-five-year period under investigation, the numbers of mothers working and cultural attitudes towards their paid employment have changed considerably in Australia, as in other Anglophone contexts. Socio-economic backgrounds have influenced both the cultural ideals to which mothers aspire as well as the financial circumstances which constrain their decision-making. In postwar Australia, for example, the stay-at-home mother was a powerful cultural figure who often appeared in magazines and movies. Nevertheless, many working-class women worked alongside mothering, as in the case of Anglo-Australian Daphne who raised her children in the inner-urban neighbourhood of Fitzroy in the 1950s while working in factories, waitressing and managing a dry-cleaning shop, supported by the childcare of her parents.

Female labour force participation climbed from 34 per cent in 1961 to 60.7 per cent in 2019.[22] By the 2010s, the cultural assumption had flipped to an expectation that women would combine paid work and care work, though my research suggests that the stay-at-home ideal was perhaps stronger in lower-income households and regional households. While the numbers of women engaged in paid employment have risen, they are still more likely to be the primary carers of their children, shoulder the bulk of the domestic work and perform most of the emotional labour of the family.[23] Mothers of preschool-aged children are more likely to be working part-time than full-time. For the most part, the growth in the numbers of mothers working has not been matched by a reduction in the hours of working fathers. Only one in twenty Australian fathers takes primary parental leave.[24] After a decades-long battle, the Australian Government introduced paid maternity leave in 2011, to be taken at eighteen weeks at the minimum wage. Partners are entitled to two weeks at the minimum wage. Despite being legally protected from discrimination and entitled to request flexible working arrangements, women still report suffering discrimination in the workforce when they are pregnant, on maternity leave and after they have children.[25] While we know something of the shifting social context within which Australian women have come to motherhood, we know much less about the emotional, relational and experiential aspects of mothering over time. Partly, this is to do with the ways in which feminist history and women's history have developed.

## Motherhood without mothers? The historiography of motherhood and the development of maternal studies

As the historical context of Australian mothering has shifted since 1945, so too has scholarly research about mothers across disciplines such as history, psychology and sociology. Across these three-quarters of a century, popular and academic knowledge, activism and tradition, and ideas and practice, have maintained a dynamic dialogue about real and ideal forms of mothering. From the late nineteenth century, Sigmund Freud's psychoanalytic theories emphasised the powerful lifelong influence of unconscious desires and fantasies developed during early childhood, implying that mothers as primary carers of children held a critical responsibility for healthy psychic development.[26] While psychology was not widely popularised in the first half of the twentieth century, this Freudian emphasis upon the maternal role complemented the maternalist thrust of first-wave feminists, who based claims for political participation in their valorised role as mothers.[27]

Psychological theories of child development influenced the early- to mid-twentieth century assumption in industrialised societies that a single primary carer – usually the mother – was best for the infant's emotional wellbeing.[28] John Bowlby's theory of the dire psychological consequences of maternal deprivation led to an emphasis on close emotional attachment between mother and child.[29] D. W. Winnicott emphasised the importance of the holding environment created by an attentive maternal figure for the development of a 'true self' in the child, though she only needed to be a 'good-enough' mother in his estimation.[30] Such theories began to work their way into popular understanding, furthered by the publication of childrearing manuals like Benjamin Spock's, which privileged a responsive and empathetic maternal style over routine and discipline.[31] Nevertheless, psychological scholarship remained more interested in how the mother's behaviour impacted upon the developing child than her own maternal subjectivity.[32]

The discipline of history had even less to say about mothering and motherhood in the first half of the twentieth century. Amateur family historians may have traced matrilineal lines within their family tree but academic history during the nineteenth and early twentieth centuries focused upon political, economic and militaristic themes in the past.[33] This was History with a capital 'H', practised by elite, white males within universities.[34] The women's liberation movement of the 1960s and 1970s exploded understandings of what counted as real history. Across the industrialised world, feminists like Anna Davin, Miriam Dixson, Shulamith Firestone, Gerder Lerner, Kate Millett and Anne Summers traced the stories of women in the past to understand the position of women in the present.[35] Some of these women were not historians per se, but activists or scholars trained in other disciplines. Their history writing had a political intent: to chart a history of female oppression and to show that women had not been only minor, subservient characters in the theatre of history. These were often angry, sweeping accounts of the domination of women by virtue of their sex.

As with much of the social history and labour history that was emerging at this time, the focus of women's history in the 1970s was on women's experiences. Partly this was a product of the women's liberation movement's focus on recounting personal experiences as a form of consciousness-raising. Partly it was a realisation that traditional sources of History – written, official documents – were inadequate to tell the stories of those, like women and the working classes, who either lacked literacy or whose written traces were not preserved. Oral history, itself a sub-discipline only recently adopted by academic historians, was an obvious early ally to women's history. Women's history and oral history worked in sympathy to resuscitate long-neglected accounts of female lives.[36]

But even many of these early accounts neglected histories of mothering. The women's liberation movement was determined to show that women could do more than mother, railing against biological assumptions that women were destined to adopt primary care of children because of their ability to gestate, give birth to and breastfeed children. Many second-wave feminist demands were focused on the non-maternal possibilities of women's lives, such as rights to equal pay, education, abortion and childcare.[37] French philosopher Simone de Beauvoir's *The Second Sex* comes close to outright hostility towards the female reproductive system and was influential across the English-speaking world after translation.[38] Based upon interviews with American women in the 1950s, Betty Friedan contended that postwar housewives and mothers felt socially isolated and personally unfulfilled in their role.[39] American feminist Shulamith Firestone argued in *The Dialectic of Sex* that women needed to be freed from their corporeal connection to motherhood by breeding babies in test tubes and raising children in collectives.[40] Many mid-twentieth-century feminists were concerned that women's biological capacity to mother had been used to justify their segregation in the domestic sphere (though this was always a partial account that ignored the dual roles that working women had long played in the home and the field, then later the factory).

The rejection of motherhood in some of these early second-wave texts has perhaps been unfairly caricatured.[41] But in response, more complex accounts of mothering began to emerge such as poet Adrienne Rich's *Of Woman Born*, which holds in tension the ambivalences of the maternal position. Rich's work suggested that while the patriarchal institution of motherhood was undoubtedly stultifying, individual experiences of mothering held the potential to be satisfying and self-actualising.[42] British sociologist Ann Oakley sought to understand the experiences of women becoming mothers in the 1970s, in a ground-breaking study in which maternal voices were privileged over her own scholarly perspective.[43] Australian sociologists similarly interpreted the rich interplay between ideal visions of the 'good mother' and quotidian maternal practice, implicitly asserting that there was something profound to be understood in the everyday domestic experiences of women.[44] In an innovative melding of psychology and sociology, American feminist Nancy Chodorow argued that women are not 'naturally' destined to be primary carers of children. Rather, boys and girls grow up in families observing that their mother is the primary carer and they in turn internalise and perform gendered roles within their own families as adults.[45] Nevertheless, there remained a suspicion within feminist thought of valorising the maternal or associating it biologically with women for fear that women would forever be limited by that role.

American philosopher Sara Ruddick's treatise on 'maternal thinking' was an attempt to move beyond this impasse. Ruddick argued that through the practice of looking after a vulnerable child who is dependent upon them, mothers (usually women) learn a particular mode of reflecting, problem-solving and acting that she termed 'maternal thinking'.[46] By separating motherhood from the body and linking it instead to thought and practices, Ruddick provided a different rationale for valuing the ethical practices of mothers without trapping them in biology. A body of literature also developed in the 1980s and 1990s which provided a sophisticated framework for understanding and valuing the ways in which women's perspectives were shaped by their cyclical, leaky, non-unitary bodies.[47]

Women's history was also beginning to question the very premises on which the sub-discipline was based – namely that there is a unitary category of woman that can be studied throughout time. Women of colour questioned whether the women's liberation movement was speaking only about and on behalf of white women's experiences. Black feminists like Alice Walker, bell hooks, Audre Lorde and Patricia Hill Collins argued that the demands of white second-wave feminists ignored the experiences and desires of black women.[48] Historians were considering questions of gender and sexuality – what these terms mean, how their interpretation has changed over time and how they can be meaningfully deployed as categories of historical analysis.[49] And perhaps most fundamentally, some began questioning epistemologically how we can begin to know anything about women's lives in the past.

Post-structuralism and post-modernism were increasingly influencing the study of history. In an influential article, Joan W. Scott questioned 'the evidence of experience' and whether there is any human experience that is pre-linguistic or existing prior to the cultural context in which it emerges.[50] Such debates precipitated a seismic shift in historical debate from social history's focus on the personal experiences of non-elites to an emphasis upon analysing cultural discourses. For women's history and maternal history, this resulted in a focus on discourses of motherhood rather than experiences of mothering.[51] During the late twentieth century and into the early twenty-first, we learnt more about cultural ideals of childrearing and medical understandings of pregnancy and birth than we did about emotional, personal or relational experiences of gestating, birthing and raising children. A burgeoning interest in the history of sexuality led to a focus upon non-procreative sexual intercourse and non-heteronormative sexual identities – and mothering, by implication, was deemed distinctively un-sexy.

At the same time, there developed a sense within popular culture that feminism had rejected motherhood. While this was in many senses an oversimplification of feminist positions, what is most influential upon cultural discourses and the daily lives of women is what a majority of people *believe* feminism has to say about motherhood, regardless of the nuances of academic and activist debates. From the late twentieth century, a popular cultural discourse developed which claimed that feminism had wrongly told women that work was more important than motherhood, or that they could 'have it all' by delaying motherhood in order to progress their careers.[52] Many non-activist women appreciated gains in gender equality but wished to disassociate themselves from what they saw as the radical, bra-burning aspects of feminism.[53]

In the early twenty-first century, a different feminist perspective on mothering has emerged globally in response to the ambivalent second-wave relationship to motherhood. These perspectives could loosely be labelled 'matricentric feminism', a term developed by Canadian feminist Andrea O'Reilly to refer to a branch of feminism developed by and speaking to the unique perspectives of mothers. Just as we have recognised over the last forty years that women of colour, lesbian women and women living with disabilities need their own forms of feminism, so too do mothers need to claim their own discursive space.[54] With rising numbers of women choosing not to have children across the industrialised world, it is increasingly evident that the discrimination long considered to be gender-based is more profoundly care-based, and most consistently felt by mothers specifically, not women more broadly. Australian social theorist Petra Bueskens has identified a new social contract in which women are freed as workers/citizens but enslaved as mothers.[55]

Australian social commentator Anne Manne critiqued the 'new capitalist mother' in 2005, referring to the ways in which neoliberalism had co-opted the messages of feminism to define gender equality as the freedom to work as hard as men.[56] The victims of this all-encompassing ideology become leisure time but especially the work of caring for the vulnerable (including children, the elderly and the disabled). In a reference to Ruddick's landmark work, Australian social theorist Julie Stephens identified the prevalence of 'post-maternal thinking' in twenty-first-century western societies. Stephens is concerned by our cultural forgetting of maternal values and calls for a re-gendering of feminism to prioritise mothering.[57] While neoliberal ideologies encourage a version of feminism in which there are no limits on a woman's freedom, the extreme vulnerability of small children (as well as the aged and disabled) begs the question: who has the capacity to care? Both Manne and Stephens are concerned by how difficult it is in the current cultural climate for women to value and prioritise their love and care for their children, what American psychologist Daphne de Marneffe calls 'maternal desire'.[58]

At the same time, psychological and psychoanalytic debates have encompassed a greater interest in maternal subjectivity for its own sake, independent of the perceived needs of the child. Daniel Stern argues that the birth of a first child also signals 'the birth of a mother', as motherhood forces a rearrangement of a woman's identity into a 'motherhood constellation' – an identity shift that is permanent and transformative.[59] Rejecting the mid-twentieth-century focus on maternal attachment and attention, Rozsika Parker instead emphasises maternal ambivalence as a natural and necessary facet of becoming a mother.[60] Psychosocial researcher Lisa Baraitser has theorised maternal subjectivity as an encumbered and interrupted form of selfhood, where what defines the mother are her experiences of being weighed down by unfamiliar objects and finding her agency in the world intermittently disrupted by the needs of a child.[61] Others such as Alison Stone, Joan Raphael-Leff and Rosemary Balsam have urged attention to the powerfully intergenerational nature of mothering a child, as matrescence engenders a repetitive return to the experience of being mothered.[62] Some sociologists and psychosocial researchers such as Rachel Thomson and Wendy Hollway have focused specifically on becoming a mother, drawing upon multidisciplinary concepts and innovative methods of qualitative research to insist that while matrescence is complex, it nevertheless deserves our efforts at comprehension.[63]

Yet few historians have yet taken up the invitation posed by matricentric feminism to understand mothering as a central and formative experience in a woman's life. Some women's historians *have* maintained an interest in the history of mothers.[64] But given the omnipresence of mothering in women's lives throughout history, mothering has been a rather minor interest of historians. In particular, it is striking that despite the recognition in psychological literature that matrescence signals a psychological transformation for the new mother, and an emphasis in anthropological and sociological literature that this is a rite of passage that permanently changes a women's embeddedness within social relations, historical literature has been rather silent on the emotional experiences of becoming a mother or the psychic transformation of new motherhood.[65] I suggest that there are several reasons why this is so. Culturally, the cloying sentimentality of the maternal ideal undercuts any sense that this is a subject of serious scholarly analysis. Politically, there remains a suspicion of the ways in which the maternal ideal has constrained women to the private sphere. Historically, the study of mothers and the family has felt a little old-fashioned and unsophisticated, associated with what many now view as the naive ambitions of early social history and women's history. For some feminists, and feminist historians, it has felt simpler to reject or ignore maternity rather than explore the possibility that there may be something complicated yet compelling about the transition to becoming a mother. This present study is an attempt to do just that. Working against assumptions that mothering is necessarily stultifying, conservative and oppressive, this book charts a history of mothering as passionate, radical and transformative. In undertaking this subversive historical project, I borrow insights from psychology, sociology and psychosocial studies – strategically adopting an interdisciplinary lens in order to study the rich and multifaceted phenomenon of matrescence.

## Foregrounding maternal voices: a methodological approach

This research has been stimulated by matricentric feminism, but also by the observation that the historiography on women's experiences of mothering is sparse. Hence my methodology is framed by a commitment to understanding mothering through the words and worlds of mothers themselves. My research has centred upon the creation of sixty oral histories with Australian mothers and then radiated outwards into archival sources where these sources were mentioned or implied by maternal narratives. By starting with intimate investigations of the lives of mothers, I aim to foreground and emphasise their thoughts, feelings and actions and use documentary sources to supplement and enrich their stories.

This methodological strategy is partially the product of a feminist commitment to listening to and valuing the perspectives of women. Internationally, women's history and oral history have shared close connections since the early days of both sub-disciplines, with feminist historians recognising that spoken narratives could often offer greater details of women's lives than written documents.[66] An oral history methodology also allows this research to focus particularly on emotional aspects of the history of mothering. Perhaps the most profound transformation a woman undergoes when she becomes a mother is on a psychic level, and one of the most effective ways to understand psychological changes is through intersubjective dialogue. In this way, the research is also a contribution to the burgeoning literature on the history of emotions – but it is important to remember that oral history has maintained an interest in emotions since its earliest days.[67]

Perhaps the greatest strength of oral history is its ability to create a dialogue between the past and the present. A written document tells us only about the time it was created (though through her interpretation, the historian creates a link to the present). An oral history is necessarily, ontologically, a source that is born of both now and then. Interviews are backwards-looking, as the interviewer's questions invite the narrator to mentally return to their past through memory. But interviews are also strongly shaped by the moment in which they are conducted, by the cultural attitudes and circumstances of both participants in the here and now. Sometimes, the actions of the past are submitted to re-evaluation in light of the present. Sometimes, past thoughts and feelings offer new illumination on events or opinions occurring now. Either way, a mnemonic bridge is created between the past and the present within the unique space of the interview. For research like mine – which aims to use the past to awaken forgotten or repressed aspects of mothering in the present – this link between now and then is invaluable.

## Constructing the sample

One of the greatest challenges for my project was not deciding whether to use interviews but deciding *which* women to interview. Decisions about participant selection and sampling shape the way a project is conducted but also the very conclusions that can be drawn.[68] My concern in analysing pre-existing historiography was that the great bulk of Australian mothers have been largely ignored in historical studies, so I determined to extend my scope broadly. This allows the possibility of comparisons between mothers on the basis of factors such as cultural background, place of residence or marital status. I approximated the diversity of the population within my sample of sixty by prioritising diversity in terms of age, cultural background, socio-economic background, educational attainment, place of residence, ability, sexuality, relationship status and number of children.[69]

I define a 'mother' expansively in my study, including women who gestate and birth a baby as well as adoptive and foster mothers who take on primary or significant caregiving responsibilities in relation to a child. However, I have deliberately limited my study to mothers rather than parents more broadly because women experience parenting in distinctly gendered ways. Partly, this is because of the deeply embodied nature of maternal experiences – including pregnancy, birth, breastfeeding, carrying and cuddling – but also because of the specific cultural scripts that attach to female parenting.[70] Mothers are subject to a set of cultural ideals and social discriminations that do not apply equally to fathers. I have not included transgender participants in this study because numbers of transgender parents were very low across the period I am studying, though this is changing in twenty-first-century Australia.[71]

Due to my aspiration to understand a wide variety of maternal experiences, I sought to include First Nations mothers in my sample. But this intention is neither straightforward nor unproblematic. Aboriginal and Torres Strait Islander peoples have been subject to intense non-Aboriginal scrutiny since the earliest moments of colonisation. Research has been predominately *about* rather than *for* or *with* Aboriginal participants. In addition, the history of Indigenous mothering is fraught and painful, as across Australian jurisdictions, colonial and later state authorities customarily removed Aboriginal children from their families, severing their connections to kin and custom. This is a traumatic history, and one that ideally would be explored by Indigenous researchers working with Indigenous communities. And yet to leave Aboriginal mothers out of my study entirely would further marginalise and silence their stories. I chose to raise these issues with Indigenous scholars, curators and health workers, seeking their advice and assistance. Three First Nations mothers took up my invitation to participate in an interview and their stories are explored in the pages that follow.

I sought participants in three case study locations. My previous research into growing up in 1950s Australia found that children's experiences were heavily influenced by the places in which they were raised, due to both the spatial and the social characteristics of those neighbourhoods.[72] Historian Angela Davis's study of motherhood in England over the second half of the twentieth century also concluded that the location in which women mothered affected their experiences of mothering.[73] I ultimately chose an inner-urban, a suburban and a regional location in Victoria in order to explore whether the contrasting physical and social characteristics of these places impacted on experiences of mothering. Fitzroy is a medium-density, urban neighbourhood that borders the Melbourne city centre on the lands of the Wurundjeri people of the Kulin nation. Since 1945, it has gentrified from a socio-economically disadvantaged area while remaining culturally diverse, including a significant urban Aboriginal population.[74] Malvern is a middle-ring, middle-class Melbourne suburb on Wurundjeri country. Since colonisation, it has been largely Anglo-Australian with significant numbers of Italo-Australian and Greek-Australian residents after World War Two.[75] Ocean Grove is a small coastal town 100 km to the west of Melbourne on Waddawurrung country. It has been socio-economically diverse throughout the period studied and after a postwar influx of European migrants has become predominantly Anglo-Australian.[76] Sometimes, I had to go outside the strict boundaries of these areas in order to find certain types of mothers I felt were important to include in my study.

In order to explore how motherhood has changed over time, I decided to focus upon the past seventy-five years of mothering, roughly the bounds of living memory. So this study begins in 1945 – as the end of World War Two ushered in a period of prosperity and peace – and continues to 2019. (As the Black Summer bushfires and COVID-19 pandemic have radically changed experiences of matrescence since late 2019, I have chosen to exclude these most recent years of Australian mothering. They are instead the focus of new research I am conducting on motherhood in the Anthropocene.) As this research is interested primarily in the experience of becoming a mother, in seeking participants, I focused on the year in which a woman first became a mother rather than her year of birth, following the expanded definition of birth cohort provided by British sociologist Rachel Thomson.[77] Thus, this study encompasses any woman who had her first child in Australia after 1945. In attempting to gain relative parity in the numbers of interviewees from different time periods, I have grouped them into three broad generations. Postwar mothers refer to those women having children between 1945 and 1969, during a time of economic security, social conservatism and political stability (see Figure 1). Second-wave mothers are those that had their children between 1970 and 1989, when the women's liberation movement challenged gendered notions of work, care and family life. Millennial mothers are those having children from 1990 to 2019, as medical and communications technologies revolutionised experiences of mothering and neoliberalism transformed expectations around work and care. Where opportunities existed to interview mothers and daughters, I seized the opportunity to explore the matrilineal inflections of new motherhood, so in some cases intergenerational differences are explored both within families and within socio-historical cohorts.[78]

**Figure 1** Postwar mother with first child, rural Victoria, 1950 (private collection)

I attempted to find equal numbers of women from each case study area and within them, roughly equal numbers from each 'maternal generation'. Within these parameters, I also attempted to maximise the diversity of my sample. I advertised in libraries, recreation facilities, schools, aged care facilities and other community organisations within each area. Primarily, women who responded to such advertisements tended to be from middle-class, English-speaking, tertiary-educated backgrounds. Perhaps these women assumed that their experiences were 'typical' and would interest an historian. Perhaps they simply possessed the linguistic competency, cultural capital and educational training to feel confident in their ability to 'satisfy' or 'impress' an academic. But I discovered that in order to create a truly diverse sample, I needed to deliberately seek out women in different places, which I did by contacting organisations representing women with disabilities, cultural organisations representing different ethnic backgrounds and organisations representing different types of mothers such as lesbian mothers and single mothers by choice. I also sought to expand my sample by snowballing: asking interviewees at the conclusion of our interview whether they knew other mothers who might wish to be involved. But while maintaining my overarching desire to interview as diverse a sample of Australian mothers as possible, I remained very conscious of the ethics of interview participation.[79] When inviting someone to share some of their most personal – and sometimes most painful – memories, it is critical that there is absolutely no pressure in forming the interview relationship. I was careful to never place even the slightest encouragement on a potential participant, cognisant of the emotional significance (and sometimes danger) of accepting the invitation to co-create an interview. This sometimes meant that my sample was less diverse than I might have liked. But I am confident that every narrator entered their interview with a consent that was well informed and freely bestowed.

## Maternographies: memories of mothering

The significance of matrescence in a woman's life story means that to invite narrators to reflect on becoming a mother is to seek permission to enter one of the most personal recesses of the self. I was aware of this when I started the research, but I became much more conscious of the profundity of my research invitation as I began interviewing mothers. Some became visibly distressed as they discussed difficult topics such as pregnancy loss, relationship breakdown or deceased parents. I began to wonder and worry about the impact of the interviews upon participants. Through a process of active reflection, I developed three strategies for safeguarding against causing harm to an interviewee when inviting them to share experiences that matter deeply to them.[80] One was to follow up with interviewees who experienced difficult emotions, to make explicit my care and concern for them and to ensure that interviews were not causing harm. Another was to conduct a self-interview, where I asked another oral historian to interview me about my matrescence. This experience illuminated the interview relationship from the other side of the microphone and allowed me to experience the sometimes vulnerable position of narrator. I have made a conscious ethical decision to render myself as vulnerable as my narrators by using quotes from my maternography throughout this book. It also served the epistemological purpose of helping me to surface and interrogate half-conscious assumptions that underpinned my research.[81] Thirdly, I sought to make clear to narrators that their interview was contributing a wider social purpose: that by sharing their personal maternography, they were contributing to my project of diversifying and complicating our collective cultural understanding of becoming a mother.

As we began creating oral histories together, I would listen with one ear to what an individual woman was telling me and with the other to what her narrative revealed of the broader history of mothering. Kathryn Anderson and Dana Jack asserted that when interviewing women, interviewers need to 'listen in stereo' to what the woman is explicitly stating as well as the feminist subtext of her words, which may be muted by patriarchal social expectations.[82] While this was an important caution in the late twentieth century, more recently, oral historian Lynn Abrams has argued that the normalisation of expressive modes, gender equality and a confessional culture have made it easier for women to tell emancipatory, feminist narratives of their lives. She calls these liberated narratives 'feminographies'.[83] Within a feminography, women produce 'self-realising and self-validating narratives in terms of lives lived and choices made as well as the frameworks for telling'. Following Abrams, in this book and elsewhere, I argue for the critical importance of *maternographies* in developing a historical understanding of mothering. Maternographies I define as narratives of mothering constructed after and influenced by second-wave feminism. They are explicitly created in opposition to the view that mothering 'is not all that interesting' or 'has not really changed much', instead foregrounding and prioritising narratives of mothering.[84]

Multiple understandings of time surfaced within these maternographies, influencing the shape and tone of memories. In their interviews about work and care with four generations across twelve UK families during the twentieth century, sociologists Julia Brannen, Peter Moss and Ann Mooney similarly discovered that temporality featured in many complex, and sometimes contradictory, ways.[85] 'Time present' referred to the moment in which the interview was conducted, which oral historians sometimes refer to as 'the time of the telling'. Personal experiences and cultural discourses in the present inevitably influence the way that the past is remembered, sometimes as an explicit point of comparison and sometimes as the normative framework against which the past is implicitly evaluated, such as when women contrasted working mothers of the twenty-first century with stay-at-home mothers of the 1950s. 'Life course time' denotes the phase that the interviewee currently occupies in their life cycle. Women who had recently become grandmothers found that their memories of early motherhood were reignited by that experience. 'Generational time' is the term Brannen et al. use to refer to cohorts of different generations born into similar socio-historical periods, acknowledging that individual memories are often shaped by collective experiences such as economic depression, warfare or public health crises. Many postwar mothers found that family life was influenced by the aftermath of World War Two, just as the everyday experiences of mothers today have been transformed by the COVID-19 pandemic. In addition to the temporal categories identified by Brannen et al., Stone examines the related category of 'maternal time':

> the mother replays her maternal past ... primarily at an affective, bodily and habitual level, by re-enacting patterns of behaviour and affective response that once circulated between herself and her own mother. These modes of maternal remembering generate a particular

form of lived time – maternal time – that is cyclical, centring on the regular reappearance of an archaic past that cuts across time, as a linear succession of moments. However ... the mother's past repeats itself with a difference. Because that past is reenacted between the mother and her child, the past is re-created in a new shape, adapted to the unique individual that the child in each case is. This ensures that the mother can only remember her maternal past in the light of this novel present, a present that bestows upon the past new meanings that it did not originally have. The maternal past returns, but never simply as it was.[86]

All of these meanings of time influenced the content and form of the multi-layered maternographies created for this research, but in this book, I will focus particularly on maternal time and generational time, exploring in each thematic chapter the narrative continuities of maternal time alongside the contextual dynamism of generational time.

Other layers of meaning and analysis are also present. There is always a tension between collective and individual modes of remembering in an interview, as there is between person narratives and cultural discourses. British sociologist Tina Miller has productively explored this nexus, analysing the subtle interplay between maternal experiences and cultural constructs, or how women 'make sense of motherhood' in relation to cultural scripts.[87] Early oral history studies emphasised the power of individual narratives to rupture dominant historical understandings, but theorisations of collective memory have also revealed the ways in which a person's life story is framed in reference to the society to which they belong. British oral historian Penny Summerfield's elaboration of composure explains that an individual usually seeks composure during the interview, both in terms of composing a life story that has internal coherence and in terms of ensuring that their personal story does not contradict our dominant collective memory of the era. This can be particularly problematic for women because public narratives of femininity are often complex.[88] One of the contributions of this research to oral history is in revealing the ways in which personal narratives are influenced by collective memory, while always containing the possibility for contradictory stories to break through.[89]

Rather than interpreting women's stories as inescapably controlled by cultural discourses, I contend it is important for feminist historians to take women's stories seriously, including their interpretations of their own lives. In particular, the deeply embodied nature of mothering provides a basis for a visceral, emotional and corporeal experience that has the potential to explode cultural constructs of what motherhood 'should' be. I have argued previously that experiences connected to strong feelings, sensory experiences or valued social relationships tend to adhere more firmly in memory.[90] Mothering incorporates all of these, in the intense emotions a mother feels about her new role, the corporeal interactions of birthing, feeding and holding, and the unprecedented type of relationship that develops between mother and child. For all of these reasons, memories of mothering achieve a special luminosity in the mind. As a distinct form of oral history narrative, I argue that maternographies require a specific methodology and conceptual framework for their creation and interpretation.

While the profundity of the experience of matrescence lends maternal memories a distinctive psychic resonance, it also poses a significant epistemological challenge. Mothering can be hard to describe adequately and therefore to remember accurately. Psychosocial researchers Wendy Hollway and Lisa Baraitser both contend that mothering is at least partially ineffable. Hollway contends that 'the identity change involved when women become mothers is perhaps the most inaccessible to language'.[91] For Baraitser, 'the maternal remains haunted by her link with the impossibility of knowing, and hence remains somewhat unspeakable'.[92] How, then, can a researcher begin to comprehend an experience as complex, as multi-layered and as indefinable as matrescence? To approach the difficult task of 'knowing mothers', both Hollway and Baraitser draw upon an interdisciplinary suite of theories and methodologies that may broadly be termed 'psychosocial'.[93] In attempting to approach maternality and matrescence, while recognising that becoming a mother is an experience that resists easy summation or simple characterisation, I have drawn upon psychosocial studies and extended its parameters historically.

I thus call my conceptual framework for this study a 'temporal-psychosocial' approach.[94] Psychosocial studies invite simultaneous consideration of the social frameworks and individual psychologies of human lives. In studying mothers, this might mean analysing cultural discourses, health services, legal protections and government policies alongside the personal, emotional and relational experiences of mothers. This research explores such social and psychological factors within a shifting temporal context of historical change. This multifaceted methodology and interpretive framework seek to slowly unfold the intricate experience of matrescence one layer at a time. As the book unfurls, each chapter will examine psychological, cultural and historical change and continuity in relation to a specific theme.

## Outline of chapters

Rather than approach this subject matter chronologically, the structure of this book follows a woman's journey into matrescence, from conception through pregnancy, birth, childrearing, shifting relationships, changing paid and unpaid work, through to the self-transformation effected by mothering. While historical studies often tend to adopt a chronological structure and emphasise change, this thematic structure instead mimics the personal transition of becoming a mother, allowing recognition of its distinctive continuities. Within each chapter, the narratives' continuities of 'maternal time' will be analysed alongside the socio-historical dynamism of 'generational time', revealing the ways in which matrescence is always both stable and shifting across locations and time periods.

Chapter 2 explores how Australian experiences of pregnancy have been impacted by wider historical changes including the ways in which birth control, sex education and ART have allowed women greater control over conception; rising surveillance of and moral discourse surrounding both maternal and foetal wellbeing; and the increasing specificity and commercialisation of maternal and infant material culture. Stories of gestation are analysed, revealing themes of conception, preparation, suffering, generation, anticipation and transition. The chapter argues that matrescence begins with gestation, that pregnancy can be understood as an apprenticeship for motherhood.

Chapter 3 identifies historical shifts in cultural discourses and health practices surrounding childbirth. While in the immediate postwar era, Australian women often experienced birth as a hospitalised, medicalised and disempowering experience, the maternity reform movement of the 1970s sought to empower birthing women with greater knowledge and control. Yet despite having access to a diversity of birth support options and childbirth education, contemporary women still report high rates of dissatisfaction, distress and sometimes trauma, while rates of medical intervention continue to rise. Close examination of birthing memories reveals consistent patterns: these narratives suggest that birth is a peak, unparalleled experience that is extraordinarily difficult to capture in words or memory. Furthermore, early motherhood is significantly impacted by the birth experience.

Chapter 4 follows these mothers through their experiences of early mothering. As health advice about infant feeding has shifted, Australian mothers have received differing levels of support and encouragement of bottle feeding and breastfeeding. Once considered a matter of maternal instinct and transmitted informally via family and friends, childrearing is increasingly seen as the province of experts. Sources of parental advice have multiplied amidst the growing popularisation of psychology, leaving mothers increasingly confused about which recommendations to follow. While cultural discourses idealise immediate bonding and a maternal devotion of limitless patience, mothers report more complex and ambivalent feelings towards their children and their new role, including anxiety, exhaustion, resentment and a passionate love that exceeds all previous bounds.

Chapter 5 considers the support available to new mothers in Australia from partners, family, social networks and community organisations since the mid-twentieth century. Postwar mothers often assumed primary, indeed almost total, responsibility for raising their children. Changing cultural values relating to gender, work and care have meant that increasingly, women enter maternality expecting to share the burden of childcare with partners, family or paid care workers. Nevertheless, many heterosexual couples are shocked by the persistent regression to a gendered division of labour between homemaking mother and breadwinning father. Attention to these maternographies reveals that matrescence consistently transforms the close relationships of the new mother, particularly matrilineal connections to her own mother. While available supports have risen over the past seventy-five years, new mothers continue to feel inadequately supported through the momentous changes of matrescence.

Chapter 6 examines changes in the balance of Australian mothers' paid and unpaid work in relation to shifting gender expectations, economic structures, government policies and personal ambitions. It considers the extent to which women have wished to engage in work outside of mothering and whether they have felt supported or constrained in following their desires. Drawing upon Ruddick's conceptualisation of 'maternal thinking', it considers whether mothers take distinctive skills back into the paid workforce. Analysis of maternal narratives reveals a dramatic shift across this seventy-five-year period. While postwar mothers felt judged by their contemporaries if they chose to engage in paid work, millennial mothers experience social disapprobation if they wish to mother their children full-time. Cultural ideals surrounding motherhood may have shifted, but moral condemnation of their choices remains constant.

Chapter 7 confronts the central question of the book: to what extent does a woman feel that her self-identity changes when she becomes a mother? While psychologists understand 'the birth of the mother' as signifying a shift to a maternal identity and anthropologists view matrescence as a significant rite of passage, an historical lens suggests that the level of personal transformation experienced by Australian women has amplified as the age of entering motherhood has increased and as motherhood has become understood culturally as a choice rather than a compulsory expectation. This chapter also considers the identification of perinatal depression and anxiety as a medical condition, asking whether the individual pathologisation of maternal distress disguises what is more helpfully understood as a failure of social supports, and obscures the fact that matrescence is always and inevitably experienced as a challenging and transformative experience.

In closing, the Epilogue connects the past to the present and future, arguing that maternographies are critical to understanding the ways in which memories of mothering shape personal experiences of and social debates relating to mothers today. Policy issues concerning mothers and families are at the heart of contemporary society: what kinds of antenatal and postnatal health services best support new mothers; what kinds of parental leave, childcare subsidies and family tax systems enable contemporary mothers to combine work and care; and what combination of partner, family, community and government supports are required to cushion new mothers against perinatal depression and anxiety. In looking to the future of mothering, I suggest that we will continue to see rising numbers of women choosing not to mother, as well as an increasing diversification of family forms and parenting styles. I also discern the early emergence of a distinctive new generational experience of maternality – motherhood in the Anthropocene – in which environmental factors exert a profound influence upon the raising of children. But even in looking to the future, the past is always close by. Remembered experiences of mothering continue to exert an influence upon the present, which is why the history of mothers remains relevant, compelling and essential in the twenty-first century.

## Notes

1. All narrators except the author are referred to by pseudonyms. All interviews are in the possession of the author. Where consent is granted by narrators, interview materials are also preserved in Museums Victoria's collections.
2. Renata Kokanović, Paula A. Michaels, and Kate Johnston-Ataata, eds., *Paths to Parenthood: Emotions on the Journey through Pregnancy, Childbirth, and Early Parenting* (New York and London: Palgrave Macmillan, 2018).
3. Marilyn Lake, 'State Socialism for Australian Mothers: Andrew Fisher's Radical Maternalism in Its International and Local Contexts', *Labour History: A Journal of Labour and Social History* 102 (2012): 55–70.
4. Catherine Kevin, 'Maternal Responsibility and Traceable Loss: Medicine and Miscarriage in Twentieth-Century Australia', *Women's History Review* 26, no. 6 (2017): 840–56; Desley Deacon, 'Taylorism in the Home: The Medical Profession, the Infant Welfare Movement and the Deskilling of Women', *Journal of Sociology* 21, no. 2 (1985): 161–73.
5. Anne Maree Payne, *Stolen Motherhood: Aboriginal Mothers and Child Removal in the Stolen Generations Era* (Lanham, Maryland: Lexington Books, 2021).

6 John Murphy and Belinda Probert, '"Anything for the House": Recollections of Post-War Suburban Dreaming', *Australian Historical Studies* 36, no. 124 (2004): 274–93.
7 Betty Friedan, *The Feminine Mystique* (New York: W.W. Norton, 1963); Carla Pascoe, *Spaces Imagined, Places Remembered: Childhood in 1950s Australia* (Newcastle upon Tyne: Cambridge Scholars Publishing, 2011).
8 Carla Pascoe, 'The Bleeding Obvious: Menstrual Ideologies and Technologies in Australia, 1940–1970', *Lilith: A Feminist History Journal* 20 (2014): 76–92; Carla Pascoe, 'A "Discreet Dance": Technologies of Menstrual Management in Australian Public Toilets during the Twentieth Century', *Women's History Review* 24, no. 2 (2015): 234–51.
9 Ann Game and Rosemary Pringle, 'Sexuality and the Suburban Dream', *Australian and New Zealand Journal of Sociology* 15, no. 2 (1979): 4–15.
10 Human Rights and Equal Opportunity Commission, *Bringing Them Home: Report of the National Inquiry into the Separation of Aboriginal and Torres Strait Islander Children from Their Families* (Sydney: HREOC, 1997), https://humanrights.gov.au/our-work/bringing-them-home-report-1997
11 Rebecca Jennings, '"The Most Radical, Most Exciting and Most Challenging Role of My Life": Lesbian Motherhood in Australia 1945–1990', in *Australian Mothering: Historical and Sociological Perspectives*, eds. Carla Pascoe Leahy and Petra Bueskens (London: Palgrave Macmillan, 2020), 179–200.
12 Some Australian laws previously restricted ART to women in married or heterosexual de facto relationships. Legal challenges in South Australia and Victoria overturned these restrictions as contrary to the Sex Discrimination Act 1984 (Cth). However, a state or territory may remove ART from their anti-discrimination laws, which the Northern Territory has done: Sonia Allan, 'Access to Assisted Reproduction', Health Law Central website, www.healthlawcentral.com/assistedreproduction/access/.
13 Ruth Pearce, 'If a Man Gives Birth, He's the Father – The Experiences of Trans Parents', *The Conversation*, 26 September 2019: https://theconversation.com/if-a-man-gives-birth-hes-the-father-the-experiences-of-trans-parents-124207.
14 Renate Klein, *Surrogacy: A Human Rights Violation* (North Geelong, Vic.: Spinifex Press, 2017).
15 Australian Bureau of Statistics (ABS), Australian Historical Statistics, Cat. No. 3105.0.65.001 (2008); ABS, Births, Australia, Cat. No.

3301.0 (2012). See https://aifs.gov.au/facts-and-figures/births-in-australia.
16 Lixia Qu, *Australian Families Then and Now: Having Children* (Australian Institute of Family Studies, 2020), https://aifs.gov.au/publications/having-children#footnote-001-backlink.
17 Lixia Qu, *Australian Families Then and Now*.
18 ABS, *Births, Australia*, Cat. no. 3301.0 (2000). See www.abs.gov.au/AUSSTATS/abs@.nsf/bb8db737e2af84b8ca2571780015701e/1e8c8e4887c33955ca2570ec000a9fe5.
19 Carla Pascoe, 'Mum's the Word: Advice to Australian Mothers since 1945', *Journal of Family Studies* 21, no. 3 (2015): 218–34.
20 Isobelle Barrett Meyering, *Feminism and the Making of a Child Rights Revolution, 1969–1979* (Carlton, Vic.: Melbourne University Press, 2022); Isobelle Barrett Meyering, 'Liberating Children: The Australian Women's Liberation Movement and Children's Rights in the 1970s', *Lilith: A Feminist History Journal* 19 (2013): 60–74.
21 Sharon Hays, *The Cultural Contradictions of Motherhood* (New Haven, CT: Yale University Press, 1996).
22 ABS, Australian Social Trends December 2011, Cat. no. 4102.0 (2011), www.abs.gov.au/socialtrends; Australian Department of Education, Skills and Employment, 'A Statistical Snapshot of Women in the Australian Workforce', www.employment.gov.au/newsroom/statistical-snapshot-women-australian-workforce.
23 Lyn Craig, *Contemporary Motherhood: The Impact of Children on Adult Time* (London and New York: Routledge, 2007).
24 Emma Walsh, 'Fathers and Parental Leave', Australian Institute of Family Studies 2018 Conference, https://aifs.gov.au/aifs-conference/fathers-and-parental-leave.
25 Australian Human Rights Commission, *Supporting Working Parents: Pregnancy and Return to Work National Review* (Sydney: AHRC, 2014).
26 Sigmund Freud, 'Female Sexuality', trans. Joan Riviere, reprinted from *International Journal of Psychoanalysis* xiii (1932), 281. See also Petra Bueskens, 'Introduction', in *Mothering & Psychoanalysis: Clinical, Sociological and Feminist Perspectives*, ed. Petra Bueskens (Bradford, Canada: Demeter Press, 2014), 1–72.
27 Seth Koven and Sonya Michel, eds., *Mothers of a New World: Maternalist Politics and the Origins of Welfare States* (New York and London: Routledge, 1993); Marian van der Klein et al., eds., *Maternalism Reconsidered: Motherhood, Welfare and Social Policy in the Twentieth Century* (New York and Oxford: Berghahn Books, 2012).

28 Bueskens, 'Introduction'.
29 John Bowlby, *Maternal Care and Mental Health* (Geneva: World Health Organization, 1951). See also Angela Davis, *Modern Motherhood: Women and Family in England, 1945–2000* (Manchester: Manchester University Press, 2012), 122–8.
30 D. W. Winnicott, *The Child, the Family, and the Outside World* (Harmondsworth: Penguin, 1973); D. W. Winnicott, 'Ego Distortion in Terms of True and False Self', in *The Maturational Process and the Facilitating Environment: Studies in the Theory of Emotional Development* (New York: International Universities Press, 1965), 140–52.
31 Benjamin Spock, *Common Sense Book of Baby and Child Care* (New York: Duell, Sloan and Pearce, 1946).
32 Bueskens, 'Introduction'.
33 Tanya Evans, 'Secrets and Lies: The Radical Potential of Family History', *History Workshop Journal* 71 (2011): 49–73.
34 Anne Curthoys and John Docker, *Is History Fiction?* (Randwick, NSW: University of NSW Press, 2009).
35 Anna Davin, 'Imperialism and Motherhood', *History Workshop Journal* 5 (1978): 9–65; Shulamith Firestone, *The Dialectic of Sex: The Case for Feminist Revolution* (New York: Morrow, 1970); Kate Millett, *Sexual Politics* (New York: Doubleday, 1970); Gerda Lerner, *The Creation of Patriarchy* (New York: Oxford University Press, 1986); Anne Summers, *Damned Whores and God's Police: The Colonization of Women in Australia* (Ringwood, Vic.: Allen Lane, 1975); Miriam Dixson, *The Real Matilda: Woman and Identity in Australia 1788 to 1975* (Ringwood, Vic.: Penguin, 1976).
36 Joanna Bornat and Hanna Diamond, 'Women's History and Oral History: Developments and Debates', *Women's History Review* 16, no. 1 (2007): 19–39; Carla Pascoe Leahy, 'Public Histories and Private Struggles: The Place of Janet McCalman's Struggletown in Australian Historiography', *History Australia* 16, no. 4 (2019): 656–73.
37 Catherine Kevin, 'Maternity and Freedom: Australian Feminist Encounters with the Reproductive Body', *Australian Feminist Studies* 20, no. 46 (2005): 3–15.
38 Simone de Beauvoir, *The Second Sex* (New York: Alfred A. Knopf, 1953).
39 Friedan, *The Feminine Mystique*.
40 Firestone, *The Dialectic of Sex*.
41 Ann Snitow, 'Feminism and Motherhood: An American Reading', *Feminist Review* 40 (1992): 32–51.

42 Adrienne Rich, *Of Woman Born: Motherhood as Experience and Institution* (New York: Norton, 1976).
43 Ann Oakley, *From Here to Maternity* (Harmondsworth: Penguin, 1981).
44 Betsy Wearing, *The Ideology of Motherhood: A Study of Sydney Suburban Mothers* (Sydney: Allen & Unwin, 1984); Jan Harper and Lyn Richards, *Mothers and Working Mothers*, 2nd ed (Ringwood, Vic.: Penguin, 1986). This thread within Australian sociology was later continued by Stephanie Brown et al., *Missing Voices: The Experience of Motherhood* (Melbourne: Oxford University Press, 1994); Susan Goodwin and Kate Huppatz, eds, *The Good Mother: Contemporary Motherhoods in Australia* (Sydney: Sydney University Press, 2010).
45 Nancy Chodorow, *The Reproduction of Mothering: Psychoanalysis and the Sociology of Gender* (Berkeley: University of California Press, 1978).
46 Sara Ruddick, *Maternal Thinking: Toward a Politics of Peace* (Boston: Beacon Press, 1989).
47 Moira Gatens, *Imaginary Bodies: Ethics, Power and Corporeality* (London and New York: Routledge, 1996); Elizabeth Grosz, *Sexual Subversions: Three French Feminists* (Sydney: Allen & Unwin, 1989); Elizabeth Grosz, *Volatile Bodies: Toward a Corporeal Feminism* (Bloomington: Indiana University Press, 1994); Roslyn Diprose, *The Bodies of Women: Ethics, Embodiment, Sexual Difference* (London and New York: Routledge, 1994).
48 Audre Lorde, *Sister Outsider: Essays and Speeches* (Freedom, CA: Crossing Press, 1984); bell hooks, *Feminist Theory: From Margin to Center*. (London and New York: Routledge, 2015); Patricia Hill Collins, 'The Meaning of Motherhood in Black Culture and Black Mother–Daughter Relationships', in *Double Stitch: Black Women Write About Mothers and Daughters*, ed. Patricia Bell-Scott (Boston: Beacon Press, 1991); Alice Walker, *In Search of Our Mothers' Gardens: Womanist Prose* (New York: Harcourt Brace Jovanovich, 1984). Australian Indigenous scholar Aileen Moreton Robinson later added her voice to such critiques: *Talkin' Up to the White Woman: Indigenous Women and Feminism* (St Lucia, Qld: University of Queensland Press, 2000).
49 See, for example, Joan W. Scott, 'Gender: A Useful Category of Historical Analysis', *American Historical Review* 91, no. 5 (1986): 1053–75; Gayle S. Rubin, 'Thinking Sex: Notes for a Radical Theory of the Politics of Sexuality', in *Pleasure and Danger: Exploring Female Sexuality*, ed. Carole S. Vance (London: Pandora, 1992), 267–93.

50 Joan W. Scott, 'The Evidence of Experience', *Critical Inquiry* 17, no. 4 (1991): 773–97.
51 Sarah Knott, 'Theorizing and Historicizing Mothering's Many Labours', *Past and Present* Supplement 15 (2020): 1–26.
52 Natasha Campo, *From Superwomen to Domestic Goddesses: The Rise and Fall of Feminism* (Bern: Peter Lang, 2009).
53 Chila Bulbeck, *Living Feminism: The Impact of the Women's Movement on Three Generations of Australian Women* (Cambridge: Cambridge University Press, 1997).
54 Andrea O'Reilly, *Matricentric Feminism: Theory, Activism, and Practice* (Bradford, Canada: Demeter Press, 2016).
55 Petra Bueskens, *Modern Motherhood and Women's Dual Identities: Rewriting the Sexual Contract* (London and New York: Routledge, 2018).
56 Anne Manne, *Motherhood: How Should We Care for Our Children?* (Crows Nest, NSW: Allen & Unwin, 2005), 258–9. See also Kathy Pitt, 'Being a New Capitalist Mother', *Discourse and Society* 13, no. 2 (2002): 251–67; Julie Stephens, 'Beyond Binaries in Motherhood Research', *Family Matters* 69 (2004): 89; Ruth Quiney, 'Confessions of a New Capitalist Mother: Twenty-First Century Writing on Motherhood as Trauma', *Women: A Cultural Review* 18, no. 1 (2007): 19–40.
57 Julie Stephens, *Confronting Postmaternal Thinking: Feminism, Memory and Care* (New York: Columbia University Press, 2011).
58 Daphne de Marneffe, *Maternal Desire: On Children, Love, and the Inner Life* (New York: Little, Brown and Company, 2004).
59 Daniel N. Stern, *The Motherhood Constellation: A Unified View of Parent–Infant Psychotherapy* (New York: Basic Books, 1995); Daniel Stern and Nadia Bruschweiler-Stern, *The Birth of a Mother: How Motherhood Changes You Forever* (London: Bloomsbury, 1998).
60 Rozsika Parker, *Torn in Two: The Experience of Maternal Ambivalence*, 2nd ed. (London: Virago, 2005).
61 Lisa Baraitser, *Maternal Encounters: The Ethics of Interruption* (London and New York: Routledge, 2009).
62 Alison Stone, *Feminism, Psychoanalysis, and Maternal Subjectivity* (New York and London: Routledge, 2012); Joan Raphael-Leff, *Pregnancy – The Inside Story* (London: Sheldon Press, 1993); Rosemary H. Balsam, 'The Mother within the Mother', *Psychoanalytic Quarterly* LXIX (2000): 465–92.
63 Rachel Thomson et al., *Making Modern Mothers* (Bristol: Policy Press, 2011); Wendy Hollway, *Knowing Mothers: Researching Maternal Identity Change* (London: Palgrave Macmillan, 2015).

64 Davis, *Modern Motherhood*; Sarah Knott, *Mother: An Unconventional History* (London: Penguin, 2020); Rebecca Jo Plant, *Mom: The Transformation of Motherhood in Modern America* (Chicago: University of Chicago Press, 2010).
65 Dana Raphael, 'Matresence, Becoming a Mother, a "New/Old" Rite de Passage', in *Being Female: Reproduction, Power and Change*, ed. Dana Raphael (Paris: Mouton, 1975), 65–72; Stern and Bruschweiler-Stern, *The Birth of a Mother*; Stern, *The Motherhood Constellation*; Tina Miller, *Making Sense of Motherhood: A Narrative Approach* (Cambridge: Cambridge University Press, 2005); Thomson et al., *Making Modern Mothers*.
66 Bornat and Diamond, 'Women's History and Oral History'.
67 Alistair Thomson, 'Indexing and Interpreting Emotion: Joy and Shame in Oral History', *Oral History Australia Journal* 41 (2019): 1–11.
68 Carla Pascoe Leahy, 'Selection and Sampling Methodologies in Oral Histories of Mothering, Parenting and Family', *Oral History* 47, no. 1 (2019): 105–16.
69 In taking this approach, I followed the methodology utilised by the Australian Generations Oral History Project in constructing a sample of 300 interviewees. See Alistair Thomson, 'Australian Generations? Memory, Oral History and Generational Identity in Postwar Australia', *Australian Historical Studies* 47, no. 1 (2016): 41–57.
70 Carla Pascoe Leahy and Petra Bueskens, 'Contextualising Australian Mothering and Motherhood', in *Australian Mothering: Historical and Sociological Perspectives*, eds. Carla Pascoe Leahy and Petra Bueskens (London: Palgrave Macmillan, 2020), 3–20.
71 I have avoided gender-neutral language such as 'parent', 'chestfeeding' or 'pregnant person' because this is historically anachronistic terminology and these are not the terms that my narrators identify with or choose to describe themselves.
72 Pascoe, *Spaces Imagined*.
73 Davis, *Modern Motherhood*.
74 Cutten History Committee of the Fitzroy History Society, *Fitzroy: Melbourne's First Suburb* (South Yarra, Vic: Hyland House, 1989).
75 Lynne Strahan, *Private and Public Memory: A History of the City of Malvern* (North Melbourne, Vic.: Hargreen, 1989).
76 Gil McKeown, *The Grove That Grew* (Ocean Grove, Vic.: Paxton Press, 1983).
77 Rachel Thomson, 'Generational Research: Between Historical and Sociological Imaginations', *International Journal of Social Research Methodology* 17, no. 2 (2014): 147–56.

78 For more details, see Carla Pascoe Leahy, 'The Mother Within: Intergenerational Influences upon Australian Matrescence since 1945', *Past and Present*, Supplement 15 (2020), 263–94.
79 Carla Pascoe Leahy, 'The Afterlife of Interviews: Explicit Ethics and Subtle Ethics in Sensitive or Distressing Qualitative Research', *Qualitative Research* 22, no. 5 (2022): 777–94.
80 Pascoe Leahy, 'The Afterlife of Interviews'.
81 Ashley Barnwell, Carla Pascoe Leahy, Signe Ravn and Sarah Rood, 'How to Put Yourself in the Story', *Narrative Now* podcast, 30 April 2021, https://blogs.unimelb.edu.au/narrative-network/2021/04/30/episode-three-how-to-put-yourself-in-the-story/.
82 Kathryn Anderson and Dana C. Jack, 'Learning to Listen: Interview Techniques and Analyses', in *Women's Words: The Feminist Practice of Oral History*, eds. Sherna Berger Gluck and Daphne Patai (London: Routledge, 1991), 11–26.
83 Lynn Abrams, 'Heroes of Their Own Life Stories: Narrating the Female Self in the Feminist Age', *Cultural and Social History* 16, no. 2 (2019): 205–24.
84 Carla Pascoe Leahy, 'From the Little Wife to the Supermom? Maternographies of Feminism and Mothering in Australia since 1945', *Feminist Studies* 45, no. 1 (2019): 100–28.
85 Julia Brannen, Peter Moss and Ann Mooney, *Working and Caring over the Twentieth Century: Change and Continuity in Four Generation Families* (Basingstoke: Palgrave Macmillan, 2004), 210–12: 3–4.
86 Stone, *Feminism, Psychoanalysis, and Maternal Subjectivity*, 8–9.
87 Miller, *Making Sense of Motherhood*.
88 Penny Summerfield, 'Culture and Composure: Creating Narratives of the Gendered Self in Oral History Interviews', *Cultural and Social History* 1, no. 1 (2004): 65–93.
89 Anna Green, 'Individual Remembering and "Collective Memory": Theoretical Presuppositions and Contemporary Debates', *Oral History* 32, no. 2 (2004): 35–44; Julie Stephens, 'Our Remembered Selves: Oral History and Feminist Memory', *Oral History* 38, no. 1 (2010): 81–90.
90 Carla Pascoe, 'City as Space, City as Place: Sources and the Urban Historian', *History Australia* 7, no. 2 (2010): 30.1–30.18.
91 Hollway, *Knowing Mothers*.
92 Baraitser, *Maternal Encounters*.
93 Others have attempted to gesture towards the inexpressibility of mothering through creative writing, music and art. See, for example: Ceridwen Dovey and Eliza Bell, *Mothertongues* (Southbank, Vic.: Hamish Hamilton, 2022).
94 Pascoe Leahy, 'The Mother Within'.

# 2

# Mother-in-waiting: pregnancy

I remember when I found out that I was pregnant: I was laughing and crying simultaneously, and maybe that's the best metaphor I could use for motherhood, possibly, that it's both so profound that you want to bawl, because it's connecting you to your mother and your grandmother and your entire family, and you know, your brother and his children. And it doesn't matter how many times people get pregnant, it's a miracle. It's a miracle that somehow, this little sperm found this little egg and there's an actual human being growing inside you. It's just – it's stupid that it can happen ... Maybe I was also crying because, you know, I was really worried that I would never have a chance to be pregnant. I don't know, maybe everyone has that fear, on some level ... I think there was relief in there ...

The other thing that I noticed really early ... [was] a sense of vulnerability. On the one hand, the thing about wanting to surf as long as possible was, I'm still independent, I still own my body, I can still do the things that are important to me, I won't be downtrodden by all these pregnancy risk narratives. Yet I felt, you know, acutely, profoundly protective of the new life inside me ... It was one of those lightbulb moments, where I realised that I felt – my fear around my physical body was different ... To realise that you could feel vulnerable about someone else, that was both you and not you, that was just – it kind of hit me, like the way that a wave of cold water will slap you in the face. I just felt really, really vulnerable.

Carla Pascoe Leahy

## Introduction

Pregnancy transforms a woman on almost every level. Most obviously, there is a physical metamorphosis. The woman's body temperature rises, her menstrual cycle ceases, her abdomen slowly expands, her chest broadens, her feet swell, her hair ceases to fall out, her nipples broaden and darken, her skin pigmentation changes and she may experience nausea, exhaustion, heartburn, varicose veins, bleeding gums and haemorrhoids. Some aspects of this physiological transformation are biological and inevitable, standing largely outside shifting cultural views of gender and reproduction. But the ways in which biological aspects of pregnancy manifest are influenced by culture, such as the fact that a rising age of first pregnancy makes it harder for the body to adjust to these changes and heightens medical risks for older primigravidae.

The metamorphosis of pregnancy is more than simply physical, however. The mother-to-be is also affected emotionally by gestation, as are the people around her. She feels the kindling of new life inside her as a kind of miracle, both commonplace and extraordinary. The rational scientific explanation of sperm meets egg seems insufficient to contain the enormity of the fact that a unique human being is forming inside her. For the first time in her life, she is not one but two. She holds another life inside her, which is of her and yet not of her. This sense of what philosopher Iris Marion Young calls 'a splitting subject' is psychologically challenging for the pregnant woman.[1] While the growing foetus is dependent upon the nurturing environment of the mother's womb and subject to the nourishment that she puts inside her body, it is not simply a part of her as her internal organs are. This person-to-be is developing a consciousness separate to hers and will one day enter the world as a separate physical entity. But for now, the woman experiences the terror of having another life form completely dependent upon her. It is a heavy weight of responsibility that grows as her womb swells.

Not all women are conscious of these potent, existential swirlings of emotion inside themselves. But they do begin to notice the ways that other people view and treat them differently. For the pregnant woman's family, if present, her parents are transported emotionally to their own experiences of becoming parents, and the urgent waiting of gestation. Their daughter may symbolically carry their own wishes for the future in the body of the grandchild within her. The woman's partner, if present, will begin to see her as a maternal being as well as a sexual being, as a mother to their child and not only a partner to them. Friends may feel affinity, envy or incomprehension: either way, they know that their friendship is beginning to change. Work colleagues may begin emotionally and professionally de-investing in the woman on the assumption that her psychological world will soon centre on something far more primal and potent than the salary and status of paid employment. The metamorphosis of pregnancy is an all-encompassing transformation. It is a rite of passage from girl to woman, from daughter to mother, from individual to dyad – which is why societies develop rituals to contain the symbolic disruption caused by this terrifying change.[2]

A woman's experiences of first-time pregnancy are influenced by her physiological symptoms, her emotional responses, her significant relationships, her material circumstances and the cultural understandings of pregnancy in which her personal experience is embedded. This chapter will consider experiences of pregnancy since the mid-twentieth century. We will firstly analyse the compelling continuities that characterise women's remembered stories of pregnancy. Several themes persistently surface in memories of gestation: stories of conception, of preparation, of anticipation, of generation, of loss and of transition. We will then examine the extensive medical, technological, legal and cultural changes that have altered the context in which women experience pregnancy. Although a woman is only officially a mother when her child is born, I will argue that these narratives demonstrate that the enormous personal changes of matrescence begin in pregnancy, if not before.

## Maternal time

While the context within which women conceive has changed significantly, there are remarkable continuities in their storied gestations across the past seventy-five years. This section will explore the recurrent themes that surface within maternographies of gestation. In many respects, stories of matrescence begin prior to conception, and are influenced by whether a woman always wanted to have children and her ideas about what maternality encompasses.[3] Narratives also carry the inflections of whether a woman 'falls' pregnant accidentally or conceives deliberately, and how long it takes her to conceive; whether there were years of longing, suffering and disappointment preceding conception.

## Preparation

Most narrators avoided the topic of conception and its role in beginning the journey of matrescence (though Connie and Patsy below are notable exceptions). Many had either forgotten the details of their first child's conception or were embarrassed to share them with me, given the sexual implications of conception. In interviews that were lengthy, candid and wide ranging, it was one of the few moments when many narrators faltered, their eyes silently wondering whether I was asking them for details of the sexual act that often precedes conception.

But women do tell stories of the rituals of preparing for a baby's arrival. These may include buying, making or lending baby clothes, furniture and other paraphernalia. These preparation activities also encompass packing a hospital bag, preparing a nursery and reading about or attending classes in childbirth education. Although the nature of infant and maternal material culture has changed, the essential meaning of these activities has not. They allow the mother-to-be to rehearse her maternality by fantasising about life with a baby. These rituals are a kind of psychic preparation for motherhood.

Lucy was Swedish-born and had her first child in 1997 in Ocean Grove. Her preparation was quite clearly about fantasising about her new maternal existence.

> I probably could have given birth at twenty weeks and the room would have been sorted. Painted. Clothes washed. Ironed. Folded. Very, very organised. I'm a super-organised person anyway, but yeah. I had everything. Everything was ready to go – my bag was packed; I had all the little jumpsuits; I had absolutely everything ... Couldn't wait to do a nursery and all that sort of thing. But yeah,

> I could remember being very, very organised. I used to go in there and think, 'Oh, hurry up ... I want to dress you in that' [laughing].

Lucy recalled her impatience to skip the interminable waiting of pregnancy – that liminal period where a woman is aware that a monumental shift is just around the corner, but she is powerless to control the timing of the process. There are very few events in life that are so charged with significance but over which we exercise so little control, except for birth and death.

Yet psychologist Daniel Stern argues that the unbearable waiting of pregnancy plays a vital psychological role as emotional preparation for motherhood. The nine months, or forty weeks, of gestation give the woman an opportunity to work through – both consciously and unconsciously – the unprecedented changes that await her. Stern theorises that this may be why mothers of premature babies can have difficulty adjusting to maternity.[4] Anglo-Australian Tessa had her first child in 2013 while living in Ocean Grove. When her baby was born prematurely at twenty-eight weeks' gestation, Tessa felt disappointment that the premature birth robbed her of the ceremonies that would have psychologically and culturally signalled her transition into motherhood.

> All of a sudden, I went from being pregnant to not being pregnant ... I never even looked pregnant ... I had a maternity bra from about week four but then my breasts never got any bigger than that. I never had to have maternity clothes. I could just wear all my normal clothes. So we don't have any of those bump pictures ... Nothing to ever suggest that I had been pregnant. Then she was so little that, yeah, she was weird. That whole process was just very odd ... We never had a baby shower ... I didn't want presents or anything like that. I just wanted to celebrate that whole process, you know, because I was so much older ... I felt like I never actually got to have any of that rite of passage thing ... We didn't have the antenatal classes ... It's funny the sort of things you look at them and just think, 'Oh, I wouldn't have had that' ... We didn't get to feel that, you know, really strong, you know, kicking and moving ... So we kind of missed those things.

Women like Tessa have not only been robbed of the cultural rituals of preparation. They have also been robbed of a full emotional gestation, giving them less time to prepare for the monumental affective changes of matrescence. Stern also suggests that for adoptive mothers, the period of waiting for a child to adopt is experienced as akin to pregnancy, in that the woman has time to emotionally prepare for her new role.[5]

Narrators who had experienced accidental pregnancies seemed to have greater difficulty adjusting emotionally to their impending motherhood, and this was reflected in avoidance of preparation rituals and lifestyle changes. Irish-Australian Caitlyn did not want to have children when she fell pregnant inadvertently in 1990. When I asked what she thought about motherhood while she was pregnant, she responded:

> I was probably scared and I was in denial ... I didn't give it a lot of thought. I worked, you know, long hours as well as commuting and then I was involved with the local netball club ... Given that I was probably in denial, I think I didn't give it much thought at all.

Caitlyn at least felt comfortable in her stable relationship with her partner. By contrast, when Dutch-Australian Katherine became pregnant accidentally in 1993, she was not intending to commence a long-term relationship with the baby's father. Her ambivalence about the pregnancy manifested in a refusal to prepare for the baby's arrival.

> I did have a very weird kind of resistance ... when I actually was about to become a mother, I completely like rebelled against the idea. Like, for instance, I didn't do any preparation. You know how people buy all this stuff and do up the nursery, I did nothing. I was in complete denial and then I remember having this dream where the baby was born and I had nothing for it and I woke up in this kind of hyperventilating anxiety attack thinking, holy shit, I've done nothing for this baby, and I was probably about maybe eight months pregnant. Miraculously, my mother turned up that day with a bassinet and a baby bath, completely full of little jumpsuits and socks and singlets and everything that I needed, that her neighbour had given her ... and it was just like, oh my God, I can relax. I shoved it all under the bed and did not look at it again until the baby was born.

As well as demonstrating her 'rebellion' against the idea of maternality, Katherine's story also demonstrates the networks of exchange, gifting and lending that flourish among mothers, grandmothers and pregnant women. In some ways, the transfer of baby care items indicates a kind of unspoken maternal peer support, a way of offering support and understanding from one mother to another, and a subconscious resistance of the commercialisation of one of the most intimate and potent rites of passage in a woman's life. Katherine's story also hints at the dark, nocturnal power of dreams. Pregnant women often have intense, vivid and more frequent dreams, a hint of the deep internal processing of profound emotions that goes on at a largely unconscious level.

## Suffering

Some women narrate memories of 'easy' or non-problematic pregnancies, remembering that they felt wonderful or 'glowing'. But a majority of narrators told stories of suffering. Sometimes, there was a measure of pride in their ability to survive the ordeal of gestation to birth a healthy child. Sometimes, there was a hint of anger, that the reality of their experience of pregnancy was so different from the cultural stereotype of the 'glowing' pregnant woman. These stories take a literary form similar to epic quest stories such as Homer's *Odyssey*, where a hero proves their worth through struggle and trials.[6] In symbolic terms, it is as though this transition passage requires suffering to enable the new maternal self to emerge.

Unlike Katherine, Anglo-Australian Heather was in a long-term relationship when she and her wife deliberately decided to become pregnant in 2012 (via artificial insemination). She found her first pregnancy unexpectedly challenging; she expected the experience to be much more special and enjoyable. But she felt supported by her colleagues in the arts sector who were brutally honest about the challenges of gestation.

> They would always refer to it like 'How is the alien?' they'd say to you, and 'how is this like foreign object growing inside you?' ... They all had these kind of stories of like it's hideous and being really honest about it ... Even though I was quite shocked that this was so horrible, I just wanted to be over, I felt supported by them. There wasn't anything you couldn't say to them about feeling shit or whatever.

German-Australian Alison also told a vivid tale of gestational suffering. But she gave her story of suffering a moral purpose through the narrative logic of her maternography. Alison explained that it took nearly three years for her to become pregnant in the

# Mother-in-waiting

early 2000s while, around her, other women seemed to conceive with ease.

> I was extraordinarily resentful of people around me that would fall pregnant. At that time, a lot of my friends were having babies too ... It was ... really hard. I was just jealous of people, you know, I just didn't want to see pregnant people and I didn't want to hear about pregnant people.

But Alison used her maternography to give meaning to what would otherwise be a meaningless and painful delay to motherhood. In her narrative, that longed-for first conception in 2004 became a necessary precondition to a difficult pregnancy, birth and early motherhood.

> There was never a reason [for their infertility issues]. So I have my own theory on it. My nanna always said ... she thought one day I would have twins. My theory is that ... having twins straight up was going to be pretty full on and so I better have *really, really, really* wanted them, and I *really, really, really* wanted them. So having a pregnancy that was really uncomfortable and I was tremendously sick for, and a birth that was not great, and then just sort of managing twins and I ... never complained once. Just surrendered to it all ... I vomited every day for nine months, including labouring. I had stretch marks so severe up to my ... boobs that they bled; it was like a tiger ... I had size 26 undies ... and they didn't fit because ... my belly was so big. I was so uncomfortable. I couldn't keep any food down. I only put on 13 kilos for a whole pregnancy and for a twin pregnancy that was quite, you know, remarkable; just because I just kept vomiting. I had blood noses. I had bleeding gums ... It was disgusting ... I just couldn't eat, couldn't sleep. I just didn't care. I just went with it [emphasis in original].

Alison's lengthy catalogue of pregnancy symptoms denotes a challenging gestation, as do her vivid descriptions of looking 'like a tiger' because of bleeding stretch marks. She also admits that emotionally she felt like 'a mess', filled with resentment and envy when other women around her conceived and she could not. As well as offering a 'reason' for the psychological and physical suffering that predated motherhood for her, Alison's maternography hints at the darker emotions that underlie pregnancy: the jealousy, frustration and resentment of women thwarted in their desire for maternality.[7]

## Generation

Stern also writes of the ways in which a woman's connections to her family change when she is becoming a mother for the first time.[8] During pregnancy, a woman becomes the 'generational pivot' between the past and the future.[9] She feels the weight of the past, and the influence of family stories of pregnancy, birth and mothering. She may feel the burden of providing a longed-for grandchild to her parents. But she may also feel more connected to her family, as her place within intra-family dynamics begins to shift. Often this link is felt most powerfully through the matrilineal line.

Petronela's story of conception in 2017 was deeply embedded within matrilineal associations as she discovered that she was pregnant while she had returned to Poland to be with her dying grandmother (her primary carer during childhood). Petronela had literally returned to her mother country and mother tongue to be with her grandmother when she found she was going to be a mother herself, and in a symbolic closing of the circle, was at the hospital in which she was born.

> It was such a surreal and beautiful experience to be there at my grandmother's deathbed while she was still, I guess, technically alive but not really, not at all conscious and within me was this little life that was, I guess, alive technically but also not conscious and it was kind of like slipping in and out of lives, it made me just really realise there is no black and white, no definitive start and stop to life. There's just this kind of spectrum of life and it was just kind of really beautiful to think that maybe there was – as one soul is kind of passing off into whatever else there's another little soul just budding here within me and so I guess I allowed myself to think that maybe there's just something of my beloved grandmother's life coming through in this new life that I'm bringing into the world and that gave me a lot of comfort in those times and even now, now I've got this beautiful little child here in my lap, I just really think of my grandmother a lot when I'm with my daughter.

Many women report that their relationship with their mother changes as they begin to enter maternity.[10] Having only ever viewed their mother from the position of a child, as they approach motherhood themselves, they begin to appreciate what it feels like to be in the maternal position. For some, this results in a greater feeling of closeness to their mother. They may also become aware, consciously or unconsciously, that their feelings about pregnancy, birth and motherhood are influenced by stories that have circulated in their own family. Their own mothers' remembered and recounted experiences are often the most potent, but also influential are the stories of other siblings and relatives.

Grief and yearning can provide powerful matrilineal connections. For Justine, the experience of losing a baby at twenty-one weeks was a devasting first experience of pregnancy. It also linked her to her deceased mother who had given birth to a full-term, stillborn child in the early 1960s and reawakened Justine's impossible desire to be able to talk to her mother about this experience. When Justine fell pregnant for the first time in 1994, she was thirty years old, living in Malvern and working long hours in advertising. Her maternography is filled with half-articulated questions about why she lost her first pregnancy to miscarriage.

> For a first pregnancy, that was extremely traumatic for me ... Of course my mother had lost her first baby but full term ... I have all these questions that I can't get answered ... My father answered some of them. But it's not the same, like, I don't think he remembered as much as he could have remembered ... But of course those things are going through your head, well, I wonder and what happened to her? ... She'd always talked about it. That's what I mean by seeing things through childish eyes because you – as a child you go, 'Oh okay, Mum had a baby before us but, you know, it didn't live'. It's just – that's it and you don't question the whys and wheres.

Justine's maternography poignantly summarises the shift in matrilineal connections that comes with matrescence. As a child relating to her mother-as-nurturer, Justine never thought to question the details of how and why her sibling was stillborn. But as a mother-to-be relating to the maternal within her own mother, she found there were many questions she yearned to have answered, not least the inexpressible question of how her mother felt and how she dealt with that heartbreaking loss.

## Loss

Loss and grief permeate many of the remembered pregnancies related by narrators. The immensely complex and painful topics of miscarriage and stillbirth deserve a book of their own. Yet it is important to acknowledge that threads of loss permeate many of the maternographies created for this research, and often colour memories of pregnancies that resulted in live births. These stories remain raw and powerful for the women remembering them even after many years, partly because of the intensity with which women emotionally invested in the foetuses quickening in their wombs, but also because these stories so often remain subterranean. Many women told me they would only reveal previous miscarriages to friends and family after they had reached a viable stage with a subsequent pregnancy, as though they did not want to jeopardise the new pregnancy. Possibly, the pain of the former loss was too great to put into words until they felt secure that their next baby would live. The history of pregnancies lost thus remains a hidden history shadowing the more visible history of pregnancies realised.[11] Yet even when a foetus is 'lost' through miscarriage, they have often started to gain personhood in the mind of the pregnant woman[12] and thus she had started the journey of mothering. If matrescence begins with conception, perhaps part of the pain of pregnancy loss is that the mother-in-waiting has experienced a partial, interrupted maternality that has not been fully realised.

Raised in rural Victoria in a Catholic, Anglo-Australian family, Brenda trained as a nurse and midwife before she fell pregnant for the first time in 1977. She told me how her painful experience of miscarriage revealed to her some of the failings of the antenatal health system.

> My first pregnancy was a miscarriage, which was a really big turning point in my life ... I was absolutely devastated to experience a miscarriage and was just so sad. But the hospital treated me with absolutely no respect, and my obstetrician – who I thought was God almighty – was really non-caring, and cold, and unpleasant. And so I had to go to hospital and have a curette, and as I stayed in hospital ... I don't even think I stayed overnight – but my experience there with the staff was just so awful, and I realised that at such a crucial, emotional time, that nobody cared about me.

As we shall see in the next chapter, Brenda describes her traumatic experience of miscarriage as a necessary precondition to her exultant experience of home birth, by forcing her to look for childbirth options outside her medical training.

# Mother-in-waiting

Brenda's experience of an uncaring health system in the 1970s was to some extent echoed by Justine's experience in the 1990s. As she fought back her tears, Justine described her naivety about both the physical process of miscarriage and the ways it would affect her emotionally.

> I didn't realise I was going to go through labour ... The birthing part is easy because the baby's so tiny. But the labouring is the same because your body ... thinks it's delivering a full-term baby. So it's doing the same amount of preparation. Then, of course, your milk comes in afterwards ... I think if it was your second or your third, you'd know more about what to expect. But because I'd never experienced birth, it was obviously quite a traumatic thing for me to experience ... I remember we had an eightieth birthday – it was probably only a few days later ... It was the first thing I think we sort of went to, and ... I can remember what I was wearing now all these years later. Because, of course, my milk came in and just, like, leaked on this beautiful outfit ... I wasn't prepared for that. I had no idea about breast pads or, you know, any of the normal mothering things ... If you'd had a close aunt or a mother close by saying, 'Oh, you better be prepared for this', but I wasn't. There was no one. You're just alone. No one telling you those silly little things.

Justine remembers that her doctor was very supportive throughout the process, but she was disappointed in the hospital she attended, which placed her in a maternity ward to recover: 'you could hear little babies crying and you saw other mothers with their babies'. She felt well cared for by some close female friends, but was also aware of a deep yearning to be with her mother, who, she fantasised, would have been able to provide her with the practical information and emotional support that she longed for.

## Anticipation

Part of the reason that experiences of pregnancy loss are so devastating is that women experience these losses as dashed expectations: of the baby they imagined in their womb and the mother they imagined they would be. Anticipation is in some senses the over-riding emotional timbre of pregnancy, as the woman waits expectantly, poised between the childless and seemingly autonomous existence she has always known and the encumbered, intertwined existence that she faintly intuits is ahead of her. Two formidable events loom in the gestating woman's immediate future: childbirth and mothering. Redolent with multiple cultural significances, primigravidae simultaneously look forward to and fear these potent events that they have never before experienced.

Anticipation of birth is something that affects all women, for the event of bringing life into the world is steeped in potent symbolism but also shrouded in mystery. In speaking of how she anticipated her first labour in 2017, Petronela wondered if a fear of birth (tokophobia) develops long before the first pangs are felt, because many women only hear negative stories.

> This is the thing that people talk about probably the most and that people fear the most ... It's fascinating that as the experience of childbirth becomes less and less risky, the more we fear it. I think firstly labour again begins in the mind months before the actual contractions start.

While labour looms large in the minds of first-time pregnant women, once childbirth is over, many women struggle to remember their pre-maternal fear. They do, however, recall their (often unrealistic) expectations of mothering. A form of black humour circulates among mothers: many laughed during their maternographies at how little they understood of what was coming during their first pregnancy.

Sometimes, stories of anticipation are blissful and idyllic. When she was pregnant in 1964, Anglo-Australian Rachel felt aflutter with eagerness for the enjoyment she imagined she would feel in mothering her child, ruefully reflecting on her ignorance of the challenges of mothering. 'I think I was pretty excited about it – I thought it was going to be all good fun, pretty dresses and things like that, taking B [child] out. I didn't realise it was a lot of hard work too.' Before she became a mother in 2012, Anglo-Australian Lily imagined mothering as a kind of contented holiday from the pressures of the workaday world.

> I thought it was just going to be wonderful ... I'd been sort of working full-time for ... nine years ... so I was ready for a break of some sort and I just thought, 'Oh I won't be working full-time. I'll be at home. I'll be able to do so much more'. Like, I'll do so much more around the house and M can just concentrate on his work and I'll just have

... all these lovely ... family times ... I just thought it was just going to be lovely. A bubble.

By contrast, Katherine, who had an unplanned pregnancy in 1993, recalls that she was more in denial of her circumstances than blissfully fantasising about life as a mother. Under the surface, she worried about whether she possessed the 'selflessness' to care for a child, and this anxiety manifested in her dreams.

> I was in complete denial ... Even though I was quite happy to be pregnant, but I still was in denial. The whole idea of being a mother at that stage was just foreign to me ... I don't want to say I was a party girl, but you know, my conception of myself was not that selflessness that being a mother requires.

> *Carla*: Do you remember what you thought motherhood would be like before you were a mum, when you were pregnant?

> *Katherine*: No. I just remember having, yeah, the crazy dreams about an egg that was in the aquarium that cracked open and thinking, 'Oh my God, it's going to drown' ... Virtually no one I knew, apart from one friend ... no one else was having children. Nobody. They were all establishing their careers, and there I was having a baby.

Katherine's sense of disavowal of her pregnancy was perhaps heightened by the fact that she felt out of step with her peers. Her focus was on what they were gaining career-wise, by postponing motherhood, rather than on what she might be gaining by taking a different path.

Welsh-Australian Sybil had her first child (narrator Ariana) in Malvern in 1979. In contrast to the narrators who felt impatient for pregnancy to be over, Sybil recalls, 'Once I realised that I was pregnant, that we were going to have a child, I was so relieved and grateful that it would take nine months'. When I asked whether this implied some apprehension about motherhood, Sybil explained:

> I think before I realised I was having a child, before that sort of really hits you in reality, that it was quite dreamy and perfect. I think once I was pregnant, I realised that life is different. It is different to be at home with your child all the time, not having colleagues around you. So it's the difference from going from a professional situation into a motherhood situation where you haven't ever done it before.

Sybil felt that her pre-pregnant vision of motherhood was a blurred, idealistic image. But during pregnancy, she began to contrast what she imagined would be the solitary, domestic life of mothering, compared to the sociability and competency she enjoyed in her paid employment as a teacher.

Many women also wonder what kind of mother they will be, and this anticipating can be blissful and positive or it can be nervous and fearful, sometimes for the same woman. Anglo-Australian Sophia worried about whether she would be a 'good' mother when she became pregnant in 1997, partially because she felt uncertain about exactly what lay ahead of her.

> You don't know what you don't know. It wasn't that I had specific fears, but it was just like, oh, am I going to be a good mother or not. I can remember my sister reassuring me and saying, 'just stop it – you're going to be fine. But, I remember being nervous about that. You never know until you have a child what that actually entails. Then, of course, leading up to the birth, you're focusing more on the birth process and not thinking at all about what happens after.

Helen grew up in the UK and the US before moving to Australia as an adult. Helen recalled fantasising about life with her baby during her pregnancy in 2012 and noticed that other people began to view and treat her differently. She also observed that although pregnancy was in her recent past (she was only a six-month-old mother when we recorded her maternography), it was hard to clearly remember that period, so overshadowed was it by the enormity of birth and early mothering.

The anticipation and uncertainty of pregnancy perhaps explains why so many intriguing superstitions surround this period. Despite a rising medicalisation of the antenatal period, some aspects of pregnancy seem to resist the certainties of science. Even in the hyper-rational twenty-first century, an almost magical aura seems to surround pregnancy and birth. This hint of the supernatural surfaces in the superstitions and 'old wives' tales' that are offered confidently to the gestating woman. Julia married an Italian-born man in the 1970s, cohabiting with his mother while they raised their three children (the first born in 1978). Julia's tense relationship with her controlling mother-in-law manifested in unsought advice about her unborn baby. 'I had indigestion one day from eating too much … She pulled me aside and she said, "Oh, you know why that is," she said, "it's because the baby's got a lot of hair and ... it's the hair rubbing against you".'

Joanna grew up in England and as an adult moved to Ocean Grove, Australia, with her husband. She had the first of five children in 1973. Although trained in medical science as a nurse, Joanna was convinced that she felt different during her pregnancies depending on the sex of the baby. 'I think carrying male babies really suited me; I felt much more emotional when I was carrying the girls, and I noticed that quite substantially.' Still now, in the twenty-first century, many narrators recall being offered unsolicited predictions while pregnant, even by strangers. These include beliefs that certain food cravings or physical symptoms signal the sex of the foetus or denote the health of the pregnancy.

## Transition

If many memories of pregnancy are shot through with themes of anticipation, some also display themes of transition. Psychologists speak of first pregnancy as a period of emotional preparation for maternity. But not all mothers-to-be are conscious that they have begun to change. Anglo-Australian Molly felt that she began changing during her pregnancy in 2012–13, that motherhood 'started when I saw the two blue lines, really'. She was conscious that her identity had previously centred upon her work and her recreation. By changing the ways that she interacted with paid employment and leisure, pregnancy marked the beginning of matrescence for her.

> Probably because the way I express myself was through going out and enjoying life or being at work. And people, the way they react with you or interact with you changes when you are pregnant, and they physically see you're pregnant. So my sense of self while being pregnant sort of changed – I was much more protective of myself, but also not going out, and sitting at home and doing things. So I had to learn to like my own company to a certain extent, and not feel that alcohol or partying ... was the way to have fun all the time. It's kind of weird to change my ways of having fun.

Molly's reference to other people perceiving or treating her differently while pregnant was mirrored in other accounts. Swiss-born Veronica noticed a dual recognition that occurred with other mothers after she became pregnant in 2007 – a sense that she had joined a club she did not previously know existed: 'It made me feel very different like other mothers, other people on the street being pregnant or being mothers would wink and in a very weird way saying, yes, you're part of the club now. You're respectable or – I don't know what it meant exactly'.

> *Carla*: I know what you mean.
> *Veronica*: You know what I mean?
> *Carla*: I get the same thing. I pass a mother and we're both pushing a pram and we give each other a little knowing smile.

Several twenty-first-century mothers talked about lifestyle changes as the most significant shift they noticed during pregnancy. Having grown up in an era where women could freely socialise, drink and have fun in public – and an era when the impacts of foetal alcohol syndrome were well known[13] – this generation usually gave up partying when they realised they were pregnant. From the moment she realised she was pregnant in 2004, Alison didn't want to go out and socialise with friends, as her focus shifted to her family-in-the-making.

Some women describe feeling more powerful emotions and a keen sensitivity to the world around them during pregnancy. Trudelle Thomas argues that the intense experience of 'two-in-one-ness' that characterises gestation and matrescence can form the basis for an increased sense of connection to the world and associated strengthening of ethical impulses.[14] During her first pregnancy in 1978, Anglo-Australian Julia recalls feeling 'sort of a heightened sense of empathy for people and animals and what not. Occasionally, I'd get a bit teary, probably because of that'. But she also remembers feeling upset that some friends didn't share bad news with her because they felt as a pregnant woman she would 'overreact'.

Anglo-Australian nurse Andrea was conscious that other people began to perceive her differently once they knew she was pregnant in 2010.

> A few of my friends from work were ... happy you're pregnant but you've changed to them forever because you used to be their buddy that you'll go out drinking with ... You know that some friendships are just going to end because the reason that you had the friendships

will no longer be there and that becomes obvious the minute you tell them you're pregnant. The doctors at work ... A few of them had said, 'I can't believe you've done this to me' ... They were almost put off that I was pregnant because I was their little go-to and made their life hugely easy at the hospital and they knew that that will have to change.

When I asked Polish-Australian Petronela if becoming pregnant in 2017 changed her, she reflected that it had shifted her whole definition of womanhood, in ways that felt puzzling and conflicting given her lifelong commitment to feminism.

As someone now with a PhD, as someone who is quite ambitious and career-oriented, as someone who has lived a fairly independent life, travelled around a lot, I've always felt quite fulfilled as an individual and as a woman but I've never felt so much like a woman than I did when I was pregnant ... I just felt so womanly, so wonderfully feminine and so fulfilled. It was incredible and beautiful and also I felt almost slightly guilty as a feminist to say for all my achievements, for all my independence, this biological feature is what makes me feel the most like a woman.

### Generational time

The cultural context in which women in Australia and other industrialised societies experience primigravidae has changed markedly since the mid-twentieth century. The story of how health professionals have interacted with pregnant women is complex and multi-layered, but overall, we can discern a growing medicalisation of the antenatal period from the early twentieth century, as enacted through increasing medical appointments and surveillance of the mother and foetus.[15] Adelaide opened an antenatal clinic in 1910, followed by Sydney and then Melbourne in 1917.[16] In 1912–14, 29 per cent of women giving birth at Sydney's Royal Hospital for Women had attended an antenatal clinic and by 1920–22, 50 per cent of women had received antenatal care.[17] By 1919, the antenatal clinic at the Royal Women's Hospital in Melbourne recorded over 500 attendances a year; by mid-1923, the figure was nearly three thousand.[18]

## Postwar mothers

Women who were pregnant in the 1950s and 1960s recall that they felt intimidated and controlled by medical professionals. Marjorie was born in a British-Jewish family and migrated to Australia in 1949. In recalling her obstetrician during her first pregnancy in 1953, she stated that, 'Dr Lemon was God', vividly remembering the unequal power dynamic between them. Having grown up in a cultural climate in which sexual reproduction was rarely discussed and naked bodies rarely seen, pregnant women in the postwar period felt deeply embarrassed by their physical examinations by medical professionals. This discomfort, coupled with the authority of medical professionals, left them ill-prepared to ask questions or challenge medical decisions. Anglo-Australian Maggie was raised in country Victoria and had her first child in 1966 in Fitzroy. She remembered that at check-ups she was told to:

> lie down on your back, put your heels together, spread your legs out ... It was a bit of a surprise the first time. I don't think I'd really thought what this was going to involve ... You're obedient; you go to a health outfit, you just sort of do what you're told.

While the medical professionals increasingly monitored the health of pregnant bodies, expectant women were offered fewer proscriptions than pregnant women are today. In this respect, the cultural ideal of the good pregnant mother has changed distinctively since the mid-twentieth century. Women who were pregnant in the 1950s and 1960s remember changing relatively little about their diet and lifestyle. The potentially harmful effects of smoking cigarettes or drinking alcohol upon the growing foetus were not yet known.[19] Postwar mothers recall medical advice about ideal weight gain but little else.

Pregnant bodies were subjected to different cultural and aesthetic expectations in the postwar years than they are today: we have broadly witnessed a shift in the visibility of baby bumps from hidden to flaunted. Attempts to obscure the pregnant body in voluminous clothing in 1950s and 1960s Australia were partially a remnant of pre-industrial customs, but also signalled a cultural discomfit with the brazen sexuality of the bump: here, clearly, was a woman who had engaged in sexual intercourse at least once. Although an intensely maternal symbol, the swelling womb also gestures to the intimate sexual act which prefigured it. Postwar maternity clothes were often handmade and not intended to exhibit the growing belly or reflect fashion trends.

The increasing commercialisation and specialisation of maternity clothes mirrors trends in the wider sphere of infant and maternal material culture in the Global North, where objects are used to prepare for the maternal role, to master daily maternal practices and to memorialise or remember motherhood.[20] From the earliest stages of pregnancy – and sometimes before conception – women are inducted into a specialised world of objects.[21] These include maternity clothes, baby clothes, prams, bassinets, cots and baby nappies (reusable or disposable). In the immediate postwar decades, these items were relatively simple. Often, handmade, durable items such as bassinets and christening gowns would be passed down in families as a material form of maternal inheritance.

Maternal material culture can also symbolise a pregnant woman's desire to look attractive or to act the part of mother. Anglo-Australian Patsy fell pregnant as an unmarried young woman in 1967. Patsy's description of her antenatal longing for a bed jacket and slippers perhaps signals an attempt to contain her anxiety about her impending birth, as well as just how unprepared for the brutal realities of birth that she was.

> When I'd go into the city, go to the hospital, I'd go past this shop with ... a pink, frilly bed jacket ... I loved it. It was in the window. I saw it for weeks and weeks, decided I wanted that one ... That's my emotions – I didn't think about the baby, I wanted this jacket ... This is a nineteen-year-old talking and I wanted pink fluffy slippers. I got them as well ... I had planned, when I was coming home from hospital, I was going to wear this pink woollen dress that fitted me and it was big, before I got pregnant.

Patsy then described how she had no childbirth education classes or other forms of preparation for what became quite a traumatic birth.

> I was in a ward where there was lots and lots and lots and lots of beds ... I was bleeding a fair bit, but this lovely bed jacket. I couldn't wait to get it on, it was lovely ... They just shoved a pad between my legs and I got off the bed to go to the toilet, pink fluffy shoes on, as I'm shuffling along ... Big long ward, the toilets were out in another part of the ward. All I could feel was blood dripping out. I looked down as my pink fluffy slippers were all covered in blood. I'm thinking,

'my poor slippers' ... The day I went home I couldn't fit into that bloody pink dress. I had to wear my dressing gown home because it wouldn't fit me – that was devastating as well.

Apart from shifting maternity clothes, another reason that pregnant bodies were less visible in the postwar decades was that women were less likely to be working while pregnant. In the 1950s and 1960s, the expectation was that women – particularly middle-class women – would leave paid employment at marriage or pregnancy. As a teacher, Irish-Australian Jane had to resign once her first pregnancy was announced in 1954. She remembers: 'I was very sad. I missed it very much'.

This experience was not unusual. It was not until 1968 that women were allowed to continue employment in the Australian public service after marriage. Maggie recalled the ways in which her promising career was compromised by her marriage in the early 1960s:

> It did annoy me, but since then I realised it was really a huge put-down. I'd got a promotion against other people in the section, and then got married – had to relinquish that promotion and relinquish my full-time position, and they took me on the next day as a temporary ... I would have lost some salary in that process ... We didn't have much money. So yes, it rankled ... so I stopped work, stayed home.

Such regulations and cultural expectations reflected a widespread view of the pregnant body as inherently vulnerable and less capable.

Postwar women also had less knowledge about and control over their reproductive functions. One of the most significant changes to pregnancy since the mid-twentieth century is the way in which cultural and technological developments have shifted the boundaries of conception. Girls and women in the immediate postwar era were offered little in the way of sex education. They were often frightened at menarche, having never had the menstrual cycle explained to them.[22] The mechanics of sexual intercourse or its relationship to reproduction was usually not clarified before marriage. Musing upon her naivety growing up in the 1940s, Maggie related that she did not realise her mother was pregnant with her sibling until she came home from hospital with a baby.

Patsy's sexual ignorance had more serious consequences for her. Born in 1948 and raised in a Catholic family in Queensland, Patsy was nineteen years of age and working in her first job when she unintentionally became pregnant, following sex with a man who told her he was infertile. Her story of conception and gestation was one of innocence followed by disgrace.

> Once Mum found out I was pregnant, I got packed off to Melbourne to the St Joseph's baby house to have the baby and then – with the plan was I'd adopt it ... When Mum found out, she took me to the doctor, 'Yeah, she's pregnant'. I'm thinking, I've only done it once, how can I be? I can't be pregnant, but hello, I was. Back in those days, because the stigma of it all, 'Oh gosh, my girl is pregnant'. Had to pack me off and send me away.

Patsy positions her first pregnancy within the framework of her youthful naivety, the wilful deception of her sexual partner and her mother's shame. Although her accidental pregnancy was arguably the result of her parents' failure to provide her with a basic sex education and compounded by the dishonesty of the father of the child, as a young, unmarried woman, it was Patsy who bore the social humiliation of their failings. In her young age at primigravida and inability to financially sustain a family without a male partner, Patsy was in some ways typical of her generation. Her lack of knowledge and control underpinned a lack of choice around the circumstances in which she entered motherhood. But Patsy's generation was on the cusp of significant changes. The introduction of the birth control pill in 1961 and the liberalisation of abortion access in the 1970s began to expand women's autonomy over their reproductive bodies.[23]

## Second-wave mothers

In response to critiques of the medicalised nature of antenatal and natal care in the 1950s and 1960s, from the 1970s, maternity care reform advocates attempted to give more knowledge and control to pregnant women.[24] They believed that reliable information about pregnancy and birth should be easily accessible for women and that women's own opinions and preferences should be respected in decisions concerning their bodies. But cultural change was slow.

Like her postwar predecessors, Macedonian-Australian Miroslava recalls feeling embarrassed by her antenatal appointments for her first child in 1975, particularly the fact that they involved a male looking at her body. 'I can remember lying on the bed, you know, with your legs sprawled open and him fiddling around and I was "argh" ... The initial examination I think was the most embarrassing.'

The maternity reform movement gradually began to change the attitudes and practices of some health professionals, in Australia as in North America and the United Kingdom.[25] Such shifts were broadly part of the women's health movement of this era and connected to the wider emancipatory aims of women's liberation. As we shall see in the next chapter, second-wave mothers were much more likely to attend childbirth education classes than expectant women in the postwar era, reflecting an increased respect for a woman's right to understand her pregnancy and birth, and an increased appreciation of the benefits of such knowledge.

From the 1970s, a greater volume of books and other resources were produced to provide women with health advice about their bodies in accessible language. The book *Everywoman* by Dr Derek Llewellyn-Jones in many ways exemplifies the aspirations of the women's health movement and was widely read by Australian women in the 1970s. Llewellyn-Jones was an Australian gynaecologist who was determined to provide women with accurate medical information in accessible language (see Chapter 3 for more on the influence of this book).[26] One of the consequences of this increased circulation of reproductive information was that women and girls gained more knowledge and control of sex and reproduction. From the 1970s, sex education increasingly entered Australian schools and homes, as in North America and the United Kingdom. A heightened comprehension of reproductive biology coupled with a wider variety, availability and affordability of birth control methods began to offer Australian women greater control over whether they become pregnant and the circumstances in which this occurred.

Along with this increased understanding of pregnancy and other reproductive functions came a subtle pressure to do pregnancy 'correctly'. Lebanese-Australian Sally recalls that she stopped drinking alcohol during her first pregnancy in 1978 and tried to eat healthily and sleep well. She consulted a book for advice about healthy diets for expectant women and young children.[27] She recalls obediently following the author's advice, even ingesting a nauseating smoothie each morning:

> Because of my interest in food, I bought this book by Adelle Davis, *Let's Have Healthy Children*, and I used to make this pretty ordinary concoction in the morning. I would vitamise an egg and I mean a full raw egg, shell and all, with lecithin and wheat germ and yoghurt and honey. In the first few months, you put it down dry retching all the way but, you know, it was going to make a healthy baby so I was up for it.

Second-wave mothers, as in other eras, reported mixed emotions concerning their rapidly shifting form. Some felt proud of and eager to display their growing belly or breasts, while others felt challenged by this rapidly changing, out-of-control body, having internalised a lifelong imperative to control and diminish the female form.[28] Looking back on her pregnancy in the 1980s, English-born Valerie contrasted her pregnant body with those on display in the twenty-first century.

> I certainly didn't look like any of these women today. I'm still a big girl and I was a big girl then and my pregnancy seemed to be all the way around me, not like this little front of body. What I don't understand is how women can stay exactly what they look like except with a pot belly like the men have and I never looked like that. Then again, we didn't wear clothes like that did we? I mean we wore maternity clothes so we stepped away from anything that was tight once we were pregnant ... Lovely big dresses, yes. I had specially made – a girlfriend made me two.

Valerie's narrative hints at the ways in which pregnant bodies were less on display in the 1970s and 1980s, resulting in a reduced cultural pressure to perform an exacting visual aesthetic of pregnancy (see Figure 2). Many pregnant women wore handmade maternity clothes or simply wore larger sizes of non-maternal fashion.

In many respects, the 1970s and 1980s were transitional decades between the handmade infant and maternal material culture of the postwar era and the mass-produced objects widely available by the turn of the century. Second-wave mothers like Anglo-Australian Julia gathered a combination of items produced by hand and purchased from shops, combining the sentimentality of handcrafted

Figure 2  Pregnant second-wave mother in maternity clothes, 1978 (private collection)

infant clothing with the convenience of mass-produced items. Julia had her first child in 1978 and had a detailed recall of the material ways in which she carefully prepared for her baby.

> The shopping and ... getting a bassinet ready and everything. We got a lot of hand-me-downs from my husband's aunty. But making clothes; my mother-in-law made some things. I did a lot of knitting ... There were booklets that you would get about layettes for babies ... So many singlets, so many night dresses ... New babies had nighties, little cotton nighties. So my mother-in-law, who was a dressmaker, made those. We made a nice cover for the bassinet ... It was a lot of fun and excitement just getting all the things ready for the birth ... I was so stuck to all the rules, you know, I had the right amount of

nighties, the right amount of bunny rugs and the right amount of everything ... I had my suitcase packed to go to hospital two months before I went, because that's what they said you should do, just in case you went into labour early.

Although Julia's first pregnancy in the late 1970s took place in an era in which many baby clothes were still knitted and sewn by hand, the emotional role of this preparation is constant, as we saw earlier in this chapter. Making and collecting items by 'the rules' allowed Julia to channel her excitement (and probable apprehension) about her new role, to feel that she was exercising some control over a transition that is largely uncontrollable.

Workforce experiences of pregnant women were beginning to shift as a result of both cultural and legislative changes. Julia's experience in the late 1970s was positive, but she told me she knew of 'other women with workplaces where they had to hide the fact that they wanted to have children, or hide the pregnancy for a while, otherwise they'd be dismissed immediately'. The passing of anti-discrimination legislation in the 1980s meant that it became illegal to discriminate against Australian women because of pregnancy, marriage, breastfeeding and similarly gendered issues.[29] Yet women continue to report workplace discrimination on such grounds today, as we shall see.

## Millennial mothers

The maternity reform movement was highly successful in winning greater autonomy and information for the birthing woman. Yet simultaneously, technological developments made it possible to survey the mother and foetus to a much higher degree than previously, and a rising culture of risk aversion within the medical profession supported the use of such technology wherever possible. The period since the 1980s has therefore seen antenatal care increasingly medicalised. Pregnant women are asked to undertake a series of tests and measurements throughout their gestation including ultrasounds, blood tests and urine tests, which test for abnormalities or illness in the mother or foetus. At regular health appointments, their blood pressure, uterus size and foetal heart rate are measured. On the one hand, this increasing antenatal surveillance has reduced infant and maternal mortality and decreased the likelihood of babies being born with severe health issues. But on the other hand, this hyper-medicalisation creates a sense that pregnancy is akin to an illness that must be carefully monitored by health professionals, rather than a sense that gestating a child is a healthy and normal function of a woman's body.[30] Having a baby is quite literally what female biology was designed to do.

Maternity reform advocates have gained a widening of antenatal care options for women including seeing general practice doctors (GPs), obstetricians, midwives and/or doulas. A rising discourse of consumer choice has driven a diversification of birthing and care options, alongside increasing encouragement of childbirth education classes and the formulation of birth plans. In some ways, women have been granted greater autonomy and control over the antenatal period, but the relationship with health professionals remains an unequal one. Many narrators in this project could not explain to me the reasons that antenatal testing is done, nor were they aware that they can exercise choice over whether the testing takes place. Sometimes, they were not aware of the subtle emotional effects of testing until afterwards.

Anglo-Australian Heather saw a private obstetrician in the public system for her antenatal care for her first child in 2012. Her opinion of the impact of continual surveillance changed over time.

> I'd go for check-ups and I was excited every time there was anything to do with the baby, like going for ultrasounds … because of this problem I was having to have ultrasounds every two weeks … At the time … I was excited every time to see the baby and make sure that things were kind of going as well as they could … I felt in the end it was sort of fearmongering in a way … I suppose I felt in retrospect, I felt like it was invasive and unnecessary and nobody was gleaning any new information.

Over the past seventy-five years, advice literature has increased in volume, formats and audience.[31] Millennial mothers report a bombardment of advice and warnings concerning the care of their incubating bodies. British sociologists Rachel Thomson, Mary Jane Kehily, Lucy Hadfield and Sue Sharpe characterise this as the expectation that doctors will monitor the inside of the antenatal body and mothers should take responsibility for the outside.[32] While there remain some mothers-to-be who avoid or ignore antenatal advice, the majority are acutely aware of the myriad ways in which pregnant women are expected to monitor their bodies. In this sense, the pressures of the good mother ideology commence in pregnancy, if not before. Women seeking to conceive are exhorted to change their diet, limit alcohol consumption, reduce stress and take vitamin supplements. 'Good' pregnant women stop smoking and drinking alcohol; avoid eating soft cheeses, gelati, sushi, certain fish and undercooked eggs; exercise a little but not too much; and minimise stress.[33] Anglo-Australian Lily reflected on the ways in which she changed her lifestyle when pregnant in 2012, using the word 'worry' multiple times in a short extract. In addition to excitement, she recalls,

> hoping that I was doing the right things for the baby growing ... Worried about what I was eating. Just whether it was safe enough for the baby. That was probably the main thing and worried about just, you know, squashing the baby or things like that ... I was really worried about being stressed. So I used to get quite stressed with work so I used to think, Oh, I hope this is not affecting the baby ... I took up yoga and I was trying to be a calmer person and then yeah, my husband and I would have arguments at different times so I used to worry about the effect of that on the baby. I probably tried to eat healthier and yeah, I definitely didn't have any alcohol ... I used to run a lot so I stopped running ... And tried to do a lot of walking.

One of the ironies for the twenty-first-century pregnant woman is the amount of anxiety expended in trying to meet rising expectations of 'good' pregnancy – the ways in which the pressure to abide by these strictures creates its own stress.

If pregnant women and their friends or family once made maternity clothes by hand, maternity clothes began to change across the industrialised world from the 1980s and by the late twentieth century, a flourishing maternity fashion industry existed. Women were encouraged to buy specialised bras, underwear and clothing, for a myriad of justifications including the health of the mother and/or foetus, the desire to be fashionable and the imperative to present a still-professional appearance when visibly pregnant at work. New synthetic fabrics and changing cultural attitudes shifted expectations of how pregnant bodies could be displayed. Clothing tightened over the 'baby bump' and the bump itself was increasingly sexualised. Instead of a period in which expectations around weight control and fashionable self-presentation were relaxed, increasingly, the antenatal period has become a time of when attractiveness standards are heightened. Sociologist Meredith Nash has charted the ways in which celebrity photo shoots and social media have influenced these rising expectations of the pregnant body.[34] The bump has been thoroughly commodified and commercialised. Pregnant women purchase expensive ultrasound imaging and ritualise the taking of baby bump photos at regular stages of pregnancy, with both types of images readily circulated to social networks. Magazines encourage women to carefully plan their labour outfit so they can look beautiful and feel comfortable during childbirth. Anglo-Australian Andrea laughed ruefully in reflecting on her decision to buy a special bra in an attempt to present an attractive maternal figure during her first labour in 2010. 'I even bought like a little top to wear as I was in labour and a nice little crop top bra thing. So I did have expectations that I would be quite okay ... Because I thought that would look really good [laughs].' Andrea's dark humour implies that her focus upon her birth outfit was perhaps an unconscious attempt to deflect her anxiety about more significant aspects of labour such as dealing with unprecedented pain and concerns about the health of her baby.

As this maternal material culture has become increasingly commercialised, a dizzying variety of options for each object has multiplied, including pregnancy multivitamins, maternity bras, maternity clothes, prams, bassinets, cots, nappy bags, change tables, breastfeeding chairs, breastfeeding pillows, baby clothes, baby nappies (reusable or disposable), nursery decorations, breast pumps and more. Connected to this diversification of material culture is the rise of speciality stores like Baby Bunting. Entering these stores and attempting to become acquainted with baby care items can feel like a culture shock for an expectant woman. Indeed, psychosocial researcher Lisa Baraitser theorises that mastery of such objects is a critical part of the adoption of a maternal identity.[35] During pregnancy, women are expected to acquaint themselves with maternity clothes and baby paraphernalia, to understand, accumulate and become accustomed to the material culture of mothering.[36]

Anglo-Australian Sophia vividly remembers this phase of her pregnancy in 1997.

> So, we went off to Baby Bunting and Cue and looked at prams and you could get so carried away. Emmaljungas were all the rage. You look at the prams now, which are just like space age compared to mine. But, it was top of the line at the time. We didn't have a nursery, as such. We only had two bedrooms, so the bassinet was going to go in the other bedroom. A friend of ours ... had this beautiful white painted wicker bassinet and she gave that to us. I remember the women who worked on the desk at the obstetrician's and being there for one check-up and ... she was saying you really don't need much. You just need the absolute essentials like a singlet and something for them to wear and nappies. She said you don't have to have these amazing cots ... you can have a draw or a laundry basket and put a towel on it and you'll be fine. That reassured me, because I think there's so much pressure that you've got to have this and you've got to have that, and you can't have that without having something else, and you could end up spending so much money.

Sophia's memory contains a range of competing narratives about material culture: both the pressure to consume commercial items to feel like a well-prepared parent, and the reassurance of more seasoned parents that only a few are essential. The gifting of a second-hand bassinet also encapsulates a continuity underlying the proliferation of commercial baby care items. While the commercialisation of pregnancy and motherhood has undoubtedly escalated since the mid-twentieth century, informal networks still flourish among mothers and mothers-to-be, where items are gifted and exchanged that are handmade, second-hand or family heirlooms. Recalling her first pregnancy in 2013, Torres Strait Islander mother Somi recalled that, 'I got lots of hand-me-downs from friends. With hand-me-downs comes a kind of unspoken invitation around that kind of support that's there'. The purchase or transfer of maternity items is part of the new mother's induction into a common culture of mothering.

Despite the passage of anti-discrimination legislation in the 1980s, women who became mothers at the end of the twentieth century recall that discrimination was still rampant. Dutch-Australian Katherine became pregnant in early 1993, while she was working part-time writing advertising features and aspiring to become a journalist.

> Then I got pregnant just as they had advertised for a cadetship, and I remember going along to the interview and saying, 'I'm sorry, but I'm pregnant', and presuming that therefore I couldn't get a cadetship, and they did not say, 'Of course you can take the job. Doesn't matter that you're pregnant'. They just said, 'Oh. Oh well'. So that was that. So my pregnancy ruined my chances, as I saw it, of getting a cadetship and becoming the journalist that I always wanted to be.

Such attitudes reflect a persistent belief that pregnancy ends a woman's serious engagement in the workforce. This unspoken assumption can come as a shock to twenty-first-century mothers, who have grown up assuming that they can combine mothering with a career. The introduction of firstly unpaid and then paid parental leave in Australia from the 1990s reflects an increasing expectation that women will return to work after having children, albeit in a predominantly part-time capacity. Contemporary mothers assume that they will continue in paid employment, with most following the model chosen by Welsh-Australian Ariana in 2010 of working until thirty-six weeks gestation and then taking one year of maternity leave. However, few fully perceive the practical and attitudinal obstacles to renewed engagement in the workforce after matrescence. Ariana described her pre-maternal expectations as 'blissful ignorance. I don't think I had any idea what was about to happen'. She assumed that,

> I'd just go straight back after I took a year off and then I'd go continue my career and continue to progress in my career. I know climb the corporate ladder sounds cliché but in a way, that's kind of the best way to describe how I was thinking is that I would just continue to progress and move forward in my career as a mum.

She went on to explain how wrong her assumptions were. For many women, pregnancy is their first taste of the differential treatment mothers receive. Some is intended as protective and respectful, such as the inclination to offer seats in public places to pregnant women. Other treatment is more clearly discriminatory, such as assuming that pregnant women will be less competent in the workplace. In the twenty-first century, a persistent assumption that women – as potential childbearers – are less career-focused still influences hiring and promotion decisions.[37]

One of the most significant changes to pregnancy since the mid-twentieth century is the way in which technological developments have shifted the boundaries of conception. A proliferation of birth control options, decriminalised abortion and family planning education and services have expanded women's ability to choose when *not* to have children. Assisted reproductive technology (ART) has extended women's ability to choose when and with whom they have children. Initially available only to married, heterosexual women, ART is now legally available to single and lesbian women as well, resulting in a broadening of the maternal population.[38]

Nevertheless, cultural understandings of appropriate motherhood lag behind what is technologically and legally possible. As opposed to the banality and frequency of accidental pregnancy among heterosexual women, Heather described to me the ways in which falling pregnant for a lesbian woman is necessarily a very deliberate act. Her access to ART in 2011 required counselling to prove her fitness as a potential parent and registering her relationship so both mothers could appear on the child's birth certificate. Even the process of accessing ART or intrauterine insemination felt deeply heteronormative.

> In order to store sperm ... you have to go through this counselling process to do that, to verify that you're fit for parenthood. That was kind of weird and uncomfortable to be honest because I feel like now it's so commonplace for people to sort of seek alternative family structures but at the time when we were doing it ... it was just that little bit less common and Melbourne IVF now have same-sex IVF doctors ... but at the time, they weren't that set up for it and it was a bit awkward ... I do remember at one point they called us and said, 'Just got a question about the storage of Mark's sperm', and we were like, 'Who is Mark?', and this woman is like, 'Your husband'. I'm like, 'Okay there's many things wrong with that. First of all, I don't have a husband, second of all our donor is not called Mark'. So there was a few things like that where it was just like my God, this is so heteronormative.

As a woman in a married, heterosexual relationship, Katerina didn't feel so culturally stigmatised when accessing ART in 2012. But she and her husband found the process physically and emotionally challenging, requiring her to cease work due to side effects while they were trying to conceive.

The rise of ART also hints at and contributes to another major shift in the cultural context within which pregnancy takes place: increasing knowledge of reproductive biology among women in industrialised societies. Connie's maternography speaks to many of these themes. Born in 1971 in Australia to Greek-Australian parents, Connie spent much of her life between the two countries before choosing to become a mother at the age of forty-two.

> It just hit me like a ton of bricks that maybe time was an issue ... Since I had a few relationships that didn't work out and made me unhappy, I didn't want to depend on someone. So, that's what kind of brought me to the idea that it's possible to do alone. I just went to ... the GP to ask about it. They referred me to a fertility specialist. I went ... to ask about how I could get pregnant ... [at] one of the IVF clinics in Melbourne. They looked at my blood results and my age and my situation and told me what were my chances and what I would have to do. They looked really slim. Straight away they said, 'You have a 7 per cent chance of conceiving'. I thought that was quite small. And because I turned forty-three during that process, my chances fell to 5 per cent and I thought that was funny in a month that that could happen.

Connie explained that after trying for two cycles, she became pregnant. Although the failed first cycle was disappointing, she was determined to try again. Connie felt that other people's responses to her decision to become pregnant as a single woman were

> mostly good ... Maybe a couple that were a bit weird ... A few were afraid to ask me about it. Which I wish they would because it's not anything, I didn't feel ashamed or weird. Some people hadn't heard of it ... There was one uncle that responded a bit weird. He was happy that I was doing it, but thought maybe I should keep it a secret and say that the father ran away and I just felt that was ridiculous. That it'd be much worse to know that you'd been abandoned than conceived in this way ... I had people, before that, tell me to go have a one-night stand and get pregnant ... And I thought that was irresponsible, unfair to both the child and the man involved.

Connie's narrative illustrates the broader legal and medical possibilities that now surround conception, as well as a greater cultural acceptance of single mothers. Her later age of first pregnancy also reflects a broad trend in western mothering, as well as enabling the financial independence that was not available to Patsy when she became pregnant while an unwed teenager. Connie came to pregnancy with a greater sense of knowledge and choice than Patsy did fifty years previously. But despite these obvious contrasts, there are also some interesting continuities. Both women attracted the moral condemnation of others around them when they became pregnant outside of a marriage. Both had to bridge the gap between their childhood fantasies of first motherhood and the more complicated realities of matrescence in their lives.

## Conclusion

Becoming pregnant for the first time is an experience that has cultural, physiological and psychological inflections. The many facets of pregnancy explain why the experience has both changed and remained constant over the past seventy-five years: while the cultural and material context of gestation has shifted, some aspects of the emotional and physical transformations of pregnancy are felt by all women. When women remember pregnancy in their maternographies, there are themes that consistently emerge: stories of conception, of preparation, of suffering, of generation, of anticipation and of transition.

Pregnancy is a complex experience for many women, that is perhaps best summed up by two images used by interviewees. Heather told me that being pregnant was like having an alien or a foreign object growing inside you. By contrast, Veronica likened pregnancy to carrying a precious jewel inside your body. In some ways, both images are true simultaneously, creating emotional tumult for the gestating woman. This is a psychologically potent period, as fantasies, denial, dreams, grief, fear, longing, envy, superstition and family inheritances swirl inside the mother-to-be. On top of this, the body is undergoing dramatic physical changes as it grows and prepares to birth a baby – and people surrounding the pregnant woman respond to her changing body and identity.

Pregnancy is often quickly overshadowed by the massive changes that accompany birth and early childrearing. But these narratives suggest that the mothermorphosis begins in pregnancy (if not before, as we discuss in Chapter 7). Pregnancy is partly a preparation for maternality, an apprenticeship for matrescence. On a corporeal, emotional and cultural level, the pregnant woman is truly a 'mother-in-waiting'.

## Notes

1 Iris Marion Young, 'Pregnant Embodiment: Subjectivity and Alienation', in *Throwing Like a Girl and Other Essays in Feminist Philosophy and Social Theory*, ed. Iris Marion Young (Bloomington and Indianapolis: Indiana University Press, 1990), 160–74.
2 For an anthropological discussion of the rituals accompanying different stages of matrescence, including pregnancy, see Raphael, 'Matrescence'.
3 Raphael, 'Matrescence'.
4 Stern and Bruschweiler-Stern, *The Birth of a Mother*.
5 Stern and Bruschweiler-Stern, *The Birth of a Mother*.
6 Joseph Campbell, *The Hero with a Thousand Faces* (Princeton: Princeton University Press, 1949).
7 Leslie Cannold speaks of similar themes in *What, No Baby? Why Women Are Losing the Freedom to Mother and How They Can Get It Back* (Fremantle: Fremantle Press, 2005).
8 Stern and Bruschweiler-Stern, *The Birth of a Mother*.
9 Hollway, *Knowing Mothers*.
10 Pascoe Leahy, 'The Mother Within'.
11 Some aspects of this shadow history are explored in Catherine Kevin, 'Maternal Responsibility and Traceable Loss: Medicine and Miscarriage in Twentieth-Century Australia'; Susannah Thompson, '"I'd Just Like to Die With a Bit of Peace": The Role of Oral History in Reinterpreting Repressed Memories of Stillbirth and Neonatal Death in Australia's Past', *Lilith: A Feminist History Journal* 16 (2007), 120–31.
12 Linda L. Layne, *Motherhood Lost: A Feminist Account of Pregnancy Loss in America* (New York: Routledge, 2003); Linda L. Layne, '"He Was a Real Baby with Real Things": A Material Culture Analysis of Personhood, Parenthood and Pregnancy Loss', *Journal of Material Culture* 5, no. 3 (2000): 321–45.
13 Janet Golden, *Message in a Bottle: The Making of Fetal Alcohol Syndrome* (Cambridge, MA: Harvard University Press, 2006).
14 Trudelle Thomas, 'Becoming a Mother: Matrescence as Spiritual Formation', *Religious Education* 96, no. 1 (2001): 88–105.

15 Catherine Kevin, 'Subjects for Citizenship: Pregnancy and the Australian Nation, 1945–2000', *Hungarian Journal of English and American Studies* 12, no. 1/2 (2006): 131–42; Meredith Nash, *Making 'Postmodern' Mothers: Pregnant Embodiment, Baby Bumps and Body Image* (London: Palgrave Macmillan, 2012).

16 Janet McCalman, *Sex and Suffering: Women's Health and a Women's Hospital* (Melbourne: Melbourne University Press, 1998) 158–9.

17 Catherine Kevin, 'Great Expectations: Episodes in a Political History of Pregnancy in Australia since 1945', in *Feminism and the Body: Interdisciplinary Perspectives*, ed. Catherine Kevin (Newcastle upon Tyne: Cambridge Scholars Publishing, 2009), 49–69.

18 McCalman, *Sex and Suffering*, 159.

19 Foetal Alcohol Syndrome (FAS), for example, was first explicitly recognised in an article in *Lancet* journal in 1973: Erica O'Neil, 'The Discovery of Fetal Alcohol Syndrome', The Embryo Project Encyclopedia, published 9 May 2011, https://embryo.asu.edu/pages/discovery-fetal-alcohol-syndrome.

20 Carla Pascoe Leahy, 'Maternal Heritage: Remembering Mothering and Motherhood through Material Culture', *International Journal of Heritage Studies* 27, no. 10 (2021): 991–1010.

21 Thomson et al., *Making Modern Mothers*, 197–234.

22 Pascoe, 'The Bleeding Obvious'.

23 A legal precedent concerning the legality of abortion was set in Australia in 1969, by the Menhennitt ruling in the Victorian Supreme Court case R v Davidson. Access to abortion was liberalised in Australian states from the 1970s through liberal court rulings and legislative reforms: Barbara Baird, 'Medical Abortion in Australia: A Short History', *Reproductive Health Matters* 23, no. 46 (2015): 169–76.

24 Kerreen Reiger, *Our Bodies, Our Babies: The Forgotten Women's Movement* (Carlton South, Vic.: Melbourne University Press, 2001); Kerreen Reiger, '"Sort of Part of the Women's Movement. But Different": Mothers' Organisations and Australian Feminism', *Women's Studies International Forum* 22, no. 6 (1999): 585–95.

25 Reiger, *Our Bodies, Our Babies*. See also Jill Barnard and Karen Twigg, *Nursing Mums: A History of the Australian Breastfeeding Association 1964–2014* (Malvern, Vic.: Australian Breastfeeding Association, 2014); Virginia Thorley, 'Middle-Class Mothers as Activists for Change: The Australian Breastfeeding Association', in *The 21st Century Motherhood Movement: Mothers Speak Out on Why We Need to Change the World and How to Do It*, ed. Andrea O'Reilly (Toronto: Demeter Press, 2011), 219–32.

26 Derek Llewellyn-Jones, *Everywoman: A Gynaecological Guide for Life* (London: Faber and Faber, 1977).
27 Adelle Davis, *Let's Have Healthy Children* (New York: Harcourt Brace Jovanovich, 1972).
28 Philosopher Susan Bordo has written of the pressures upon women in capitalist, patriarchal cultures to maintain a slender body shape that does not take up space or assert itself as a physical presence: Susan Bordo, *Unbearable Weight: Feminism, Western Culture, and the Body* (Berkeley: University of California Press, 1993).
29 The Sex Discrimination Act 1984 and the Affirmative Action (Equal Opportunity in Employment Act) 1986.
30 Emily Martin, *The Woman in the Body: A Cultural Analysis of Reproduction* (Boston: Beacon Press, 1987).
31 Pascoe, 'Mum's the Word'.
32 Thomson et al., *Making Modern Mothers*.
33 Nash, *Making 'Postmodern' Mothers*, 154–60; 175–76.
34 Nash, *Making 'Postmodern' Mothers*.
35 Baraitser, *Maternal Encounters*, 122–50.
36 Alison J. Clarke, 'Maternity and Materiality: Becoming a Mother in Consumer Culture', in *Consuming Motherhood*, eds. Janelle S. Taylor, Linda L. Layne and Danielle F. Wozniak (New Brunswick: Rutgers University Press, 2004), 55–71.
37 A 2014 survey found that 49 per cent of Australian women experienced workplace discrimination during pregnancy, parental leave or on their return to work: Australian Human Rights Commission, Supporting Working Parents: Pregnancy and Return to Work National Review.
38 See Chapter 1 for a fuller explanation of ART access in Australia.

# 3

# The birth of a mother: labour and childbirth

I think that the stories of birth that we grow up hearing affect our expectations around birth and whether we are scared of it … Particularly because healthcare professionals ask us about our mother's experience of pregnancy and birth and tell us that its relevant … She [mother] described the pain as excruciating … So, I grew up knowing that it was really hard …

It's really hard to prepare yourself for birth, because it's not like any other experience that you have in your life. I think that I probably would have gone in quite naively if it wasn't for the experience of my sister-in-law … Many women that I've spoken to assume that they can trust their healthcare system … that if they go to the appointments that they're supposed to go to, do what the health professionals say to them, then they should have a good birth experience. What they don't realise is that that definition of good is really slippery … Within a hospital system, that means a live mother and a live baby. For some women, those things happen, but their experience is horrible … It just made me realise that if you wanted to have a birth with less intervention, which is what I wanted, you have to actually fight quite hard for that …

Both of my children were born two days after their due date. I remember that, towards the end, it felt like one of the hardest things I'd ever done, because it's like one of the biggest things that will ever happen in your life, and there's only the vaguest sense of time and date set around it. I found the waiting really hard, the uncertainty …

What was amazing about the experience was that G [partner] and I didn't need anyone else. This woman [midwife] could see that, so she just kind of gave us space … For hours, I was squeezing, stamping, making noises and I felt like the biggest challenge was …

my internal dialogue. Not telling myself that I couldn't do it, that was the hardest thing. Not letting that idea come into – well, it was there, but not enunciating it, when I was exhausted ... [Afterwards] I felt very proud of myself and proud of G, and proud that we'd come through that together ... I felt like we'd endured something enormous, and that in a weird way, the intensity of that experience was almost appropriate to the profundity of bringing a new life into the world.

Carla Pascoe Leahy

## Introduction

Apart from our own birth, which we do not remember, and our own death, which we cannot anticipate, no other event in our human lives brings us as close to mortality as childbirth. Both the miracle of new life and the threat of infant or maternal death hang over the event, endowing it with a profundity equalled by few other moments in the life cycle. By blurring the boundaries between the sacred and the profane, birth signals danger in symbolic terms and is thus contained by multiple rituals across different cultures.[1] Across all human societies, birth is one of the most significant rites of passage,[2] representing both a discontinuity and a bridge. The infant is a wholly new person, who changes the shape of all the social groupings around them. For the mother, birth signals the end of pregnancy and the beginning of caring for a child, and she has a new social status alongside a new role and responsibility.[3] Birth is a seismic event; it shakes the foundations of a mother's life, sending ripples across every aspect of her existence.

Yet birth notices tend to sanitise the profundity and violence of this event. A mystique continues to envelop this natural yet miraculous physiological process that humans share with other mammals. Although childbirth is now commonly depicted in television, film and other media, it remains mysterious and dreaded, so that 'labour begins in the mind months before the actual contractions start', as narrator Petronela mused.

How can we begin to approach comprehension of birth? Oakley described it as 'the agony and the ecstasy'. She wondered whether this is an event which defeats words, suggesting that descriptions provide only 'clues, signposts' and statistics provide but a 'partial picture'.[4] Rachelle Chadwick urges attention to the 'fleshy materiality', the corporeality and embodiment, of 'birthing bodies'.[5] Knott provides a series of anecdotes and metaphors distilled into verbs: 'leaning, squatting, straining, callout to lovers or mothers or gods, panting, pulling, pushing'. Paraphrasing poet Sharon Olds, she concludes that 'giving birth is a glistening verb'.[6] Perhaps what is most clear is that birth resists understanding. Our metaphors, based as they are on comparison, fail us when confronted with an unparalleled life event. As Thomson, Kehily, Hadfield and Sharpe conclude, 'as an initiation into motherhood, birth is only partially narrated within the common culture'.[7]

Despite the rise of childbirth education across the industrialised world in the second half of the twentieth century, women continue to report feeling unprepared for labour, that it was not what or how they expected. Many feel disappointed in their birth experience, some even traumatised by it. This chapter explores Australian women's experiences of birth since 1945. Multiple aspects of labour and childbirth have changed over this three-quarters of a century, including where, how and with whom women birth; the degree of choice, information and preparation offered to the birthing woman; and the level of medical interventions and types of technology utilised. Despite this, many narrative themes persist across this period: that women feel unprepared for birth; that they struggle to convey what it feels like; that many feel dissatisfied or violated in its aftermath; and that birth experiences have a profound impact on early motherhood.

## Maternal time

Within the maternographies that we constructed together, childbirth was the narrative climax to many women's storied memories of becoming a mother. It constituted a dramatic peak between their pre-maternal lives and the profound shift of active mothering. Despite considerable changes to the birthing context across the past seventy-five years, thematic continuities persisted as women laboured to make sense of birth. Many of these interview themes from multiple generations of Australian women are similar to those which arose in Oakley's mid-1970s study in the UK. She described: 'The problem of *recognition* – *is* this labour, *is* this a contraction; the clash of *expectations* and *reality* – now I know how it feels, I know how I expected it to feel; the question of *control* – am I doing this myself or are other people doing it to me?'[8]

Throughout the maternographies recorded in this research, women told me that they found birth immensely challenging, that it did not meet their expectations, that they did not feel fully prepared and that they did not feel in control. Women's perceptions of birth were influenced by the personal stories and cultural scripts around them. There was considerable psychic traffic from the outer to the inner experience of birth. Although their recollections of birth were vivid and detailed, women also found it difficult to adequately capture and convey their experiences to others.

### *Feeling unprepared*

One of the most powerful continuities in women's descriptions of birth across different generations is that their experience did not match their expectations. Despite the rise of childbirth education classes, discussed below, women consistently described themselves as unprepared for labour and explain that it did not play out in the manner they anticipated. In her interviews with British women in the 1970s, Oakley similarly found a gulf between expectations and reality: 42 per cent of her narrators said birth was better than they expected and 47 per cent said it was worse than they expected.[9] In an Australian study conducted in 1989, 61 per cent of primiparous women said labour pain was worse or much worse than expected.[10]

When narrators explain that they felt unprepared for the shock of childbirth, this begs the questions: what were their expectations and why were they unrealistic? Mothers told me that their expectations of birth were shaped by cultural discourses circulating in their society, by the information given to them by health professionals and 'experts' and by personal narratives shared by family and friends. Polish-Australian Petronela eloquently summarised the ways in which expectations of birth are constructed within a woman's socio-historical context. For contemporary Australian women like Petronela, who had her first child in 2017, this means that birthing expectations are constrained by a lack of prior personal experience and distorted by limited cultural scripts.

> So obviously it was something that is looming on my mind as I think it looms in the minds of all first-time mums, partly because we just don't have an experience of childbirth prior to actually going through it ourselves unless we're there assisting in the births of our sisters or friends. As children, we don't get to see our mothers giving birth to our younger siblings or anything like that. It's something that we don't have any personal experience of it till I went there. So, I think that's partly why it looms large, and partly because that's all we talk about. It's sensationalised, I think, in some ways, and at the same time, felt sanitised, almost, in terms of the images that we see presented in movies and on TV. So, basically, there's just no realistic images that we are presented with.

As Petronela points out, most women have no direct experience before their first childbirth, and although we now talk about birth and see it depicted in different media, these images of birth remain censored and unrealistic.

While a growth in childbirth education, particularly from the 1970s, has meant more women enter birth with an expectation of what is to come, some narrators felt that this information was not entirely realistic. Anglo-Australian Carol's first child of six was born in 1974. She recalls her anger at a physiotherapist from her childbirth education class who suggested labour is not painful if you breathe properly.

> I've never forgiven her to this day ... They invited you to come to these prenatal classes and she said ... 'You won't experience pain, it's just a level of discomfort'. And when I was in labour, I thought ... I could strangle that woman if I ever met her. That's a terrible thing to do ... You're telling somebody it wasn't really pain, it was just discomfort. If you get your breathing techniques right, that's all it will be and it can be quite a pleasant experience ... I could murder her.

For Carol, the gulf between her expectations and the extraordinary pain she felt during labour generated significant fear, for she wondered whether something was terribly wrong if her labour was hurting so much more than her classes had led her to anticipate.

> It was just excruciating and I – the thing that I really look back on and I feel resentful about was because I'd been misled about this concept of the level of pain, and it was excruciating, I thought – I remember thinking if it is this painful there is something wrong, the baby's not going to survive this ... I do remember at one stage thinking I don't care if we both die, but that was – just let it all finish, and I was horrified later on when I thought back and thought, did I really think that? But I did.

As well as being influenced by cultural representations and expert advice, expectations of birth are also affected by personal stories that circulate within families and among friends. Welsh-Australian Ariana's anticipation for her first birth in 2010 was influenced by her mother, narrator Sybil's, memories of childbirth – though in hindsight, this was not a helpful guide.

> I just expected to copy my mum which was fast, easy, no pain relief, over and done within half an hour, out the door, which is basically what Mum told me her labour was. I don't know whether it was but she believes it was like that. So she said that I came out basically on the freeway and she was holding my head in and that when they arrived at Francis Perry House, they told Dad to go and wash his hands and by the time he walked back in, I was out. So I had this idea that that is how I was going to have my first baby. It did not go that fast and it was not that easy. I actually said to my dad when he walked in ... 'Why didn't you tell me it was horrendous? It was so bad. I was in so much pain', and Dad said, 'No one's telling you. No one is ever going to tell you that' ... I'm going to tell my child that it hurts a lot.

For some women, their sense that they were inaccurately prepared, or even actively misled, leads to a sense of resentment and betrayal. We see hints of this in Ariana's maternography, and it was stated overtly by Swiss-born Veronica in relating the story of her traumatic first birth in 2007.

> First time around, I didn't get all the information I wanted to get. I feel like there's a little bit of a taboo around becoming a mother and delivery. Everyone is so positive and you're so full of hormones that you're very positive yourself. Then you go through labour ... I felt traumatised after delivery ... You go into a room, two people and after ten hours, there's a baby and everyone is happy about that. But no one talks about what happens in that room. I did feel that people had lied to me ... I felt betrayed in a way.

Exacerbating the sense of betrayal that some women feel is that this occurs in a situation in which they felt at their most vulnerable. In fact, the mother is doubly vulnerable for she feels called upon to defend both her own interests and those of her infant.[11] Overcome by extremes of emotional and physical sensation, birthing women speak about the importance of being supported by people they trust during labour. Women feel anxiety as the mysterious event of birth approaches, an event shrouded in cultural silences and mystery. Many try to deal with this anxiety by arming themselves with information – they semi-consciously seek to prepare in order to give them some sense of control over what they dimly perceive may be an uncontrollable experience. Childbirth education materials imply that through digesting information, women can gain agency over the birthing experience. But once they are in labour, many women feel a distressing sensation of being overwhelmed. For some, this was feeling physiologically out of control, with gushing amniotic fluid or uncontrollable bowel movements. For others, this meant emotionally unregulated, in words or emotions. Anglo-Australian Andrea recalls that during her labour in 2010, she could not understand what anyone was saying except for her husband, as though she had lost the power of language. Losing physical or emotional control can be confronting to a modern woman raised to prize composure and rationality. But there is another sense of control which Oakley identifies: 'Am I doing this myself or are other people doing it to me?'[12] Miller suggests that this sense that control of birth is taken over by experts is particularly challenging for women who have experienced agency in the world of work.[13] In anticipating birth, some contemporary women fantasise that pain relief may help them regain control of their birth.

## Inexpressible

There is a persistent thread throughout these maternographies that women did not feel they had been accurately warned about the extremities of childbirth. Partly, this is because birth stories come up against the boundaries of the expressible, in multiple senses. Due to its association with sex, genitalia and extremes of physical and emotional experience, birth is not a topic that falls readily into polite conversation. Public references such as birth announcements generally sanitise the experience. Anglo-Australian Sophia's newspaper announcement of her first birth in the mid-1990s followed a common pattern.

TSANG – CHARLES
To Sophia and Ray a daughter
SARAH CATHERINE
Born March 16, 1997. Both well.[14]

Social media announcements in the twenty-first century echo this expurgated language: 'We are delighted to announce the arrival of our baby daughter Avy at 6:50pm on Wednesday 23 November. Mum and bub both doing well'.[15] These carefully worded, habitually formulaic statements gloss over what is often hours of pain, screaming and blood, obscuring the heroic battle fought by the birthing mother to bring new life into the world. In attempting to respect the privacy of the mother, public announcements can work to erase her accomplishment: that she has travelled to the outer rim of human experience and survived, returning the same yet not the same. Birth is transformative.

Pain is in many ways indescribable – and because it cannot be entirely shared with or wholly comprehended by another, it generates loneliness, disappointment and alienation in the sufferer.[16] People who have suffered immense physical and psychological pain may feel an anxiety that the listener cannot possibly begin to understand what they are trying to communicate.[17] Yet there are commonalities of expression and patterns of meaning in these birth stories if we listen attentively and empathetically. Israeli psychologist Gadi BenEzer identified thirteen possible signs of trauma within a narrative, including silence, loss of emotional control, emotional detachment and repetitive reporting in minute detail.[18] Many of these signs were present within the birth stories shared with me, particularly a level of extraordinary detail – though detailed recall can also accompany an event with personal significance but no traumatic associations.

In sociologist Arthur Frank's germinal work on the 'wounded storyteller', he identifies three narrative patterns among the stories of illness he analyses. In the chaos narrative, he discerns 'the anti-narrative of one thing happening after another without connections that would turn brute sequence into story'.[19] Some of the birth stories related in these maternographies are a form of chaos narrative: there is a happy ending (a live baby), but the birthing women cannot reconcile that positive outcome with the pain and suffering that precede it, with the implication sometimes being that the suffering was not a necessary precondition to the outcome.

When it came time in their maternography to tell their birth story, many women did so in a rush, almost without drawing breath, as though they feared interruption, or they feared their courage would falter if they hesitated. Numerous women had an unusual level of recall about their births, particularly their first birth. There was often an extreme level of detail not present in other parts of their life story. It seemed that the completeness of the story was important to them: they felt that every detail deserved to be told, and in the strict temporal order that it occurred. We relived their often challenging birth experiences together. I have included Anglo-Australian Heather's birth narrative almost in full to demonstrate the detail typical of many birth stories and give a sense of the specific recurring patterns of childbirth narratives. Heather had her first child in 2012. In this extract, she recalls doing everything she thought were the 'right' things to do but still found herself having a birthing experience that felt out of her control after she was induced at thirty-six weeks.

> I'd done acupuncture the week before and all of this kind of stuff … So I'd done all this prep, I'd been drinking the raspberry tea and everything and trying for it to be good. Then when he put the gel on that night, it was a Tuesday night, he said that I was already like 2.5 centimetres dilated … So he felt like it was going to work. So there was a lot of celebration about that. Then they put the monitor on and he was quite tacky and there was some sense of like I'm not sure about this – maybe we need to get him out in caesarean and I'm like 'ugh, okay'. Then it settled down so he decided to admit me instead of going home but L [her partner] wasn't allowed to stay which was where it all fell apart. That was the first trauma. I'm one of those people that just never argues with people – I like to just maintain the peace. So I was like okay, if that's the rules that's the rules, but inside I was beside myself. I didn't want her to go; I felt terrified. I suppose medically she was my support and they were just taking her away. So I just went into total panic mode. She left and then I started having this horrible pain and it just wasn't going away

and in the calm birthing class, they had said contractions kind of come and then they go like waves. I wasn't having that – it was just this one long sustained pain and then I felt like he wasn't moving anymore. So I was on the phone to L and she was like, 'well you have to tell the nurse', and I was like, 'I don't want to bother them'. It was like something stupid at the time. I was like, 'I don't want to bother them, L', and it's like if you have pain you need to tell them. So I got them in and then they couldn't feel the baby so then they took me back down to the birthing suite – called L back. He came at like 3:00 in the morning and broke my waters and it was really nothing much really happened. I was having a few contractions but nothing like much. Then at 9:00 he came and put the drip in, 9:30, the syntocinin drip, and the midwife that I had at that time was really horrible. They put the drip in and literally like it must have been a minute later I vomited and then was on all fours screaming and she said just because you vomited doesn't mean I'm not going to turn the drip up. So she turned the drip up and then I was trying to push at that point and they're like, 'don't push'. Sometimes the baby's head just is like on your – so you feel like it's on your rectum or whatever and it makes you feel like you need to push but don't push, and I was like I don't have a choice. I was saying to L 'I definitely can't do this, I need an epidural', and they were like, 'there's no epidural', and they were like, 'there's no epidural', like they're with twins or something, which I've since heard they say often to people. There's no epidural and L is saying to the midwife you have to check, you have to check her and they're like, we don't want to check her, she's still like hours off, we're not checking her but she can have gas or whatever. So while they were setting that up, L got really angry at them and said you have to check, and he was crowning. So they got me up and the baby was born half an hour later, so the whole birth was like forty-five minutes and very traumatic because I ripped, I had a terrible tear, and the pain – like it came on so fast that there was no time for my body to kind of prep for it and it was just in shock and it was horrible. So yeah, I would say my birth wasn't like a pleasing kind of experience. But it did have all – you know, as soon as it was done it was amazing, I was happy as Larry, but the actual birth itself was – yeah, full on.

There are many disturbing themes in Heather's story that have echoes in other birth narratives shared with me. She speaks of her desire to do the 'right' things to have a 'good' birth (including acupuncture, raspberry tea and calm birth classes) with the implication that none of these seemed to help when she was in labour.

She speaks of the critical importance of a trusted birthing support person to provide emotional support and advocate for the birthing woman (in this case, her wife L, who is also a doctor). And her testimony is evidence of the devastating effect of health professionals who either do not trust the subjective accounts of birthing women or are uncaring in the face of their distress. This is part of the substance of Heather's birth story. But the form in which it is told is also revealing. There is a high level of detail about the actions and words of the key actors in the story – Heather, her partner, the obstetrician, the nurse and the baby – which is related in chronological order. Medical and 'rational' terminology drawing upon pharmacology (gel, syntocinin, epidural) and anatomy (cervix, rectum) is interspersed with subjective and affect-laden language of physical and emotional responses (trauma, panic, vomit, angry, tear, pain, shock). This is a violent clash between two worlds – of medical knowledge and power and the birthing woman's subjective experience – and the power dynamics are clearly not equal. Heather tries to find a moral point to her tale of suffering by pointing to the end result: a healthy baby. But the question of whether her experience could have been more 'pleasing' remains unresolved. Her memory is ultimately, like many other birth stories, an anti-narrative of chaos in which the narrator strives but fails to find an overarching meaning.

There are several possible reasons why birth stories are often different to the other sections of a woman's maternography and feel raw, unrehearsed and untidy. Firstly, many women have not had an opportunity to fully give voice to their experience of birth before. Birth stories push at the limits of what can be comfortably stated in conversation: they are messy, visceral, primal and often involve nudity and bodily fluids. Michelle was born in Mozambique in 1979 to Dutch parents and grew up in regional Australia. She had her first child in 2013 and described her experience as 'violent'. It was a like a crime scene, she recalled, with blood on the walls and in pools on the floor.

> I always knew it was going to be difficult so when it happened it was difficult but it was short and sweet. So I was induced. I was ten days over so they induced me and it happened all of a sudden, like in an hour and a half she was out. But it was because there was no time

for it to stretch and whatnot, I just had lots of rippage. I lost a lot of blood, over a litre of blood. I had drips in my arms and just gas for painkillers. So I had quite a traumatic experience but I think T [partner] was there the whole time and he was just awesome. He was just so relaxed. My mum and dad actually ended up in the surgery as well and Mum was really supportive, warming my feet up and just made the traumatic experience an enjoyable one as well if that makes sense? It was a lot of connection and you've got this child on your chest straight away that's looking up at you and laughing almost, smiling at you. So with that balance, I think it was not something that I would look back on and say that was horrible. I see it as a beautiful moment as well.

Secondly, I think birth narratives exhibit these patterns because of a complex contradiction inherent to the experience of birth. Birth is a peak emotional and physiological experience. Few women will have faced such extremes of emotion before, from the desperate grappling with unprecedented pain, to the despair of feeling that they cannot cope, to the elation of witnessing the child they have created within their body emerge into the world, and the rush of maternal devotion, that unparalleled type of love that a mother feels for her child. Katherine was born in Western Australia in 1965 to Dutch-Australian parents. Although she had doubts about motherhood when she unintentionally became pregnant in 1993, she had a relatively straightforward labour and remembers experiencing transcendent emotions after the birth.

> It was just this amazing thing, like to produce this baby out of your own body. I still think it's the most freaky thing in the world, having done it twice ... It was just like instant love and bonding ... So all my kind of denial just flew out of the window and I just went instantly into mother mode. I was there.

Some women see the so-called 'baby blues', or feeling flat a few days after birth, as a response to the extremes of emotional and physical intensity experienced during childbirth. Michelle described the aftermath of birth as akin to 'coming down' after recreational drug-taking and partying.

> I sort of felt like ... I'd been to a three-day party and I was sort of coming down. So you had your little pill or whatever and you come down and everything becomes – the light becomes more intense and your body's just throbbing but knowing you've had an awesome

three days. So emotionally, I sort of felt like I was on a comedown a little bit but not in a bad way. It was like you know what I've been through some tough times and I've just got to recover now. So emotionally, I was just sort of like, I've had a child, let's enjoy it. But my body was exhausted.

After the exhilaration and intensity of meeting her child for the first time, it is in some ways proportionate to feel despondent in the aftermath. In addition to these intense emotional roller coasters, few women will have felt their body under such pressure before for such an extended period of time, the flesh twisting, contorting and releasing in the struggle to bring what is inner to the outer.

In the maternographies we co-create, I sense that women desperately want to put these peak experiences into words. Yet at some level, the intensity and profundity of this event escape language and cannot be entirely voiced. Oakley asked: 'How can the experience of childbirth be described? Does it defeat words? Or is it twisted by being trapped *within* words so that an event powerfully experienced is reduced to a technical account, a recitation of medical manoeuvres?'[20] Anthropologist Emily Martin analysed the ways in which medical language describing childbirth influences the ways in which women experience and perceive it, unpacking the metaphors of production used to describe the baby as 'product', the woman as 'labourer', the uterus as 'machine' and the doctor/midwife as 'management team'.[21] If the incomparability of birth render it challenging to describe in words, medical metaphors seem to increase women's sense of alienation from and lack of agency over the process of childbirth. For example, Anglo-Australian Tessa scoffed at her medical diagnosis of an 'incompetent cervix' leading to her premature birth in 2013, but she lacked alternative language through which to claim her childbirth experience as her own. The ineffability of birth also makes it difficult for memory to accurately encompass the enormity of the experience. Many women reflect that they cannot perfectly recall the quality and intensity of the pain of childbirth, because it is different to other physical sensations.

## Consequence

While many women feel unprepared, dissatisfied and out of control during birth, these difficult birth experiences are not simply forgotten or rendered unimportant by the arrival of a live, healthy baby. Rather, birth memories remain vivid and influential for months and even years afterwards. Australian health researchers Stephanie Brown, Judith Lumley, Rhonda Small and Jill Astbury found that birth remained significant for women eight months later.[22] They discovered that 'the events and experiences of pregnancy, birth and the early postnatal period have significant associations, both positive and negative, with depression after birth'.[23] Returning to interview participants in her childbirth education classes fifteen to twenty years later, US researcher Penny Simkin discovered that childbirth is etched deep within memory even after many years have passed.[24] Furthermore, the impacts of birth experiences cast long shadows. As we shall see, my interviews with Australian women found that negative birth experiences had a profound effect upon early mothering. Simkin's research also suggests lingering effects upon self-esteem and self-confidence.[25]

Birth is arguably an inherently shocking experience. Oakley found that: 'Birth is a trauma in every sense of the word. Physical lacerations ensue, but the mind and the emotions are wounded as well by the immensity of the physical sensations felt and by their meaning: another human being. "Shock" ... appears over and over again'.[26] Some birth narratives also exhibit patterns of post-traumatic stress disorder (PTSD), though the possibility that birth can cause this kind of trauma has only been recognised in recent decades. While postpartum PTSD was first identified in 1978, widespread acceptance of the condition's existence is still developing. One Australian study found that at four to six weeks after birth, 5.6 per cent of women satisfied PTSD diagnostic criteria, with another 22.6 per cent exhibiting some symptoms. Severe pain and obstetric interventions (especially emergency caesareans) were associated with PTSD.[27]

In the women I have interviewed, some maternographies go beyond the inherently shocking nature of birth and describe postnatal symptoms which sound a lot like PTSD. According to the American Psychiatric Association's Diagnostic and Statistical Manual, symptoms of PTSD include mentally reliving the trauma, feeling a generalised numbness towards the external world and a state of 'hyper-arousal' to particular stimuli, especially those associated with the original trauma.[28] Irish-Australian Caitlyn had the first of three children in 1990. She remembers that she felt 'relieved' when her lengthy and excruciating first labour finally ended, but that it haunted her for long after. Caitlyn had trouble sleeping after the birth and when she was able to sleep, she had recurrent nightmares in the form of flashbacks to her birth. She experienced what she believes was untreated perinatal depression and was reluctant to give birth again.

> It's a bit like the chicken and the egg, isn't it? You know, like, would I have been better if I'd have had an easier birth? Would I have been able to cope with her better? Or did I not cope with her because I had the traumatic birth, you know? It certainly defined our family because I didn't try for another child for another four years. I was petrified. We were both so scared.

Heather, whose long birth story we heard earlier, similarly felt haunted by her birth experience in 2012. The stitches from her tearing became infected and she developed haemorrhoids, which meant that every time she tried to open her bowels, she felt like she was giving birth again, triggering severe panic attacks. Tessa, who spent months watching her premature baby in a humidicrib in 2013, told me that she experiences panic whenever she hears noises similar to the warnings and beeps in the neonatal intensive care unit.

Although not all women experienced birth trauma, many felt shocked – that it wasn't what they expected and that their trust had been abused – either because others had not been fully forthcoming about birth, or because they did not feel respected during labour. This relates to the final reason that I believe birth narratives take a specific format. Frank explains that the telling of a painful event is a form of testimony where the person listening is transformed into a witness.[29] I sometimes felt while hearing these birth stories that they were expressed as a form of testimony and that they contained an ethical imperative insofar as I was being called upon to bear witness. But what is the psychological importance of bearing witness to trauma or pain? Herman explains that one of the common emotional responses of trauma survivors is a sense of guilt – they wonder if they bear some responsibility for their trauma, if they could have acted differently to prevent or ameliorate their pain. The survivor seeks compassion from the listener to hear her story and to help her mourn her losses.[30] Part of achieving her sense of justice and recognition for a wrong suffered, I suspect, is for her testimony to be publicly heard by an attentive and sympathetic listener. There is thus an ethical significance to capturing birth stories: in this instance bearing witness is as important as documenting history.[31] For those who have survived crises, telling their story to an oral historian helps to validate and make sense of their experience through the process of narration.[32] While oral historians are not therapists, telling a trauma story can be the first step towards healing.[33]

Ultimately, I concluded that in preserving and transmitting such detailed narratives of childbirth in their maternographies, some women were calling upon me as interviewer to bear witness to the intensity of their ordeal. In a society which sanitises the experience through coy birth notices and in which most people do not ask for the graphic details of one's birth, many women want and need someone to bear witness, to acknowledge the extremity of what they have endured.

## Generational time

If maternographies demonstrated connections to the cyclical patterns of maternal time, they were also clearly embedded within the more dynamic frameworks of generational time. During the first half of the twentieth century, pregnancy, childbirth and motherhood were increasingly subject to medical technology and supervision. Social reform movements in this era valorised motherhood through a lens of maternalism, leading to the introduction of the maternity allowance, antenatal care, infant welfare centres and free kindergartens.[34] Antenatal clinics opened at many Australian hospitals in the interwar period and maternity wards were gradually used by a wide cross-section of the population, as gestation and labour were increasingly believed to require medical supervision and support. There was very much a triumphalist narrative of medical progress among doctors, and a condescension towards women. The influential New Zealand doctor Truby King argued that 'In one sense it would be very much better for women if they never knew they were pregnant until, say, a month before the actual event of childbirth. The great mistake most women make is being frightened, indeed terrified, of the agony they suppose they will suffer in giving birth to children'.[35] Indeed, the predominant interwar attitude was that 'confinement' will be easier if women 'carry on their household duties' and lead 'a busy, contented, sensible life, refusing to listen to upsetting "old wives' tales," and thus keeping their minds free from doubts and fears ... Thinking right is just as important as living right'.[36]

## Postwar mothers

By the mid-twentieth century, birth was a much more medicalised event than it had been at the start of the century. Such shifts were taking place within the context of a demographic boom fuelled by migration and rising birth rates. These social factors added to a heightened emphasis on family, homemaking and child-raising,[37] but the baby boom also strained the capacity of the public health system, leading to overcrowded and understaffed hospital wards. At the women's hospital in Brisbane, the annual number of births in the postwar years averaged nine to ten thousand, with up to four hundred patients at a time crowded into accommodation built for 274.[38] At the Women's Hospital in Melbourne, total annual admissions doubled from eight thousand in 1945 to sixteen thousand in 1955.[39] By the end of the 1950s, almost all Australian childbirth took place in a hospital and was preceded by antenatal care.[40]

In the 1950s and 1960s, the main focus of medical efforts during childbirth was the foetus. As birth was seen as dangerous – an illness to be managed rather than a natural process – there was a tendency towards obstetric intervention. In this context, it was difficult for women to control the ways in which they laboured.[41] Popular culture reinforced the idea that modern medicine had made childbirth safe and obviated the need to suffer. One Victorian woman wrote to the *Australian Women's Weekly* (AWW) in 1959 stating that, 'Childbirth is an entirely natural process, and the skilled care now available for mothers cancels out the need to state "both well" in birth notices'.[42] Another wrote in 1946, asserting the advantages of pain relief in childbirth:

> Very little has been done to alleviate the suffering of mothers, except in a few big city hospitals; but we women are to blame because of our own apathy. I have been told by women of the older generation, who themselves have suffered at childbirth, that anything worthwhile has to be paid for ... We should ... see that women in all parts of Australia are given the right of painless childbirth, as a necessity, not a luxury.[43]

Women who gave birth in the postwar decades remember labouring in fairly unsupportive circumstances, being offered little preparation or choice, being attended by unsympathetic nurses and doctors and denied the support of husbands or other support people. Marjorie grew up in London in a Jewish family of Eastern European background before migrating to Australia as an adult. She gave birth to her first child in 1954 and recalled feeling intimidated by her Melbourne obstetrician and his nurse.

> It was a lot of hierarchy and women were intimidated ... by the medical profession. Particularly young expectant mothers. And expectant was the operative word, because we didn't know what to expect ... And when I got to the hospital, you know, R [husband] took me and I was in labour then, with my little case, and Sister met us at the door and she said, go now Mr F, and he went ... She put me in a lovely room ... overlooking treetops and everything and I remember lying there thinking, I'm on my own. I'm doing this totally alone. No mother there, no R, nobody that I could talk to, to rub my back. Sister came in, 'Yes, how are you doing Mrs F?' Yes. I remember saying once, 'I'm not doing this now, I'm going home'. And she turned to the other Sister ... and she said, 'Mrs F's going home, Sister', and she said, 'oh right'. And like, they didn't comfort me, if you like. They told me to be quiet. I was shouting – I was – a long labour and she was a big baby, 8 lb 10 oz, and she said to me, 'Be quiet!', and I did ... We were very compliant.

Marjorie's birth narrative illuminates the ways in which postwar mothers felt daunted by the authority of health professionals and were given very little information about labour. The superior and unsympathetic mode adopted by many doctors and nurses reinforced expectations that birthing women were to be compliant and docile. Many birthing women were inculcated into cultural attitudes that did not encourage them to see themselves as possessing rights to information or control. The absence of a support person left them feeling lonely and vulnerable.

Birthing women were generally not given information about what to expect in terms of pain or medical procedures. When a labouring woman came into hospital, her pubic region was shaved and she was given an enema no matter how advanced her contractions.[44] At Melbourne's Royal Women's Hospital, she might be offered heroin, morphine, pethidine, chloral hydrate or nitrous oxide during labour and anaesthesia for delivery.[45] Cultural and historical expectations govern what are considered suitable ways to give birth, including whether emotion should be displayed and whether a woman should be passive or active. In the 1950s, middle-class Anglo-Australians felt that displays of emotion, even amidst extreme pain, were inappropriate.[46] Anglo-Australian Eve reported with a measure of pride that she was determined to labour quietly when she had her first baby in 1950.

> There was another girl in the next room having a baby and she made a lot of noise ... I was settled and off they [the nurses] went ... They popped in every now and then to see how I was going because there was only two people on duty. Because of this other girl, I became a little bit frightened and they said ... 'she's just one of those that make a lot of noise'. So I thought, 'Okay, I'm not going to do that. This is an important part of my life. I'm not going to make a fuss about it' ... One nurse came in and I was on my hands and knees and she said, 'What are you doing?' I said, 'It's more comfortable this way'. She said, 'Get back on your back. This is the way we want you'. So I did. So then the doctor rushed in and barely had time to wash his hands. My baby was born at five to twelve ... I had it before that other girl. She was still making a noise when I was having my baby.

In Eve's story, hospital staff clearly conveyed that the appropriate way to give birth involved lying on one's back silently – a far cry from the 'active birth' principles of movement and vocalisation which millennial mothers are now encouraged to adopt. Eve's birth story has a moral lesson too: that 'making a fuss' simply prolongs labour.

Postwar nurses considered migrant women to be noisier and many disapproved. Sometimes, a migrant woman was slapped to be quiet.[47] There was little appreciation of the fact that many migrant women for whom English was not their first language may have struggled to understand all that was communicated to them, adding an extra layer of fear and confusion to an already difficult event.

When June migrated from Germany in 1952, she had very little English. It was sometimes baffling trying to make sense of a foreign maternity care system in which overcrowded conditions stretched the sympathy of hospital staff.

> There were six of us in one room. Three there, three there and we were all nearly at end and the midwife, she went like a sergeant from one corner of the other and she said, 'stop whinging, won't be long. It's not your turn yet. Don't scream so loud'. You could hear and see everything. So primitive.

If postwar mothers sometimes felt intimidated by the militaristic conditions prevailing in hospitals, they nevertheless appreciated the ways in which strict rules gave them an opportunity to rest. Overcrowded conditions meant that few women received personalised care during or after labour. Hospital stays lasted at least a week, with babies kept in a central nursery and only brought to the mother for four-hourly feeds. Visiting hours were limited and strictly enforced. Many postwar mothers like Marjorie felt that this system gave them an opportunity to properly recover from labour.

> [In hospital,] they took the baby away at the last feed at six and you never saw the baby till six in the morning. And it was marvellous. You were rested. Your milk came in ... Doctor came in every couple of days. 'How are you doing?' ... and your husband was allowed in visiting hours. Never outside of visiting hours.

## Second-wave mothers

Childbirth and parenting organisations which developed in Australia in the 1960s began to question some of these practices, such as the Association for the Advancement of Painless Childbirth, later the Childbirth Education Association, and the Nursing Mothers Association of Australia.[48] The childbirth reform movement was influenced by organisations which had developed overseas such as the National Childbirth Trust in the United Kingdom and the International Childbirth Education Association.[49] But they were perhaps most influenced by English doctor Grantly Dick-Read, who was the first to popularise the idea that childbirth pain is psychogenic through his book *Natural Childbirth*.[50] Dick-Read believed that fear and tension increased pain for women in labour so advocated relaxation techniques. His ideas were taken up and publicised by Dr Phyllis Cilento in Australia.[51] There is influence of fledgling interest in these concepts as early as 1951, when one article described childbirth 'as a natural, even a joyous process', comparing the prenatal woman to 'an athlete for an important indeed a vital champion event'.[52] Another article on 'natural' childbirth suggests that there was indeed rising interest among doctors and nurses, but that few hospitals had yet subscribed to the philosophy. Natural childbirth was described as the conviction that through special preparation and training, birth could be less painful, removing the need for anaesthetic.[53]

Such beliefs can be understood as part of a rising interest in psychoprophylaxis, also known as 'natural' childbirth, in the mid-twentieth century: the idea that the pain of childbirth can be managed through techniques like breathing. Drawing on Soviet practices, Dr Ferdinand Lamaze began popularising such techniques in France, and they became the most well-known method of prenatal education in the US.[54] Other ideas associated with psychoprophylaxis are Frédérick Leboyer's 'birth without violence' and water birth, advocated by Michel Odent, both of which emerged in France in the 1970s before spreading to the US and beyond.[55] From 1971 to 1973, childbirth preparation courses grew to encompass 25 per cent of US hospitals and by the end of the decade, such classes were offered nearly universally.[56]

Particularly from the 1970s, there was growing criticism of the medicalisation of birth among both feminist scholars and birth activists.[57] Maternity reformers challenged many of the practices prevalent in the postwar era, arguing that women should be both physically and psychologically informed. There was a new emphasis on preparation, and on the emotions which accompany birth, as well as a respect for the preferences of the birthing woman.[58] In a survey conducted by the Childbirth Education Association in the mid-1970s, 86 per cent of mothers who had babies in Sydney maternity hospitals were dissatisfied with their treatment.[59] Women were sceptical of the necessity of enemas, pubic shaving, induction, pharmacological pain relief and episiotomies, and wanted their husbands to be present, to not be confined to a bed during labour and to be able to hold their baby after birth.[60] Lebanese-Australian Sally had her first child in 1978 and remembers that she was influenced in her desire to breastfeed and have a 'natural' childbirth by maternity reform advocates like the Nursing Mothers Association of Australia. She recalls that, 'There was a view at the time that birth had been medicalised and that male specialists were controlling the experience. The home birth movement was an attempt for women to gain control of the experience'.

But many of these new ideas took time to be embraced. Reading women's magazines across these years, both support for and resistance to this birth revolution is evident. In 1966, the idea that fathers should be present at the birth of their children was still controversial. A British doctor disparaged the practice as 'keeping up with the Joneses – wives ask their husbands to remain with them purely because their friends or other members of their families have done it ... It's become a status symbol'. She believed that 'husbands who watch their wives give birth may find it a shattering experience and one they'll regret the rest of their lives'.[61] The 1968 edition of the *Better Homes Baby Book* similarly counselled that 'many doctors feel that you will relax more and rest better if your husband is not present'.[62] In 1970, another doctor asserted the view that husbands are a useful psychological support for their wives because 'the wife is keen to put on a good show for him and anxious to please him'.[63] By 1977, doctors were not the only authorities whose advice was sought on this issue, with one article quoting a woman explaining her desire to have her husband by her side. The same article talks about 'pregnant parents', in a clear shift in language and emphasis from seeing the woman as the only person pregnant and birthing to viewing it as something experienced by both people in a couple.[64]

By 1970, new attitudes about choice and information in healthcare are evident, such as the idea that doctors should tell women more about what to expect during labour and encourage them to attend childbirth education classes. One article critiqued doctors who did not adequately prepare pregnant women for labour. 'Perhaps, suggests a lecturer in obstetrics, it's something to do with that peculiar Australian attitude, "You'll be right, mate." An expectant mother should ask her doctor how much pain she can expect during labor and what he plans to do to relieve it'.[65] The Royal Women's Hospital produced a film for new parents, attempting to demystify the processes and places of birth, in recognition of the fact that hospitals can be intimidating.[66] Books such as the immensely popular *Everywoman* by Australian doctor Derek Llewellyn-Jones detailed childbirth experiences and options. Llewellyn-Jones aimed to provide women with accurate and accessible medical information about their bodies, echoing the ambitions of the women's health movement. *Everywoman* was considered radical at the time, for trying to make childbirth more comfortable and less interventionist, encouraging fully informed choices and supporting paternal presence in the labour ward. Llewellyn-Jones believed that:

> A woman has the right to be informed about the methods available to relieve the pain associated with labour ... Whichever method she chooses, it is the duty of those helping her during childbirth to inform her of the progress of her labour, to obtain her co-operation and to treat her as a participant in a wonderful process.[67]

Sally found reading *Everywoman* was a useful preparation for her first experience of childbirth in 1978, though she laughed as she remembered her disappointment that birth was not the orgasmic experience she had been led to expect. She also found that her expectations for the role of her partner during birth did not play out quite as they had anticipated as a couple.

> My husband was extremely enthusiastic ... They were to be your partner in the labour and, you know, they were to carry your wishes should you become too exhausted or whatever to be able to communicate them and so on. And I had said, 'Look, I reckon I can handle anything but I don't want to be in stirrups' ... So when the doctor came in ... there was signs of foetal distress and he walked in putting his gloves on and he said, 'We're going to have to get this baby out quickly. Can you put her legs in the stirrups?', and R [husband] leapt to his feet and said, 'No, she doesn't want to be in stirrups', and the doctor looked me in the eye and he said, 'It would make the delivery easier', and I said, 'Yes' [laughs]. So R was just deflated like a balloon. This was his big moment but as I said to him afterwards, the doctor could've come in and said, 'We need to amputate your left leg', and I would've said, 'Yes'. Whatever it took to finish it off I would've agreed to.

Part of the maternity reform movement's critique of medicalised birth was that hospital environments were sterile and unwelcoming. While some women were attracted to the idea of home birth, hospitals decried them as dangerous, offering instead the concept of a birthing centre as a compromise. The Director of Nursing at the Women's Hospital in Sydney scathingly critiqued the idea that hospitals were places where women's preferences were not regarded:

> It's idiotic to push aside all our new knowledge and try to cope at home. I wonder why some women imagine that if they come into hospital they'll have to fight for what they want. That's ridiculous. We're here to answer questions, to give advice, to give support, to do all we can to make birth a wonderful experience. It's our job to care for the community.[68]

The first birthing room opened in the US in 1969 and had proliferated to a thousand within a decade.[69] Australia's first birth centre opened at the Women's Hospital, Crown Street, Sydney in 1979, and in the next year, birth centres were set up at the Royal Women's Hospital and the Queen Victoria Medical Centre in Melbourne, and the King Edward Memorial Hospital in Perth. Advocates claimed that these centres felt more homely and less surgical, and meant that it was not necessary to move birthing women between labour wards, delivery wards and recovery wards. They were designed to 'cater for women wanting to have their babies "naturally" in a family-like environment, with their families around them'.[70]

While birthing centres were rising in popularity, some women nevertheless chose home birth because of concerns about the philosophy and practices of maternity hospitals. Brenda was born in 1953 and as a trained midwife, she had always assumed she would nominate obstetric, hospital care for her births. Her first pregnancy ended in miscarriage and she found the cold, unsympathetic response of health professionals deeply troubling. On the basis of this experience, she decided to have a home birth when she fell pregnant again in 1978. Brenda's is one of the very few wholly positive stories of birth recounted in these maternographies.

> Here were all these beautiful people talking about birth in a really positive way. And they spoke about their birth experiences in a way that I had not heard before. I hadn't seen birth happen that way in my midwifery training, and certainly the stories that I had heard from my mother were very different, because fathers weren't even allowed in the hospital – in the labour ward – and my mother, I think, was

quite drugged for her births, and never ever gave me the impression that it was anything positive ... And when I had my baby – E [child] – I had the most beautiful labour, and the best birth. It was just the most incredible experience of my life, I have to say. Exhilarating ... there was nobody bossing me around; nobody telling me what to do. I took complete control over the whole situation. I had a longish labour – I had quite a long second stage; in hospital, I would have definitely had a forceps delivery. You know, who knows – a caesarean – God only knows what. I didn't have any drugs ... and it was an amazing experience. And so I started off my life with E in this amazing position of feeling totally empowered and full of joy.

Brenda describes the ways in which her relatively negative expectations for birth were shaped by her training as a midwife and the birth stories shared by her mother. But Brenda's experience of home birth was very different: she felt empowered and in control, which set the tone for her earliest experiences of mothering.

Accompanying this growing attention to the preparation, support and environment surrounding childbirth was a greater interest in the psychological experience of birth: firstly the mother's, then the father's and finally the baby's. The idea of 'bonding' became popularised: that families need 'private time' after birth because 'there is already much evidence to suggest the benefits in later life of this extra early maternal contact'. Gradually, the removal of babies to nurseries separate from the mother was replaced by the concept of 'rooming in': that mothers and babies should spend their hospital stay in the same room. This shift reflected the idea that being together was important for the emotional development of the baby, for the relationship between mother and child and for the establishment of breastfeeding. One article asserted that: 'Those first hours and days are the most important in establishing a happy and strong relationship between mother and baby'.[71]

The theory that the trauma of being birthed can scar a person for life was discussed in a 1977 *Women's Weekly* article on rebirth therapy, explaining the theories of Arthur Janov (*The Primal Scream*) and Frédérick Leboyer (*Birth Without Violence*).[72] The article claimed remarkable advantages for children born using gentler methods:

Already children born by Dr Frederick Leboyer's revolutionary methods, designed to introduce a baby to its new environment as gently as possible in dim lights and silence, the newborn infant rocked in a warm bath to echo the womb are showing above-average intelligence and remarkably equable personalities.[73]

While on some levels such discussions display evidence of a concern for the birth experience of the mother, they simultaneously added to her growing catalogue of worries. Mothers were warned that induction is traumatic for a baby because it is ejected from the womb before it is ready, that medical interference such as anaesthesia or caesarean results in a child who cannot complete any task and that mothers of premature babies who spend time in intensive care may have trouble establishing a relationship with their child when it finally comes home with them.[74]

At the same time as these maternity reforms were occurring, some issues remained contested. The topic of pain relief in labour remained fraught, with one doctor claiming it was 'masochistic' to refuse medication during childbirth: 'Some women are "hung up" on pain in labor, the doctor said. "It's a masochistic thing – if they are not suffering pain, they feel they aren't having the baby properly." I'm not clear where this need for pain comes from.'[75]

Despite efforts to de-medicalise birth, interventions were rising in an era of increasing medical technologies and risk aversion. The use of technology expanded in maternity wards from the 1970s and continued into the 1980s, including induction, foetal monitoring, caesarean section and epidural anaesthesia.[76] Historian Paula A. Michaels explains how these contradictory developments could occur simultaneously – with efforts to increase the autonomy of the birthing woman occurring at the same time as medical intervention accelerated:

> These concessions to the American consumer allowed hospitals and physicians to blunt the impact of challenges to their monopoly of control over birth … With the challenges posed by home birth and midwifery neutralized, within the walls of the hospital the medicalization and pathologization of childbirth continued apace.[77]

The 1970s saw a 'phenomenal rise' in the use of induction in hospitals, with the number of articles debating their use suggesting a level of controversy about these practices.[78] In the UK, deliveries in National Health Service hospitals that were induced climbed from 15 per cent in 1965 to 41 per cent in 1974. Obstetricians claimed that induction reduced perinatal mortality, shortened labour and resulted in healthier babies.[79] But it appears that maternal satisfaction with such practices was low. In a large-scale survey in Britain, only 17 per cent of mothers who were induced wanted the same procedure if they had another birth; 40 per cent of women said they desired more information about the procedure and the reasons for its use beforehand.[80] By 1980, one in six Australian babies was born by caesarean section, with some problematising these rising rates and asking whether the procedure was medically necessary in all cases.[81]

Across the second half of the twentieth century, there was a changing discourse around maternal desires and needs in childbirth. In the immediate postwar era, a strongly paternalistic tone prevailed and medical opinions dominated debates, with women advised to simply trust their doctors. By the 1970s, activists were contributing to a rising discourse of rights and then consumerism, insisting that women need to be fully informed and give their consent to birth practices. Australian Valmai Howe Elkins asserted that parents were 'unaware of their rights in childbirth ... They blindly accept any rules hospitals or doctors lay down, regardless of whether these rules conflict with their own ideas on childbirth'.[82] She felt that 'it is time pregnant parents started to see themselves as consumers shopping for a product instead of victims of uncomfortable and undignified hospital procedures'.[83] From the late 1970s, birth took on a heightened moral meaning for mothers. As motherhood was increasingly viewed as a choice, childbirth became an experience with heightened personal and social significance.[84]

## Millennial mothers

Since 1990, the Australian birth experience has been characterised by a paradox: despite rising critique of a highly medicalised and interventionist model of birth, and increasing evidence for the alarming impacts of biomedical and technocratic childbirth, we have moved further and further away from physiological or vaginal birth with minimal interventions. In the late 1980s, a series of government reviews of maternity services were conducted, partly because of rising costs but also because of women's critiques of maternity care.[85] One 1989 Victorian study reported that most women giving birth in Australia had some form of intervention: only 11 per cent of women surveyed gave birth vaginally without major obstetric procedures such as induction or augmentation of labour, forceps or vacuum extraction, or stitches due to an episiotomy or tear.[86] One-third of the women in this study were dissatisfied with their intrapartum (birth) care.[87]

This trend continued in the twenty-first century. In 2007, 32 per cent of Australian births were by caesarean, 25.3 per cent were induced and a further 20 per cent were by augmented labour[88] (see Figure 3). By 2017, only 58 per cent of Australian women who gave birth in a hospital or birth centre were satisfied with their birth experience, with dissatisfaction associated with instrumental birth (with forceps of vacuum) or caesarean section.[89] How can we make sense of such high rates of dissatisfaction after birth? Perhaps it is at least partly explained by the disjuncture between what women expect from birth and what occurs, between what they want and what takes place. Miller's interviews with British

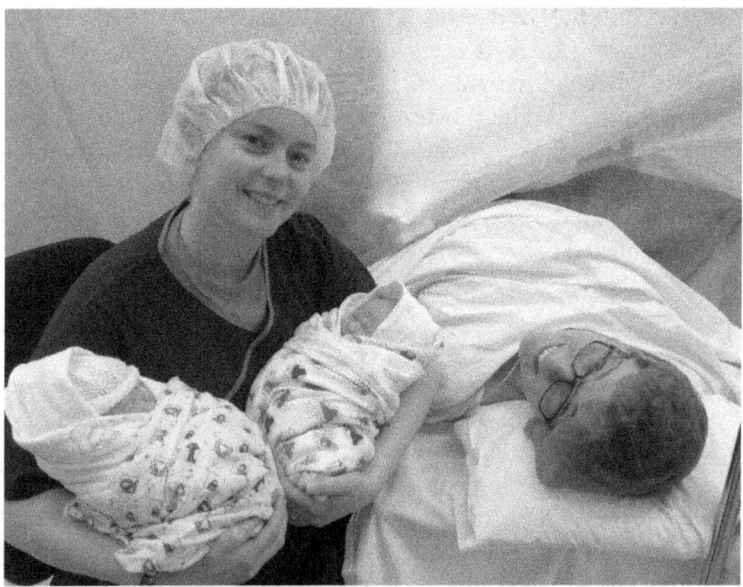

Figure 3 Millennial mother with co-mother and newborn twins immediately after caesarean birth, 2015 (private collection)

mothers in the early 2000s found that birth was overwhelmingly not how women had anticipated and birthing women felt that medical professionals and other mothers had not adequately prepared them.[90] As the number of births that women experience decreases, the idea of 'succeeding' at birth or having a 'good' birth has arguably become more important. The Australian birth rate had dropped from 3.6 births per woman in 1961 to 1.85 in 1989 and down to 1.74 in 2018.[91] As early as 1983, Australian sociologists Crouch and Manderson argued that the image of 'good' birth conveyed by popular media – free of drugs or intervention – is such a circumscribed ideal that many women fail to meet it, leading to guilt and anxiety.[92] Similarly, Miller's study found a prevalent perception that 'good' mothers produce a 'good' birth without pain relief, while simultaneously, women fearful of the many unknowns in birth were seduced by the promise that medicine could create a safe, predictable experience.[93]

Indeed, millennial mothers in Australia have been confronted by a complex contradiction when approaching birth. The ideal of a 'natural' childbirth is still powerfully influential for many women, who learn about non-medical pain relief strategies such as breathing, visualisation, movement, meditation and massage. They may read books by experts such as physiotherapist Juju Sundin or doula (birth attendant) and childbirth educator Rhea Dempsey and attend childbirth education classes run by midwives that offer strategies which prioritise physiological birth.[94] Most mothers-to-be attend some form of childbirth preparation course, and some also attend classes on prenatal yoga, active birth, calm birth, hypnobirth and more. Almost all mothers bring a support person or persons to their labour, most commonly their partner but also perhaps a relative, friend or doula. Most women create a birth plan with the encouragement of their supporting health professionals, in an effort to give the birthing woman some autonomy over her experience of labour. There have been attempts to diversify birthing options for Australian women, recognising that not all women negotiate the maternity care system from the same starting point, and that women have a diversity of linguistic and cultural needs when giving birth.[95] Birth for HumanKind (BfHK) is a nonprofit organisation founded in 2014, through which volunteer doulas support vulnerable mothers experiencing disadvantage, especially those lacking family or community support.⁹⁶ Birthing on Country models are maternity services developed to support Aboriginal and Torres Strait Islander women to birth in ways that are connected to community, country and Indigenous ways of knowing. In 2015, the Australian College of Midwives, the Congress of Aboriginal and Torres Strait Islander Nurses and Midwives (CATSINaM) and CRANAplus signed a joint position statement supporting the establishment of Birthing on Country models of care in Australia.⁹⁷

But simultaneously, rates of medical intervention have continued to rise steadily to the point where Dempsey estimates that only 1 to 5 per cent of Australian births are now free of intervention.⁹⁸ Such interventions may include induction, episiotomies, vacuum or forceps extraction, caesarean section, pain relief medication such as gas, pethidine and epidural, and the use of synthetic oxytocin to expel the placenta. Increasing interventions are generally explained by the fact that obstetricians are trained to be risk averse and to prioritise the safety of mother and infant over the rather difficult-to-measure question of maternal satisfaction with birth.⁹⁹ Perinatal mortality has unquestionably decreased over the past century. But this incongruity between what many women expect and desire from their birth and what actually happens leaves many feeling confused, upset and guilty. As up to one in four women report dissatisfaction with their experience of childbirth, books such as *How to Heal a Bad Birth* have emerged to help women cope with feelings of acute disappointment.¹⁰⁰

Perhaps the intervention that leaves the greatest imprint on the birth experience is the caesarean section. Approximately one-third of Australian births are now via caesarean¹⁰¹ yet the 'too-posh-to-push' stereotype that this is an easier birthing option is not the experience of most of these women. Not all mothers who give birth via caesarean have a negative experience. Anglo-Australian Kira was advised to have a planned caesarean in 2015 because she was pregnant with twins. Her relationship of trust with her obstetrician and the amount of information she was given helped her to feel positive as she anticipated her birth. 'I just completely trusted her [obstetrician], because she would just give me all the information, and then let me make the decisions, but she didn't pretend – she just gave it to me how it was.' During the caesarean section – which had to be rushed when Kira started going into spontaneous labour – the support of her wife and health professionals helped Kira feel safe throughout this new and potentially scary experience.

> Had lovely nurses, about a million people in the room. I thought M [obstetrician] did an amazing job of little things like, you know, I had to sign all those forms that you have to sign before surgery, when she'd kind of just say little things like you're going to have your babies tonight, like you're going to meet your babies soon, and just making it feel less like you're having this clinical procedure, and more like something really exciting was going to happen ... It was this weird thing, where I think I was having trouble with maybe – this still isn't real ... It was the first time in my life that I was experiencing pain and something really positive was going to come out of it, so I was quite – like, the midwife said to me the next day, I did not think you were going to theatre. Both of you were so chilled out.

After a caesarean birth experience where she felt informed, respected and supported, Kira felt 'ecstatic' and 'on cloud nine'.

But most experiences of caesarean birth narrated to me were not so positive. Greek-Australian Connie chose to become a single mother via IVF, giving birth in 2014 via planned caesarean due to her low-lying placenta. Connie found the experience of her caesarean frightening and it influenced her early feelings of detachment towards her baby.

> I wasn't thrilled I was having a caesarean and when I got there in the morning and they prepped me and put in the bed and were going to wheel me in, the anaesthetist came in and briefed me and just told me a couple of things and I began to cry in fear ... So, look, the birth, it took ten minutes, twenty minutes. That was weird. They cut me and it took no time. So, I found it really weird and disturbing but I had to accept that as my way ... It was like this at the beginning with him. It's not that I didn't want him, I wanted him and I loved him. But, it's like I held him but I didn't know who he was. I only know this because later only when we grew on each other and bonded, after that did I feel differently and I thought, I was still holding you like an object that I didn't know what to do with.

Connie's experience is not unusual. An increasing body of research has been critical of the consequences of births with high levels of intervention, finding that they make it harder for the mother and child to bond emotionally, result in greater breastfeeding difficulties and can leave mothers feeling traumatised and reluctant to give birth again.[102] Despite decades of research into the importance of continuity of care and minimal interventions for the birthing woman's experience and recovery, we have failed to extensively incorporate such evidence into maternity care.[103] Oakley eloquently expresses one of the emotional risks of intervention: that it has the potential to undermine a mother's sense of presence, authority and control over her birth:

> The most pernicious memory a mother may be left with is that she simply was not there: she missed the experience, and was a mere spectator during one of the most important dramas of her life ... Any kind of medical 'assistance' ... runs the risk of turning the mother into passive object rather than active subject.[104]

As a consumer choice discourse has gained ascendancy in Australian maternity care, critiques have emerged that it overemphasises the autonomy of birthing women, who can only 'choose' the circumstances of their birth amidst entrenched regimes of medical power and knowledge.[105] In the twenty-first century, the Human Rights in Childbirth (HRiC) movement has instead turned to the legal language of rights, with recognition of the existence of 'obstetric violence' increasingly codified in law.[106] In the past two decades the existence of postnatal PTSD has been recognised (PNPTSD), that women can experience trauma in birth that has a continuing impact.[107] Of women globally, 20 to 48 per cent describe their birth experience as traumatic.[108] Some researchers have argued that the trend towards Australian women seeking what are seemingly polarised birth options – freebirthing at home without medical care and elective caesarean section in the absence of medical reasons – are both symptoms of a failed maternity care system, with birthing women fearing the consequences of attempting physiological birth within contemporary Australian hospitals.[109]

Yet others maintain that the safe delivery of a healthy baby should always be prioritised over the qualitative experience of the birthing mother. In 2013, Tessa became pregnant at forty-three years of age. Her baby was born at twenty-eight weeks and struggled for life in a neonatal intensive care unit, before Tessa was finally able to bring her home three months later. As a result of coming face to face with the very real possibility of infant death, Tessa is grateful for what twenty-first-century medicine can achieve and critical of women who complain because they cannot have their idealised birth.

I get really annoyed with, you know, if I read or hear about women saying, 'Oh, my birth was traumatic because ... the CD player wouldn't work to play my whale music. My husband forgot the patchouli oil', and all that crap. That makes me just want to – I just, yeah, struggle with that. But then ... we have a very good friend who lost a twin while we were there at the hospital and, you know, I look at that and just think, wow, we had no issues. We had no dramas. Our experience was not on a continuum that stressful and that traumatic. We brought home a child. And stillbirth ... I just can't even fathom now how people deal with that.

Tessa's experience of birthing a premature infant has given her a vivid, and emotionally difficult, insight into the ways in which the shadow of infant or maternal death haunts the labour ward, a perspective that many millennial mothers are now fortunate to avoid. She feels frustrated with women who wish to control the circumstances of their birth and minimise medical intervention, insisting that the health of mother and baby are all that matter, ultimately. And this distinction between two incommensurable factors – the mortality of mother and child and the quality of the birthing experience – creates a gulf that is near impossible to bridge.

## Conclusion

Across far-flung cultures and time periods, childbirth is an event of profound individual and social significance. Many Australian women across the past seventy-five years have simultaneously anticipated and feared this labour of love, surrounded as it is by mystique, half-truths and taboo. While maternity reform advocates have shifted both preparation for and expectations of birth, and changes to the birthing environment and inclusion of support persons have occurred, striking continuities in narrations of birthing experiences persist. Regardless of medical advances, birth remains a trial by fire in women's maternographies. Although we have witnessed rising attempts to better educate women for childbirth, most still feel that they were underprepared – that their experience does not match their expectations. Notwithstanding attempts to personalise and humanise birth, many women still feel disappointed in its aftermath. Across a spectrum from unprepared and dissatisfied to acutely traumatised, what is striking in these maternographies is how few birth narratives are unreservedly positive.

On the surface, the ways in which Australian women experience birth have changed significantly in the past seventy-five years. From knowing almost nothing of what to expect, women have been offered increasing knowledge and preparation through childbirth education. A rhetoric of choice and control has emerged that is exemplified by the introduction of the birth plan, though many of these documents remain aspirational at best. There have been attempts to soften the environment in which birth takes place and to ensure that every birthing woman may have a support person if she wishes, though such reforms have not changed the fact that many feel they are in a hostile and unsupportive environment. Perhaps most strikingly, despite critiques of technocratic birth, medical interventions have continued to rise.

But the critical factor is not solely how challenging one's experience of birth is, but also whether a woman has the opportunity to share, interpret and move on from her childbirth. Birth continues to push women to the limits of what they can endure. Although not always comfortable listening, it is crucially important that women are given the space and opportunity to tell their birth story – and that they are properly heard. Birth narratives are often silenced by cultural expectations. But my experience of co-creating these maternographies suggests that women want and need to have these stories heard. They have battled at the very edges of endurance and often have an unmet emotional need to find recognition of that battle. Although birth is an unprecedented, peak experience that resists containment by language or memory, it is nevertheless critical that women are offered an opportunity to narrativise their labour – because experiences of early mothering are radically shaped by the upheaval of birth and its aftershocks.

## Notes

1 Brigitte Jordan, *Birth in Four Cultures: A Crosscultural Investigation of Childbirth in Yucatan, Holland, Sweden, and the United States*, 4th ed. (Prospect Heights, Illinois: Waveland Press. Inc., 1993); Mary Douglas, *Purity and Danger: An Analysis of Concepts of Pollution and Taboo* (London: Routledge, 1966).

2   Arnold van Gennep, *The Rites of Passage*, trans. Monika B. Vizedom and Gabrielle L. Caffee (Chicago: University of Chicago Press, 1960).
3   Mira Crouch and Lenore Manderson, *New Motherhood: Cultural and Personal Transitions in the 1980s* (Yverdon, Switzerland; Camberwell, Vic.: Gordon and Breach, 1983), 29.
4   Oakley, *From Here to Maternity*.
5   Rachelle Chadwick, *Bodies That Birth: Vitalizing Birth Politics* (London and New York: Routledge, 2018).
6   Knott, *Mother: An Unconventional History*, 56. Sharon Olds, 'The Language of the Brag', *Satan Says* (Pittsburgh, PA: University of Pittsburgh Press, 1980).
7   Thomson et al., *Making Modern Mothers*, 19.
8   Oakley, *From Here to Maternity*, 85.
9   Oakley, *From Here to Maternity*, 105.
10  Brown et al., *Missing Voices*.
11  Oakley, *From Here to Maternity*, 85.
12  Oakley, *From Here to Maternity*, 85.
13  Miller, *Making Sense of Motherhood*, 77.
14  Names and date have been changed to protect Sophia's anonymity, but the pattern of the birth notice has been retained.
15  Anonymised birth announcement from social media, 2013.
16  Elaine Scarry, *The Body in Pain: The Making and Unmaking of the World* (New York: Oxford University Press, 1985); Veena Das, *Life and Words: Violence and the Descent into the Ordinary* (Berkeley: University of California Press, 2007).
17  Lawrence L. Langer, *Holocaust Testimonies: The Ruins of Memory* (New Haven: Yale University Press, 1991).
18  Gadi BenEzer, 'Trauma Signals in Life Stories', in *Trauma and Life Stories: International Perspectives*, eds. Kim Lacy Rogers, Selma Leydesdorff and Graham Dawson (London and New York: Routledge, 1999), 29–44.
19  Arthur W. Frank, *The Wounded Storyteller: Body, Illness, and Ethics* (Chicago: University of Chicago Press, 1995).
20  Oakley, *From Here to Maternity*, 85.
21  Martin, *The Woman in the Body*.
22  Brown et al., *Missing Voices*, 59.
23  Brown et al., *Missing Voices*, 134.
24  Penny Simkin, 'Just Another Day in a Woman's Life? Women's Long-Term Perceptions of Their First Birth Experience', *Birth* 18, no. 4 (1991).
25  Simkin, 'Just Another Day in a Woman's Life?'.
26  Oakley, *From Here to Maternity*, 105.

27 Paula A. Michaels, Elizabeth Sutton and Nicole Highet, 'Violence and Trauma in Australian Birth', in *Australian Mothering: Historical and Sociological Perspectives*, eds. Carla Pascoe Leahy and Petra Bueskens (Cham, Switzerland: Palgrave, 2019), 239–55, 241.
28 Selma Leydesdorff et al., 'Introduction: Trauma and Life Stories', in *Trauma and Life Stories: International Perspectives*, eds. Kim Lacy Rogers, Selma Leydesdorff and Graham Dawson (London and New York: Routledge, 1999), 1–26.
29 Frank, *The Wounded Storyteller*.
30 Judith L. Herman, *Trauma and Recovery: The Aftermath of Violence – From Domestic Abuse to Political Terror* (New York: Basic Books, 2015), 15–16.
31 Shoshana Felman and Dori Laub, *Testimony: Crises of Witnessing in Literature, Psychoanalysis, and History* (New York: Routledge, 1992).
32 Mark Cave and Stephen M. Sloan, eds., *Listening on the Edge: Oral History in the Aftermath of a Crisis* (Oxford: Oxford University Press, 2014).
33 Leydesdorff et al., 'Introduction: Trauma and Life Stories'.
34 Philippa Mein Smith, *Mothers and King Baby: Infant Survival and Welfare in an Imperial World 1880–1950* (Basingstoke: Macmillan, 1997); Pascoe Leahy and Bueskens, 'Contextualising Australian Mothering and Motherhood'.
35 M. Truby King, 'Women Need Not Fear Childbirth', *Australian Women's Weekly*, 11 November 1933, 11.
36 King, 'Women Need Not Fear Childbirth'.
37 Pascoe, *Spaces Imagined*.
38 Reiger, *Our Bodies, Our Babies*.
39 McCalman, *Sex and Suffering*, 256.
40 McCalman, *Sex and Suffering*, 251–2.
41 Crouch and Manderson, *New Motherhood*, 31, 33.
42 Letter from Mrs Dorothy Pilkington, Moe, Victoria, 'Childbirth Worries Are Out of Date', *Australian Women's Weekly*, 3 June 1959, 26.
43 Letter from Mrs. N. Randall, Port Kembla, NSW, 'Demand for Painless Childbirth', *Australian Women's Weekly*, 9 February 1946, 27.
44 Reiger, *Our Bodies, Our Babies*, 2.
45 McCalman, *Sex and Suffering*, 286.
46 McCalman, *Sex and Suffering*, 256.
47 McCalman, *Sex and Suffering*, 256, 262.
48 Reiger, *Our Bodies, Our Babies*, 44, 49.
49 Reiger, *Our Bodies, Our Babies*, 37–8.
50 Michaels, *Lamaze*, 3–4, 18–19.

51 Reiger, *Our Bodies, Our Babies*, 41.
52 'Training Yourself for Child-Bearing', *Australian Women's Mirror*, 21 November 1951, 16.
53 'What Is Natural Childbirth?', *Australian Women's Mirror*, 13 June 1951, 16.
54 Reiger, *Our Bodies, Our Babies*, 42; Michaels, *Lamaze*, 120.
55 Michaels, *Lamaze*, 8–9.
56 Michaels, *Lamaze*, 120.
57 Susan Duncan, 'Childbirth as You Want It', *Australian Women's Weekly*, 15 June 1977, 4–5; Elisabeth Wynhausen, 'Birthing a Revolution', *Australian Women's Weekly*, 8 August 1979, 20. See also Crouch and Manderson, *New Motherhood*, 38.
58 Valmai Howe Elkins, 'The Rights of the Pregnant Parent', *Australian Women's Weekly*, 12 April 1978, 52–5.
59 Duncan, 'Childbirth as You Want It'.
60 Howe Elkins, 'The Rights of the Pregnant Parent'.
61 'At Home with Margaret Sydney', *Australian Women's Weekly*, 23 February 1966, 49.
62 R. Quatermaine and M. Street, *Better Homes Baby Book* (London and Glasgow: Collins, 1968).
63 Jean Debelle, 'Childbirth, 1970-Style', *Australian Women's Weekly*, 25 November 1970, 57–9.
64 Duncan, 'Childbirth as You Want It'.
65 Debelle, 'Childbirth, 1970-Style'.
66 Tina Harris, 'New Film Prepares Parents for Childbirth', *Australian Women's Weekly*, 9 April 1980, 83.
67 Llewellyn-Jones, Everywoman: A Gynaecological Guide for Life.
68 Eileen Alderton, Carol Veitch and Kim Douglas, 'Homebirths', *Australian Women's Weekly*, 29 October 1980, 12.
69 Wynhausen, 'Birthing a Revolution'.
70 Alderton et al., 'Homebirths'.
71 Jeanette Kostelac, 'Rooming-In: An Intense Joy', *Australian Women's Weekly*, 23 April 1980, 144.
72 Arthur Janov, *The Primal Scream. Primal Therapy: The Cure for Neurosis* (New York: Dell Publishing, 1970); Frédérick Leboyer, *Birth without Violence* (New York: Knopf, 1975).
73 Anne Woodham, 'Can You Be Born Free? An Investigation into Rebirth Therapy', *Australian Women's Weekly*, 28 December 1977, 12.
74 Woodham, 'Can You Be Born Free?'
75 Debelle, 'Childbirth, 1970-Style'.
76 Michaels, *Lamaze*, 128.
77 Michaels, *Lamaze*, 143.

78 See, for example: 'Birth Inducing: Good or Bad?', *Australian Women's Weekly*, 18 August 1975, 49; James Wright, 'Inducing labour: A Medical Controversy', *Australian Women's Weekly*, 20 September 1978, 32.
79 Wright, 'Inducing Labour: A Medical Controversy'.
80 Wright, 'Inducing Labour: A Medical Controversy'.
81 Joan Rattner Heilman, 'Challenging the Old Ideas on Caesarean Births', *Australian Women's Weekly*, 12 November 1980, 95–6.
82 Duncan, 'Childbirth as You Want It'.
83 Howe Elkins, 'The Rights of the Pregnant Parent'.
84 Crouch and Manderson, *New Motherhood*, 44–6.
85 Reiger, *Our Bodies, Our Babies*, 6.
86 Brown et al., *Missing Voices*, 54.
87 Brown et al., *Missing Voices*, 58.
88 Australian Department of Health, National Maternity Services Plan (2010), www1.health.gov.au/internet/publications/publishing.nsf/Content/pacd-maternityservicesplan-toc.
89 Safe Motherhood for All Inc., Women's Experiences of Birth Care in Australia: The Birth Dignity Survey (2017), www.safemotherhoodforall.org.au/wp-content/uploads/2017/05/Dignity-Survey-Safe-Motherhood-for-All-Circulated.pdf.
90 Miller, *Making Sense of Motherhood*, 90.
91 Crouch and Manderson, *New Motherhood*, 28; Carla Pascoe Leahy and Petra Bueskens, 'Contextualising Australian Mothering and Motherhood', 3–20, 10.
92 Crouch and Manderson, *New Motherhood*, 60–4.
93 Miller, *Making Sense of Motherhood*, 75, 77.
94 Juju Sundin and Sarah Murdoch, *Birth Skills: Proven Pain-Management Techniques for Your Labour and Birth* (Crow's Nest, NSW: Allen & Unwin, 2007); Rhea Dempsey, *Birth with Confidence: Savvy Choices for Normal Birth* (Fairfield, Vic.: Boat House Press, 2014).
95 Ruth DeSouza, Regulating Migrant Maternity: Nursing and Midwifery's Emancipatory Aims and Assimilatory Practices', *Nursing Inquiry* 20, no. 4 (2013): 293–304.
96 Birth for HumanKind, 'Our Story', https://birthforhumankind.org/about-us/our-story.
97 Australian College of Midwives, 'Birthing on Country Project', www.midwives.org.au/birthing-country-project.
98 There are no official figures available for intervention-free childbirth, but Dempsey arrives at this estimate by analysing available data: Rhea Dempsey, 'What Does It Mean for Birthing?', Birthing Wisdom, www.birthingwisdom.com.au/mean-birthing/.

99 Melanie K Jackson, Virginia Schmied and Hannah G Dahlen, 'Birthing Outside the System: The Motivation behind the Choice to Freebirth or Have a Homebirth with Risk Factors in Australia', *BMC Pregnancy and Childbirth* 20, no. 254 (2020).
100 Melissa Bruijn and Debby Gould, *How to Heal a Bad Birth: Making Sense, Making Peace and Moving On* (Kenmore, Queensland: Birthtalk, 2016).
101 Australian Institute of Health and Welfare *National Core Maternity Indicators* (Australian Government, 2021), www.aihw.gov.au/reports/mothers-babies/ncmi-data-visualisations/contents/labour-and-birth-indicators/caesarean-section.
102 Haylee Fox et al., 'Evidence of Overuse? Patterns of Obstetric Interventions during Labour and Birth among Australian Mothers', *BMC Pregnancy and Childbirth* 19, no. 1 (2019): 226.
103 Human Rights in Childbirth, Submission to *Free & Equal: An Australian Conversation on Human Rights* (Australian Human Rights Commission, 2019).
104 Oakley, *From Here to Maternity*, 112.
105 Monica Campo and Kerreen Reiger, 'Maternalism to Consumerism and beyond? Mothers and the Politics of Care in Childbirth', in *Australian Mothering: Historical and Sociological Perspectives*, eds. Carla Pascoe Leahy and Petra Bueskens (Cham, Switzerland: Palgrave Macmillan, 2019), 257–78.
106 Michaels, Sutton and Highet, 'Violence and Trauma in Australian Birth'; Campo and Reiger, 'Maternalism to Consumerism and Beyond?'.
107 Michaels, Sutton and Highet, 'Violence and Trauma in Australian Birth'.
108 Madeleine Simpson, Virginia Schmied, Cathy Dickson and Hannah G Dahlen, 'Postnatal Post-Traumatic stress: An Integrative Review', *Women Birth* 31, no. 5 (2018): 367–79.
109 Hannah Dahlen, Bashi Kumar-Hazard and Virginia Schmied eds., *Birthing Outside the System: The Canary in the Coal Mine* (New York and London: Routledge, 2021); Helen M. Haines et al., 'The Influence of Women's Fear, Attitudes and Beliefs of Childbirth on Mode and Experience of Birth', *BMC Pregnancy & childbirth* 12, no. 55 (2012); Jennifer Fenwick et al., 'Why Do Women Request Caesarean Section in a Normal, Healthy First Pregnancy?', *Midwifery* 26, no. 4 (2010): 394–400.

# 4

# Mother love: mothers and their children

It seems preposterous that this little person that was growing inside you is suddenly in front of you ... It's like a combination of feeling like you're meeting them for the first time and feeling like you're meeting someone you've known for a long time, but meeting them face to face. I know that I'm lucky, because I know that not all women get to feel this at the moment of birth, but I did love her completely and immediately, more than anything I'd ever loved before ...

The first time I held S [child] in my arms was the first time I really felt like a mother, but then, once you know what being a mother feels like and you look back, you realise that it's been a slow, gradual process throughout your pregnancy. Some of that stuff I was talking about before, about having to sacrifice your own needs to someone else, but even bonding ... I started to love my child while she was in my womb, and feel like I knew her ...

I just remember that night, being like, wow, this is the first reality check to motherhood, because I've never been this tired in my life, but I have to get up and service this little baby straight away. I just remember being shocked by how noisy babies are, even when she wasn't crying. They're like little wombats – they're just snuffling and grunting. I barely slept, even though I've probably never been that tired in my life. I remember that, and I remember feeling acutely the sense of responsibility. Like, oh my God, it's my responsibility to keep you alive, and much more than it is G [partner]'s, because I want to breastfeed, so it's actually my body that is responsible for keeping you alive ...

I didn't understand how much of the dance between a parent and a child is influenced by the child's personality, just as much as the parent's, and that the method you end up adopting, which is constantly changing anyway, is actually a compromise between their needs and preferences and yours.

Carla Pascoe Leahy

## Introduction

After childbirth, a woman meets her baby for the first time. Although the infant already knows the sound of a birthgiving mother's voice and has literally taken shape inside her body, this is the first time that they have met as separate individuals. What was one has become two, although for a short time the cord connecting them remains intact. The infant is officially a person unto themselves – their birth and name are registered by the state and they have citizenship bestowed upon them. With the birth of her child, the woman is now suddenly, formally, a mother. She will forever bear the title of Mum, Mama, Mother or Ma. And she vaguely intuits that life will never be the same again. Daphne de Marneffe calls these maternal emotions 'maternal desire': the passionate attachment of mothers to their children in a relationship that is fulfilling and self-actualising for both.[1] There is a deep primal power to the intensity of the emotional experience of mother love, an emotion that is so wholly unique that the pre-maternal woman could not fully fathom it.

What happens to the mother and child after childbirth, when the oneness of pregnancy splits into twoness? How does the new mother feel about her new role and her child? How do those feelings within her, and the influence of external forces, influence how she interacts with her child? Much has changed since the mid-twentieth century in the historical context in which women come to motherhood. But although many things change in the experience of becoming a mother, there are some powerful continuities. Newborns are eternally vulnerable, utterly dependent upon their carers for food, warmth, shelter and care. The primitive, instinctual needs of these tiny creatures remain demanding and exhausting to satisfy. The vulnerability of the woman entering maternity is another constant – her exhaustion, her desperation, her exultation and her passionate love for her child. This chapter will explore change and continuity in the relationship between mother and child, and the ways in which mothers have chosen to raise their children, since the mid-twentieth century.

## Maternal time

In this chapter, we will look closely at the experience of adjusting to motherhood in the early days after birth, including the quality of maternal love, or what it means to be responsible for another human. (Building on this discussion, Chapter 7 will consider the extent to which motherhood changes a woman.) Within their maternographies, women groped hesitantly towards descriptions of what mother love feels like. In remembering day-to-day practices and experiences of mothering, certain themes arose recurrently: that matrescence is emotionally intensive, accompanied by a sense of vulnerability and responsibility, corporeal and sensory, experiential, interrupted and encumbered. A mother's relationship with her baby paradoxically wavers between the sacred and the profane, the quotidian and the miraculous.

### *Intensity and bonding*

One of the first things that many birthgiving mothers experience after their child is born is a flood of intense feelings. In the maternographies created for this research, I asked narrators how they felt immediately after birth. Their answers varied, but interestingly, many sound like descriptions of romantic love at first sight. For Dutch-Australian Katherine, who fell pregnant unintentionally in 1993, meeting her child face to face removed many of the doubts she had felt during her pregnancy. I asked her 'do you remember how you felt at the moment of birth?', and she told me she felt 'instant love and bonding'.

> It was like instant transformation from this kind of mixed up – I wasn't so mixed up ... I went from I don't know what to do with my life, I don't know what my meaning, my purpose is in life, and it was like, I know what my purpose is in life. This is really straightforward. This is it ... So yeah, we really did walk through the door that we didn't even know was there. It's like, holy shit, this is another experience altogether.

In Katherine's narrative, the force of the love that she feels for her newborn child is immediately transformative. She describes a passionate devotion that literally eclipses her worries, overwhelming them with a sense of ontological purpose. While in Chapter 2 I argued that for birthgiving mothers, matresence often begins during pregnancy (whether consciously or not), in Katherine's maternography, pregnancy was a time of uncertainty and anxiety which was resolved through the powerful emotions which accompanied birth. In this regard, Katherine's birth story reflects recurrent tropes in contemporary cultural discourses, where there is a strong idealisation of the first moment that mother and child meet after birth, when bonding is supposed to be instantaneous.[2]

But not all narrators described the kind of ecstatic, immediate bonding experienced by Katherine. Women exhausted or traumatised by their births often took some time to feel such positive emotions. Anglo-Australian Andrea had her first child in 2010. After a long and difficult labour, she did not feel able enjoy a sense of emotional connection with her newborn immediately after birth.

> They put T [child] on me the night she was born and I was disinterested. It wasn't that I didn't love her. I felt that instant, oh my God I love you, but I was so disinterested because I was feeling so unwell. I thought I'm going to vomit on her and I did keep saying get her off, just get her off … You know how you hear those stories where they're just sitting on you – I didn't want it. I said give her to S [husband].

Andrea's maternography undermines the cultural script of instantaneous adoration, as she felt too exhausted and nauseated to bask in pleasant feelings of love with her child.

If immediate bonding was not experienced by all mothers, it was also not confined to birthgiving mothers. Some adoptive mothers also describe feeling an instantaneous love for their children. Anglo-Australian Grace adopted two infant sons in 1962 and 1963, respectively. She described an instantaneous and ardent attachment to her first child.

> *Carla*: How did you feel, when you first met J [first child]?
> *Grace*: Oh, absolutely bowled over. Absolutely beside myself. I couldn't put him down; couldn't stop kissing him. B [husband] always said that, 'You couldn't stop kissing him'. No, I was just

absolutely overcome. In fact, I couldn't almost bear him to be out of my sight, you know, and in fact I hardly went out, for about three months.

Experiences such as Grace's show that motherhood is not necessarily natural, inevitable or biologically based. Anglo-Australian Daphne's experience was similar. When Daphne married her husband in 1949, she took on the role of mother to his sister's illegitimate child, before having a biological son in 1954. In her maternography, there was no distinction in the force of her maternal love for both sons, connected to her by marriage and by blood respectively.

## *Vulnerability and responsibility*

Alongside the powerful emotions of early motherhood, the new mother finds herself in a position of enormous vulnerability and unprecedented responsibility. Birthgiving mothers must endure the immense physical and emotional challenges of childbirth – what many describe as the most difficult thing they have ever done – and then immediately assume responsibility for a helpless new being who is utterly dependent upon them. Ironically, this occurs at a time when the new mother herself feels vulnerable and in need of care, still recovering from the physical and psychological extremes of birth. Katerina, who grew up in Ecuador and the US in the 1980s, reflected on the fact that while she anticipated challenges in childbirth, she had not conceived of the reality that there is no time to recover when the responsibilities of motherhood are assumed instantly.

> Nobody tells you what – your body is just – the recovery. They tell you about that moment when you're delivering and pushing and all of that, but they don't tell you about how you might bleed for six weeks, or they won't tell you how you have no abdominal muscles whatsoever. They don't tell you what it's like if you have stitches down there – they don't tell you [laughs] ... And then you know the demands of a newborn are pretty hardcore. I think maybe it's for the first time you just realise how fragile they are, you have such a sense of responsibility for their life, you know, and their wellbeing. I think you're just dealing with all those emotions and those realisations and then you're physically trying to recover, but then you're completely sleep-deprived.

In many ways, the hardest lesson of matrescence must be learnt immediately after birth: that motherhood entails sacrifice, as the new mother's needs are subjugated to that of the baby. English-born Valerie struggled to adjust to matrescence in 1984 because, as she explained, a mother has to put herself in the background while caring for a dependent infant. Exacerbating the challenge of this position is the fact that a newborn's demands are unpredictable and ever-changing as the child develops. Many narrators described challenges in learning to look after their baby, including sleeping and breastfeeding difficulties. For some, their difficulty managing these issues impacted negatively on their confidence and sense of self. Valerie found early motherhood difficult because

> I wasn't in control and I'm a bit of a control freak, [so] I lost a lot of confidence, yes. It was only when she got older and I had probably a bit more freedom away from her and independence again because she wasn't with me twenty-four hours a day, that came back up again, probably not as much as it ever was before ... I think it was just becoming involved with a child, which you had to do. You can't just categorise them or bring them out when you want to. They're there all the time. So you put yourself in the background while you're looking after these tiny, precious creatures.

Valerie sums up the way that caring for an inherently vulnerable being is an intimidating and unrelenting responsibility for the first-time mother, and the ways in which women can feel like they have failed the test of motherhood.

### Corporeality

Mothering is a corporeal experience from its earliest moments. Pregnancy and birth are highly embodied – perhaps the most intensely physical experiences it is possible for a woman to feel. For birthgiving mothers, the act of conceiving, gestating, birthing and breastfeeding a baby transforms their physical body in unprecedented ways and triggers vividly corporeal experiences. But regardless of pregnancy or breastfeeding, mothering is an embodied practice in which quotidian tasks of carrying, changing, cuddling and comforting require the body of the mother to conform and adapt to the body of the child. This embodied practice is constantly changing as the size and needs of the child change.

Such profound embodiment often feels at odds with our twenty-first-century world of digitally mediated intimacies. Narrators marvelled at how like animals they felt upon becoming mothers, newly conscious of how little separates humans from other mammals on the planet. Anglo-Australian Hazel was taken aback at the primal ferocity of the feelings evoked when her first child was born in 1989, drawing upon metaphors from the animal kingdom to try to explain her novel sensations.

> I was very surprised by things I've not felt before, like the extremely protective feeling when the child's born ... Almost the images that you get from the animal world like the lioness ... This very basic feeling of wanting to protect, look after, look out for your child.

In addition to birthing, the act of breastfeeding struck many new mothers as intensely animalistic, a quintessentially mammalian way of nourishing infants that connected humans to the more-than-human world. Katherine characterised breastfeeding as 'natural' and 'earthy'. Her experience of breastfeeding her first baby in 1993 felt like an emulation of her own mother's maternal style, and a contrast to her mother-in-law's maternal behaviour and perspectives.

> My parents were very much about family and love and whatever, and that's a natural thing. So breastfeeding came very easy, for instance, because that's what you do. You just breastfeed because that's your whole purpose ... When E [child] was three months old, my husband's parents came to visit and she [mother-in-law] had a completely different approach to mothering ... His mum had that ... fifties scientific kind of structured approach to mothering ... To her it was all too icky and body and nakedness and all that kind of stuff, whereas my mum was like, 'Oh, it's so beautiful that you're there nursing baby and that's how God made us' ... So it was a completely opposite approach to mothering and I'm so glad I had my mother having that very sort of natural, earthy – that's kind of a bit of a Dutch thing as well. There is quite a strong earthiness to the Dutch culture. So that was good and that made me embrace it.

In Katherine's narrative, emulating her mother's 'natural', 'earthy' and 'peasant' approach to mothering helped her feel more comfortable with her new role, in contrast with her mother-in-law's discomfort with activities like breastfeeding. Despite this characterisation, many narrators, like Valerie above, did not necessarily experience their interactions with their children as 'natural' or 'easy', with many encountering breastfeeding and sleeping difficulties with their infants.

Whether they found matrescence effortless or difficult, many women described motherhood as an entry into a new world of sensory experiences. Entering maternality was an induction into novel smells, sounds, sights and sensations. In an article from 1977, writer Marina Warner described the ways in which mother love is mediated through a myriad of sensory intimacies.

> A thousand thrills will soon be yours which perhaps no one else can share: yours is the thrill of holding your baby for the first time; of stroking his head; of feeling the push of his little button nose into your neck; and of experiencing the vicelike grasp of his tiny hands around your fingers. To others he may seem unattractive, and even to you momentarily, but he becomes more beautiful each minute. You will watch him purse his lips, mouth open in bird-like fashion, as he gropes for his first meal. You will enjoy the hundreds of vague noises he makes: the squeaky sounds of satisfaction after he has been fed, almost like the creaking of a new leather saddle; the tiny rusty-hinge noises; the little piglike grunts; and the cooings of contentment. The first beginnings of a smile will probably be yours alone.[3]

While it is perhaps no longer true to say that 'no one else can share' these sensory intimacies – as fathers and partners have taken on more of the care of children – the immersion in the wonder of a new life is perhaps intrinsic to matrescence. This careful, close engagement with the intricacies of another human being connects to another aspect of maternal love that narrators documented – a sense of mindful observation.

## Observation and attention

As she experienced matrescence in 2012, Heather became aware that through 'watching and listening' carefully to her child, the practice of mothering was slowly changing her on fundamental levels. Heather was born in 1981 and raised in Sydney by adoptive parents. She now lives in Melbourne with her wife. In describing her shifting relationship with her creative work, Heather spoke of how motherhood had changed her.

> A sense of kindness and care and things that I'd always had but it was sort of – yeah, it was bigger and I listened more, definitely ... Found myself watching and listening a lot. I feel like that came from that early motherhood of like learning to kind of listen to cues. I actually found early motherhood, I remember feeling it like it was a really big creative act ... So much about instinct and the unconscious. All of those things really played out in that first year and so I became more sensitive.

Heather's descriptions here of how mothering changed her are in many ways reminiscent of philosopher Sara Ruddick's argument about the ways in which 'maternal thinking' can change a woman. Ruddick offers a model for thinking about how maternal subjectivity is learnt through the daily care of children rather than being innate or instinctive. For Ruddick, maternal thinking is a conscious, reflexive mode of thinking and behaving that women (and others including non-birthgiving parents such as fathers, co-mothers and adoptive mothers) can learn through caring for children. In striving for the preservation, growth and social acceptance of their children, mothers develop a certain ethical relationship to the world and a uniquely maternal way of reasoning.[4]

In addition to enhancing her observation of her child, Heather explained that matrescence increased her mindful observation of her local neighbourhood.

> The thing that has surprised me about motherhood was a newfound obsession with walking – I just walked everywhere. He screamed in the car, he didn't scream as much in the pram, it was just simple like that. I just loved being outside. Everything slowed down – I noticed nature more – I became really obsessed with the seasons and the weather and would walk in every weather, rain, hail or shine kind of thing. We had the dog, which was a lifesaver because I had to get out of bed and walk him every morning which was actually a really amazing thing because as soon as I was outside, I felt good, blood flowing, it was just really good ... I would kind of do the same walk every single day and I would notice particular things that were different on the walk and yeah, I suppose it was sort of like a much more attention to detail that I had never experienced before.

Although her daily walks through nearby streets and parks were motivated by the desire to calm a screaming child and exercise the family dog, Heather found that the long perambulations had benefits beyond the practical and immediate. She found that 'everything slowed down' and she cultivated an enhanced 'attention to detail', implying that this mindful observation shifted her relationships to everyday time and local places. In other words, matrescence has the potential to shift a woman's very understandings of time and space.

## Interruption and encumberment

Psychosocial researcher Lisa Baraitser also theorises that maternal subjectivity is an interrupted and encumbered subjectivity.[5] Being constantly interrupted in her attempts to finish tasks or to complete conversations can leave a new mother with a sense of fragmented subjectivity, when no thought, word or action feels fully realised. New Zealand-born Māori mother Avril became a mother in 2013. Avril reflected on how mothers adapt to persistent interruption, and how her friends without children found it much harder to maintain a consistent thread of conversation during disruptions: 'Mums can have conversations while children are making noise and stop and start a conversation. It's a skill that mothers have. But if you've not had a child, it's really disruptive. It's like, I can't do this'.

The encumbered nature of mothering that Baraitser describes stems partly from the ways in which caring for a small child is a deeply embodied experience, but also from how the new mother is weighed down or challenged by unfamiliar objects. In Chapter 2, we discussed the ways in which pregnancy constitutes an induction into an unfamiliar world of goods. Mothers-in-waiting practise for and emotionally prepare for motherhood through the creation and acquisition of infant care items. Once a baby is born, mothers begin a process of mastering the use of such unfamiliar objects (such as buckling a car seat, unfolding a pram or changing a nappy), but being able to perform competent mastery in public can generate considerable anxiety for some time.[6] While there have been historical changes to the types of objects which mediate the relationship between mother and child, their psychological importance as technologies of relation remains relatively constant. These relational objects such as feeding bottles, breast pumps, baby slings and baby carriers are designed to replicate the embodied interactions between mother and child, and their success depends upon how effectively they imitate the actions of breastfeeding and gestation in the womb.[7] Infant care items are also social signifiers in that a new mother's choice of different material culture – be it cot, high chair, pram, clothing or toys – signals her affiliation with different parenting philosophies. For example, use of reusable cloth nappies generally signals a desire to practise eco-friendly or sustainable parenting. Once inducted into the common culture of motherhood, new mothers quickly learn how to decode the meaning of such signifiers.

Across these maternographies, mothers spoke evocatively about what it felt like as they began active maternal practices of caring for a child. They offered vivid descriptions of the unique and transformative quality of maternal love. Several themes emerged which are reflected in academic literature on maternal subjectivity: that new motherhood is emotionally intense, embodied, observational, interrupted and encumbered.

## Generational time

While these maternographies demonstrate that many aspects persist, in other ways, the mother–child relationship has changed over time. It has partially shifted in response to changing patterns of gender, work and care, such as a growing involvement of fathers in the daily care of children, increased workforce participation among mothers and the rising availability of paid childcare. These trends will be discussed further in Chapters 5 and 6. Another significant trend has been the upward shift in the age at which a woman first has children and a downward shift in the number of children she has overall – leading to a shorter 'maternal window' in which a woman is actively caring for preschool-aged children.[8] Postwar mothers like Eve had her first of eight children when she was nineteen years of age, and Jane had her first of eleven children when she was twenty-three years of age. By the 1970s, it was more common to have three children, like Brenda, who had her first child at twenty-five years of age. For millennial mothers, the average age at which women start having children is now over thirty and more women are having only children, like Connie and Tessa, who both had a single child at the age of forty-three. This section tracks shifts in the historical context, cultural discourses and material circumstances of mother–child relationships, in terms of both childrearing advice literature and the everyday practices of individual mothers.

## Postwar mothers

Perhaps the most prominent historical shift in the past seventy-five years has been in the sources and content of childrearing philosophies and practices. Child-raising strategies have broadly shifted from discipline and routine to affection and expressiveness, in line with shifting psychological discourses abut children, though there remained considerable diversity of approaches across all generations of parenting. In the immediate postwar decades, a concern about the negative impacts of 'maternal deprivation' as conceived by John Bowlby was mobilised to foment concern about the lifelong psychological harm caused by a less than attentive mother.[9] But by the late twentieth century, the importance of maternal ambivalence was acknowledged: that a mother cannot and should not be omnipresent.[10]

Across this seventy-five-year period, the sources of childrearing advice have broadly changed from experiential knowledge shared verbally among female relatives and friends, to a profusion of 'expert' information accessible virtually and instantaneously. Historical studies have demonstrated that childrearing advice directed towards mothers has steadily increased across Australia, Canada, New Zealand, the UK and the US since the late nineteenth century and that such advice reflects changing cultural understandings of ideal childhood and parenthood.[11] This shift towards 'mothering deskilled' during the early to mid-twentieth century in Australia was particularly a feature of middle-class family life.[12]

Baby health and infant welfare centres began to spread across Australia from the early twentieth century, originally as not-for-profit ventures started by charitable maternalist reformers, then as part of the public health system. In Victoria, the first Baby Health Centre began in Richmond in 1917, followed by the establishment of a clinic and Model Training School for the Baby Health Centre Association at the Women's Hospital in 1918–24.[13] Medical experts argued that expert advice was necessary to reduce infant mortality and to train mothers in appropriate childrearing strategies. But historian Phillipa Mein Smith argues that it is not clear whether the infant welfare movement was the primary cause of the decline in infant mortality – rather, this trend commenced before the introduction of the centres.[14] Further, it was not until the late 1930s that attendance at Victorian infant welfare centres reached two-thirds of new babies. Mothers did not always follow the advice of infant welfare nurses and their services tended to be utilised by middle-class and skilled working-class mothers, rather than more disadvantaged families.[15]

Although it would be tempting to assume that an increase in 'expert' parental advice in the mid-twentieth century immediately undermined mothers' confidence in their innate abilities, a belief in maternal instinct was still relatively prominent among postwar mothers interviewed. These new mothers of the 1950s and 1960s recall seeking and sharing advice among female relatives and friends. They did not recall referring to expert advice manuals frequently. Anglo-Australian Eve did not consult any books with her first baby in 1950 because she believed that raising children came naturally: 'In my generation, we believed in mother's instinct. And I just assumed that when I had a baby that I'd know what to do with it ... So there was no anxiety ... And I just knew that I could always call on my mum if things went wrong'. This confidence that motherhood is instinctual has gradually eroded over the past seventy-five years, replaced by a conviction that mothering must be learnt. A counter-discourse of scientific motherhood gained ground in the postwar decades, as is evident in this maternal and child welfare manual from 1942:

> Experience too has demonstrated that MATERNAL INSTINCT ALONE IS INSUFFICIENT EQUIPMENT FOR A MOTHER TO UNDERTAKE THE RESPONSIBILITY OF FEEDING AND CARING FOR A BABY. Mothers are slow to accept this. The tendency is to regard maternal instinct as all-sufficient. But, in every sphere of human endeavour it is TRAINING that counts [capitals in original].[16]

Childrearing advice books asserted that a mother's behaviour could have profound impacts upon the psychological development of the child, but this influence was understood in rather punitive terms: that she must guard against 'spoiling' or indulging her child. In 1941, Australian psychologist Irma Schnierer wrote that a mother

> should never be guided by love only. From the very first day of his life she must train him to regular feeding hours and not spoil him by indulgence; she must let him cry between meal-times until he knows his 'time-table' ... Even the very young child is exactly aware of what he can achieve by crying and screaming and what not! He does not 'think' of course, in the usual sense of the word, but he is impressed by his 'training' and he has a good memory. He does not forget your indulgence if you gave in on one or several times during his earliest life, and he will use this remembrance to his own advantage in the future.[17]

This sense that babies must be disciplined to follow the dictates of the mother could be stressful for new mothers attempting to adhere to professional advice. Eve had eight children, the first born in 1950. Initially, she tried to follow the directives of the nurses who had cared for her in hospital after her birth although she found this upsetting.

> Taking the baby home – the matron said to P [husband] and I, 'You've got a perfect baby, don't spoil her'. It was the worst advice we ever had, you know. I'd live by the rules and she'd cry before it was time to feed her and ... I'd be crying with her and waiting ... for the four hours to finish. I'd go up the other end of the room and put the radio on then I'd rush out the moment the time was up to feed her. By this time, she might be asleep.

The advice received by Eve echoes Queensland health advice from 1949, that 'Every baby comes out perfect, the way they are treated effects how they turn out'.[18] Postwar mothers tended to initially follow the guidelines laid down by doctors, midwives and nurses, though with subsequent children, they were more likely to ignore advice with which they disagreed. Interviews in other Australian states also confirm that mothers had a variety of responses – including adoption, adaptation and rejection – to the information provided by maternal child health nurses.[19] Eve explained that although she originally tried to follow the four-hourly feeding guidelines laid out by health professionals, when that did not work for her, she began to feed her baby more frequently.

Part of the reason that postwar advice was not always strictly adhered to was that information such as infant feeding advice was confusing and contradictory. Doctors and nurses officially supported breastfeeding, but advice and practices in hospitals and infant welfare clinics worked against it.[20] Staff in maternity hospitals expected that women would breastfeed, and yet the advice they gave and the practices they followed undermined successful feeding, such as giving women drugs during childbirth, separating mothers and babies after birth, sterilising nipples before and after each feed, restricting the number of minutes a baby could feed on each breast and feeding babies infant formula during the night.[21] Postwar hospitals tended to follow the philosophies popularised during the interwar period by New Zealand doctor Truby King, who recommended keeping infants to strict feeding and sleeping regimes and restricting overly affectionate modes of interaction so as not to adversely affect the child's character. He wrote that, 'The most reliable modern experience and research shows that even during the first month feeding every four hours suits most babies and no normal baby needs feeding more often than four hourly'.[22] Consistent with such recommendations, in hospitals, infants were kept in a nursery and brought to the mother for four-hourly breastfeeds. Overnight, babies were bottle-fed by nurses to allow the mother to rest. Many postwar mothers appreciated the sleep and rest they received in hospital. But when Eve obediently followed such prescriptions with her first child, her breastmilk 'just dried up' after six weeks. From 1945, breastfeeding rates declined until they reached their lowest point in 1971, when only 26 per cent of babies were breastfed at three months of age and only 9 per cent at six months.[23]

After going home from hospital, postwar mothers received parenting advice from nurses at infant health centres (see Figure 4). This advice was delivered during frequent visits: postwar mothers were told to attend appointments every week for the first three months and every fortnight until twelve months of age.[24] (By 2019, Victorian appointments had been reduced to six appointments in the first year of life.) While there has been much subsequent criticism of the inflexible regimes advocated by these nurses, some mothers felt reassured and supported by this regular, 'expert' advice.[25] Nurses were trained in the ideology of scientific mothering and encouraged mothers to follow firm routines. Postwar appointments emphasised vaccination schedules and growth charts, as evidenced

## Mother love

Figure 4 Mothers and babies at the Drouin Infant Welfare Centre, Victoria, circa 1944 (photo by Jim Fitzpatrick, National Library of Australia U-429–122)

in the booklets mothers kept and showed me during interviews. Infants were weighed at every appointment and if their weight gain was considered less than optimal, mothers were advised to supplement breastfeeding with formula feeding. Though considered a preventative health measure to promote healthy weight gain, such advice was later critiqued as contributing to a decline in infants still breastfed at three months of age, from over 50 per cent in 1943 to around 25 per cent in 1967.[26]

Anglo-Australian Maggie had her first of two children in 1966 in Fitzroy. She recalls that her nurse's advice undermined successful breastfeeding.

> 'And what are you feeding her?' And I said, 'Well, I'm feeding her myself'. She said, 'Yes, I know, dear – but what are you giving her?' And I said, 'Well, I'm breastfeeding her'. And she said, 'Oh, you brave little woman. You brave little mother' … My kids were always much lower weight than all the others, and the Sister wasn't too happy with

them. She kept on a bit about ... maybe we should have a test feed, and maybe we should top her up, and things, but I was very resistant ... I kept away pretty much by then, just went for the vaccinations and so on ... Just as well I wasn't easily upset at all ... But she said, 'Skin and bone, Mrs P.'. Really, that's awful.

Maggie felt fortunate that her convictions were strong enough to counteract the nurse's warnings. But other mothers she knew found their confidence in breastfeeding shaken by visits to the nurse.

It was not only health advice that contributed to declining breastfeeding rates in the postwar era, but also cultural attitudes and personal opinions. A woman's desire to breastfeed is often shaped by matrilineal influences,[27] as is evident in Patsy's maternography of becoming a mother in 1967. As a young woman of nineteen, she was heavily swayed by her mother's opinion that formula feeding was preferable to breastfeeding. Patsy clearly remembers the strength of her mother's assertion and its influence upon her: 'I didn't breast-feed because my mother ... was a pretty strong woman ... She was adamant that I was not going to breastfeed and I can't remember the reasons why ... I did bottle-feed T [child]'. Bottle-feeding was often viewed as a more scientific, hygienic and modern way to feed babies in 1950s and 1960s Australia. It was also supported by a cultural discomfort with breastfeeding's association with nudity and sexuality. Such associations meant that breastfeeding in public was unacceptable, and exposing one's breasts seen as indecent. Recalling her experiences with her first child in 1953, English-born Marjorie said:

> A few of us were breastfeeding at the same time ... and we'd go in another room and shut the door ... in front of the other men. R [husband] saw me breastfeeding because I'd lie in bed and he'd sometimes go and get L [child] and bring her into me, but ... it was a private thing between you and your baby.

Such attitudes were reinforced by health professionals. As late as 1972, a mother recalled being asked by a maternal and child health nurse to go into a separate room to feed her baby when she was at a playgroup.[28] The scientific approach to motherhood also prioritised the measurable, which worked against breastfeeding. Mothers whose babies were constantly weighed and who were advised that they needed additional fluids and the early introduction of solids were anxious for the reassurance that a bottle provided, where they knew exactly how much milk their baby was getting.[29]

Expert advice offered to postwar mothers about infant sleep was also regimented and punitive. For example, Schnierer's 1941 book on *Making Childhood Happier* took an unsympathetic approach to children's fears or need for comfort during the night.

> Children who do not fear the darkness in their bedroom become less timid than others and they are better prepared for life. You shouldn't indulge your child when he asks you to leave the light on ... mostly it is not fear which makes the child ask for the light to be left on but a means to attract attention. Mummy comes to the bedroom, and sits down, consoles the darling and tells stories. So the little tyrant gets what he wants ... Many a mother goes so far as to take a crying child – not only a baby – into her own bed. That is the worst thing you can do. The child becomes quiet, of course, but his education will be very difficult later on, for he will be so spoilt that you never can make good what you have ruined in his early childhood.[30]

Two attitudes are prominent here: that a mother must guard against permanently 'ruining' her child through overly affectionate treatment and that children will seek to cynically manipulate their parents if given the opportunity.

In her regular newspaper column in the 1950s, infant welfare nurse 'Sister Alice' similarly recommended that 'From the first week of his life, train baby to sleep well by establishing good sleeping habits and you will avoid many sleeping problems'.[31] To guard against manipulation by their baby, mothers were told that any failure to sleep through the night was their own fault. 'Sleeplessness to the young child is usually caused by not being trained to sleep to a room alone or by bad practices, such as rocking to sleep, the use of a comforter, or baby being given attention and picked up each time he cries.'[32] Although nursing advice may have undermined the idea of maternal instinct, it remained a key theme among advice literature that would continue to resurface across the next seventy-five years. In the postwar years, there was an increasing interest in childrearing theories based upon Freudian psychology.[33] In a shift away from scientific, regimented motherhood, experts such as Benjamin Spock, Maurice Bevan-Brown and John Bowlby argued that babies should not be raised by clocks; rather, mothers should become attuned to their individual and ever-changing needs. Although critics labelled such ideas overly permissive, they gradually grew in influence. Bowlby's theories of attachment and maternal deprivation became the basis for the conviction that insufficient love from a primary caregiver would cause permanent emotional damage to a child. Popularisation of such notions of child development influenced the cultural belief that mothers should be responsible for their children's psychological wellbeing, further entrenching the ideal of the stay-at-home mother and a reliance on childrearing experts.[34]

In 1946, a book was published that spearheaded an explosion of advice literature in the decades to follow. Spock's *Common Sense Book of Baby and Child Care* was first published in the United States but quickly spread around the world. Spock advised mothers to follow their instincts with his famous words: 'Trust yourself. You know more than you think you do'. He argued that routines could be a helpful guide but did not need to be slavishly adhered to, and that displays of love would not spoil a child's character.[35] The influence of Spock's ideas was immediately discernible, such as a 1950 article by 'a mother and a doctor', who urged empathy rather than punishment when children encountered problems such as bed-wetting, thumb-sucking or rule-breaking:

> It is not natural for a young child to behave extremely well all the time. High spirits, the keen desire to explore new fields, and the urge for physical activity: all of these are bound to cause some kind of upheaval … Children need a happy, relaxed and untroubled home atmosphere where love and affection flourish and where parents are kind and understanding.[36]

Despite the increased publication of such parenting guidance after 1945, very few postwar mothers remembered consulting professional childrearing advice. However, this was to change as their children came to parenthood in the 1970s and 1980s.

## *Second-wave mothers*

These more permissive and responsive attitudes continued to grow in influence into the 1970s. Second-wave mothers sought information on childrearing from a range of sources, both informal and formal. When asked where she received advice on parenting in 1975, Irish-Australian Penny told me:

> Certainly, friends and family. Especially friends who'd recently had babies. My mother as well, definitely. I was always an avid reader. There were plenty of books going round the family about childrearing and birthing. Also having a good doctor and ... we had parent nights and pre-visits to the hospital.

A 1989 survey asked new mothers which sources of advice they found helpful, and two-thirds appreciated the advice of their mothers, friends and sisters.[37]

Like their postwar predecessors, many second-wave mothers reported that they had had experience looking after children before they become a mother, either their siblings' or friends' children, giving them valuable hands-on skills before they had their own children. As we saw in the previous chapter on birth, mothers in the 1970s and 1980s increasingly believed in the importance of access to reliable information to make fully informed choices. There was also a rising view that 'good' mothering meant following expert advice, with more and more new mothers turning to books for parenting information. When she had her first child in 1974, Dutch-born Mary recalled that 'everyone I knew had the Spock book' – though she contrasted this reliance on a single tome with the approach of her daughter-in-law a generation later, who had a coffee table covered in childrearing literature when she became a mother.

When she had her three children in the late 1970s, Penny read the *Better Homes Baby Book* and found Penelope Leach's *Your Baby and Child* especially helpful. Leach is a British psychologist who first published her advice in 1977 and whose updated books remain in print today. She advises against strict schedules and placing too much faith in 'experts': 'Rearing a child "by the book" – by any set of rules or predetermined ideas – can work well if the rules you choose to follow happen to fit the baby you have. But even a minor misfit between the two can cause misery'.[38]

While postwar mothers like Eve often cited the influence of their own mothers, they did not often mention the influence of their peer group. Second-wave mothers relied on both. Many mothers of the

1970s and 1980s report seeking out and listening to the advice of their own mothers. Mary remembers that:

> I used to talk a lot to my mum about it ... I think if you're happy with your own upbringing and how you became the person that you are, when you grow up you see that it comes from having a good childhood so you appreciate what your parents have done.

Childrearing advice was also coming from new sources which challenged the assumption that expertise only resided in health professionals. Influenced by the La Leche League in the US, the Nursing Mothers Association of Australia (NMAA) (later the Australian Breastfeeding Association) was formed in 1964 by a group of suburban, middle-class mothers concerned that the advice of health professionals might be contributing to declining breastfeeding rates.[39] As one childrearing author wrote in 1975, 'the expectant mother who wants to nurse her baby often meets discouragement on every hand: from relatives, hospital nurses and even paediatricians'.[40] By the 1970s, NMAA had formed local chapters in many areas, which became important sources of information and support for new mothers. Their breastfeeding advice literature was read by women across Australia, including interviewees Sally and Penny. Groups like NMAA contributed to a shift in attitudes in the 1970s, as it was gradually realised that breastfeeding on demand rather than by a schedule encourages a mother's milk supply.[41] This also influenced hospital regulations: while demand feeding was only permitted in 14 per cent of Victorian hospitals in 1977, by 1984 it was 'actively supported' in 87 per cent of hospitals.[42] By 1980, it was claimed that breastfeeding rates were higher than they had been in decades.[43]

## Millennial mothers

Since the 1990s, the amount and diversity of parenting advice has grown, at the same time as the perceived importance of listening to experts has risen. Consequently, many new millennial mothers report feeling overwhelmed by the quantity and contradictory nature of this advice, and concerned about the consequences of failing to master or implement it. Former maternal and child health nurse Robin Barker was obviously responding to such concerns when she first published her popular book *Baby Love* in 1994:

> Babycare information is everywhere. Around the globe there are thousands of books that cover the same information as this book. 'Parenting' magazines are flourishing, along with classes on breastfeeding, sleeping and settling, introduction of solids, discipline and so on and so on. Yet, the most common phrase heard from the lips of new parents, especially new mothers, is still, '*Why didn't anyone tell me it would be like this?*' ... After years of working with families and babies, however, I am convinced that there is no way to totally prepare anyone for the incredible event of the birth of their baby and what follows. An element of mystery remains, which is impossible to anticipate or provide for. No two babies are alike, no two mothers or fathers are alike. This is why, despite the avalanche of information available covering the whole spectrum of babycare from 'attachment-style babycare—never put your baby down' to 'strict routine-style babycare—never pick your baby up', no one can tell you what it will really be like *for you* [italics in original].[44]

She concludes that the only truisms in childrearing are that babies are unpredictable, and it is often impossible to fully understand or 'solve' issues with sleep, feeding and crying.

If new mothers were drowning in infant care advice in the early 1990s, this trend has only increased in the decades since. In the last thirty years, vast changes to information and communications technologies have transformed Australian lives, including the uptake of computers, the development of the internet and the permeation of smartphones. It is within this context that millennial mothers are consuming childrearing advice. Anglo-Australian Sarah located most of her parenting information online when she had her first child in 2013, appreciating the convenience of guidance available at any time of the day or night: 'Number one was the internet. So much trawling the internet for things. Next thing was I had a lovely girlfriend who'd had a baby the year before so I'd talk to her ... I had a couple of books, but I didn't really turn to them much'. When she conceived in 2012, Anglo-Australian Molly preferred to download relevant apps on to her smartphone, like a pregnancy app that sent her weekly updates on the development of her foetus.

The experiential advice of older generations of women, such as their own mothers, is less trusted by many millennial mothers, though they will seek out informal advice from their contemporaries, such as friends or mothers' groups. This seems to be largely because the proliferation of expert advice, combined with the frequency with which it changes, undermines the seeming relevance of the experiences of previous generations of mothers, which are dismissed as 'old wives' tales'.[45] Sarah explained that she would seek advice from her mother or mother-in-law only after exhausting other avenues of information, and partly to humour her relatives.

> I think with the grandparents, they have this confidence and this sense that they know so much but it was thirty years ago and I think they really forget. So I still ask them things more to include them than because I actually want their information … [My husband's] dad, when he was crying, said, 'Get a dummy and dip it in honey'. I was like, 'Honey is on the list of things not to give them!'

The increasing prevalence of professional childrearing advice and a growing sense that mothering requires expert training has perhaps made advice from their own mothers seem less relevant or trustworthy to millennial mothers. Molly is aware that she is influenced by her mother's parenting style while also mistrusting explicit recommendations as 'old wives' tales'.

Dutch-Australian Michelle had a different relationship to her mother's advice. Although Michelle reflected on the ways in which expert advice has changed since her infancy, she found this a source of interest rather than a reason to mistrust her mother's advice. Michelle found that she was actively reflecting on her experiences of being mothered as she learnt to mother in 2013.

> Once F [child] was born, I have to say I was calling Mum up on a regular basis … Just getting her to talk about her experiences and stories of, like my dad changing my first nappy or what did you do, sleep her on her back? You know, Mum used to sleep us on our tummies, whereas now it's all about sleeping the babies on their backs. I think when we were children, or babies, things were a little bit more relaxed than what they are possibly now … Yeah, I did speak to Mum quite a lot in the first few weeks. And she came over a few times as well and stayed the night. She was a great support … She never really told me you should do it this way or that way. She was just always there for me.

One of the issues for millennial mothers is the sheer volume of information which confronts them. It can be challenging to distinguish between the confusing and conflicting variety of books, websites, apps and other sources, particularly for inexperienced and sleep-deprived new parents. Beginning with conception (and even before), there are ample books and websites tracking gestation, such as the popular American tome *What to Expect When You're Expecting* or the humorous Australian book *Up the Duff*.[46] After their birth, mothers are confronted by an ever greater diversification of childrearing advice reflecting a wide spectrum of parenting philosophies, from attachment parenting and co-sleeping advocates like Pinky McKay to strict routine and controlled crying advocates like Tizzie Hall.[47] Just as confusing as this expert advice is the unsolicited informal advice from family and friends. American-born Katerina felt intimidated by the avalanche of advice confronting her as a new mother in 2013:

> You've got all this stuff on the internet. You've got grandmothers that have a certain approach ... And you kind of have to learn to sift through that information and kind of put in your pocket. Oh, this might be useful. Save that for later ... Or I'm just going to discard that and move on. So I think that part's particularly overwhelming. And when you're a new mum, you don't necessarily know what's good advice and not for baby care ... But I think earlier on I didn't have that confidence or that sense of boundaries. And I think as he's getting older and you've kind of gone through the physically exhausting part in some sense, I've been able to communicate that better and have made certain choices and decisions about my parenting style.

Many mothers describe a similar process: they draw upon a range of advice from people they know and 'experts' while remaining sceptical and learning through experience. They start out their mothering journey feeling tentative and unsure, but gain confidence through daily trial and error. Eventually, they come to know their child and to learn their maternal style, though this knowledge is dynamic as the child grows and its needs change. This learning of maternal styles echoes the ways in which Ruddick describes the development of 'maternal thinking': a specific expertise and relationship to the world that mothers gain through the daily care of children.[48]

Māori mother Avril found that one method of navigating expert advice is to ask other mothers what sources they trust. Of her first pregnancy in 2013, she recalled:

> During my pregnancy, I really avoided too much information. So my midwife gave me things that I needed to know, as I needed to know them ... Once I became a mum, I've read a lot more. And it's usually from friends that have recommended. So [one friend] recommended *The Wonder Weeks* book, which I found very useful. Another friend recommended *Save Our Sleep*. I found that very useful ... And the website that the maternal child health clinic recommended ... Also mothers' group. Just asking questions and everyone going, 'Oh yeah, I've experienced that last week'.

These books which friends recommend to Avril are popular in twenty-first-century Australia. *Save Our Sleep* was written by Australian-based 'expert' Tizzie Hall. Her routine-based prescriptions promise to help babies sleep through the night from a young age, with schedules commencing in the second week after birth. Though her routines have been criticised as contradicting health advice to demand-feed young babies, Hall defends her methods as producing happier, easier babies.

> Debate still rages over the benefits of demand versus routine feeding but the fact remains that babies thrive on routine and the security of knowing that their needs are being met in a consistent way. In my experience, babies who are given a defined daily routine are more content. They tend to adapt to life more easily than those who are conditioned to making demands and then expect their parents to meet those demands every time.[49]

By contrast with Hall's methods, which are based on her own experiences of babies, *The Wonder Weeks* by Dutch researchers Hetty Vanderijt and Frans Plooij is based upon research with infants. Vanderijt and Plooij argue that all babies have predictable times of growth and development when they will become fussier. Knowing these 'wonder weeks', they argue, means that parents can be reassured that there is nothing wrong with their baby and they do not need to change their caregiving routines.

> This book focuses on the eight major leaps that every baby takes in her first 14 months of life. It tells you what each of these developments mean for your baby's understanding of the world about her and how

she uses this understanding to develop the new skills that she needs at each stage in her development ... Parents can use this understanding of their baby's developmental leaps to help them through these often confusing times in their new lives.[50]

If books like *The Wonder Weeks* are designed to reassure parents that their baby is developing appropriately for their age, peer support groups perform a similar function for parents. New parent groups, colloquially known as 'mothers' groups', have become more common since the 1990s. Usually, they commence when a local maternal child health nurse links a group of new mothers in the same neighbourhood with babies of the same age. Often, groups continue to socialise after nurse-facilitated sessions cease. When they work well, mothers' groups can help new mothers sift through conflicting childrearing advice through discussions about personal experiences. Remembering her experiences with her Fitzroy-based mothers' group in 2013, Molly recalled:

> Eventually, when we went to mothers' group at the centre and I heard [the other mums] talking ... I thought, Oh crap, I think I'm doing everything wrong. And they said, 'don't get your baby to sleep through breastfeeding', and I thought, I do that. 'Don't do this.' 'I do that.' ... So I listened to what [the other mums] were saying and I spoke to [them] for advice and I thought what I was doing was fine. And then once it wasn't fine, I changed it.

Generally, millennial mothers regard the recommendations of books and websites as more accurate and trustworthy than the opinions of friends or family. Yet they nevertheless discovered, just like previous generations, that the shared experience of motherhood could be powerfully bonding. With her first child born in 2013, English-born Helen found that:

> [During my pregnancy, I] trusted the reliability of books rather than people ... Whereas that kind of did a wonderful shift after ... he was born. Still I was a book worm and I would read what is this ... And then as that started to not work ... It just started to really make me feel great to talk to people and see that no one is the same.

The expansion of the digital realm into all facets of contemporary life has had mixed outcomes for millennial mothers. While it has no doubt led to an increasing spread of 'experts', some with more dubious claims to expertise than others, it has also offered mothers an opportunity to speak for themselves and offer their own advice to their peers, as well as to mock unattainable mothering ideals.[51]

Overall, the sources and content of childrearing advice have changed considerably since 1945. Millennial mothers have sometimes told me of the importance of their mothers' group for providing advice, support and company, while others felt more ambivalent about such peer support groups. The extent to which women rely on the advice of their own mother has decreased over the seventy-five-year period I am studying, with millennial mothers more likely to search the internet than call their mother. One legacy of the maternity reform movement has been that some perinatal women feel more empowered to question the authority of health professionals or their parents. However, the democratisation and proliferation of childrearing advice that has occurred through the internet can be a double-edged sword.

## Conclusion

There is both powerful continuity and significant dynamism in the mother–child relationship over the last seventy-five years. In their maternographies, women evocatively described the intensity of their feelings for their child, the vulnerability and responsibility of the new mother's position and that maternality felt overwhelmingly corporeal, interrupted, encumbered and experiential. Some things, it seems, have not shifted in the sensations of mother love and the fundamentals of mother–child interactions.

But the extent to which new mothers are imagined to need external or expert guidance has certainly increased, judging by both the maternographies collected and the evidence of childrearing advice literature. During her interview, postwar mother Eve reflected on twenty-five years of volunteering at the Women's Hospital in Melbourne, where she witnessed a shift from an assumption motherhood is natural to an assumption that women need professional advice and training.

> I was almost the last of the mothers that mother's instinct was to be relied upon and you were confident and you went ahead. It was the beginning of ... an influx of knowledge and people wanting to know ... everything that was going on and wanted to be informed about everything ... I think there's too much information out there

now. I think it can be confusing for a lot of mothers. I did voluntary work at the women's hospital for a long time and ... when I first volunteered, there was about oh, a half a dozen books on mothering, right, and on childcare. By the time I finished there were three shelves of pamphlets on everything you could think about. I would see young mothers come in and they'd be anxious and they'd be confused and they'd be wondering – they'd be anxious about the baby. It was such a big responsibility.

Eve's reflections gesture to a wider cultural shift from a belief in maternal instinct to a belief that good mothering relies on expert knowledge. While advice concerning scientific mothering increased significantly in the interwar and immediate postwar years, these interviews suggest that maternal reliance upon professional advice lagged several decades behind. Advice has mirrored changes in childrearing fashions, from regimented and emotionally distant parenting through to emotive and responsive styles, to the contemporary polarisation of parenting philosophies. While mothers once sought the advice of their own mothers, they now doubt so-called 'old wives' tales'. While postwar mothers may not have been granted a great deal of information about pregnancy, birth or childrearing, millennial mothers are inundated with a proliferation of purportedly expert advice. The conundrum today is not how to access information but which sources and types to trust (and when to ignore the 'experts').

Ultimately, while childrearing philosophies have shifted in different time periods, they are always contested and subject to moral judgements. Sally Maushart argues that despite the proliferation of expert advice, women are less prepared than ever before for motherhood, citing a yawning chasm between expectations and reality.[52] But it is hard to separate the influence of advice from the value of support, and the mother's relationship with her child from her relationship with others around her. While it is true that some mothers struggle when the advice they are offered is not applicable to their baby, what is perhaps more important is the support they receive from those around them. While the mother's relationship with her child is the most transformative aspect of the mothermorphosis, she also finds that her relationships with nearly everyone else in her life undergo a profound change, as we shall see in the next chapter.

## Notes

1 de Marneffe, *Maternal Desire: On Children, Love, and the Inner Life.*
2 Reading magazine articles across the past seventy-five years, it appears that the term 'bonding' came into prominence in the 1970s, and began to inform women's expectations of birth and the ways that they make sense of childbirth experiences. One magazine article wrote that 'Bonding is the awkward new name for the private time the family has together after the birth': Wynhausen, 'Birthing a Revolution', 20.
3 Marina Warner, 'Motherhood: Just an Ordinary Sort of Miracle', *Australian Women's Weekly*, 16 November 1977, 51.
4 Ruddick, *Maternal Thinking.*
5 Baraitser, *Maternal Encounters.*
6 Miller, *Making Sense of Motherhood.*
7 Pascoe Leahy, 'Maternal Heritage'.
8 Lixia Qu, Jennifer Baxter and Megan Carroll, 'Births in Australia: Facts & Figures' (Australian Institute of Family Studies, 2022), https://aifs.gov.au/facts-and-figures/births-australia.
9 Bowlby, *Maternal Care and Mental Health.*
10 Parker, *Torn in Two.*
11 Katherine Arnup, *Education for Motherhood: Advice for Mothers in Twentieth-Century Canada* (Toronto: University of Toronto Press, 1994); Julia Grant, *Raising Baby by the Book: The Education of American Mothers* (New Haven, CT: Yale University Press, 1998); Jessica Nathanson and Laura Camille Tuley, eds., *Mother Knows Best: Talking Back to the 'Experts'* (Bradford, Ontario: Demeter Press, 2009); Christina Hardyment, *Dream Babies: Childcare Advice from John Locke to Gina Ford* (London: Frances Lincoln, 2007); Paula S. Fass, *The End of American Childhood: A History of Parenting from Life on the Frontier to the Managed Child* (Princeton, NJ: Princeton University Press, 2016); Harry Hendrick, *Narcissistic Parenting in an Insecure World: A History of Parenting Culture 1920 to Present* (Bristol: Policy Press, 2016); Sue Kedgley, *Mum's the Word: The Untold Story of Motherhood in New Zealand* (Auckland: Random House, 1996).
12 Deacon, 'Taylorism in the Home: The Medical Profession, the Infant Welfare Movement and the Deskilling of Women'; Kerreen Reiger, 'Mothering Deskilled? Australian Childrearing and the "Experts"', *Community Health Studies* 10, no. 1 (1986): 39–46.
13 McCalman, *Sex and Suffering*, 159.
14 Mein Smith, *Mothers and King Baby*, 244.
15 Mein Smith, *Mothers and King Baby*, 245.

16 Victorian Department of Public Health, *Maternal and Child Welfare Manual* (Melbourne: Department of Public Health, 1942).
17 Irma Schnierer, *Making Childhood Happier* (Melbourne: Woman's World, 1941), 26–27.
18 Queensland Health Education Council, 'Health Service: Your New Baby Is Unique', *Queensland Times*, 17 May 1949, 4.
19 Wendy Selby, ' "Raising an Interrogatory Eyebrow": Women's Responses to the Infant Welfare Movement in Queensland, 1918–1939', in *On the Edge: Women's Experiences of Queensland*, ed. Gail Reekie (St. Lucia, Qld.: University of Queensland Press, 1994), 80–96; Virginia Thorley, 'Australian Mothers' Decisions on Infant Feeding: An Historical Analysis of Public Health Advice, Marketing, and Other Factors Influencing Their Choices, 1900–2000' (PhD, Brisbane: University of Queensland, 2007); Virginia Thorley, 'Assumptions and Advice: Mothers and Queensland Well-Baby Clinics. A Review', *Breastfeeding Review* 22, no. 1 (2014): 23–30.
20 Reiger, *Our Bodies, Our Babies*; Virginia Thorley, 'Feeding Their Babies: Infant Feeding Advice Received by Queensland Mothers in the Postwar Period, 1945–1965' (MA, Brisbane: University of Queensland, 2000); Brown et al., *Missing Voices*, 105.
21 Brown et al., *Missing Voices*, 105.
22 Truby King, *Feeding and Care of Baby* (London: Macmillan, 1921).
23 Brown et al., *Missing Voices*, 105.
24 Barnard and Twigg, *Nursing Mums*.
25 Kedgley, *Mum's the Word*, 171–2.
26 Nursing Mothers' Association, 'Decline in Breastfeeding at Three Months, 1943–67, Victoria', *NMA Newsletter* 4, no. 5 (1968): 7.
27 Joel Negin, Jenna Coffman, Pavle Vizintin and Camille Raynes-Greenow, 'The Influence of Grandmothers on Breastfeeding Rates: A Systematic Review', *BMC Pregnancy and Childbirth* xvi, no. 91 (2016): 1–10.
28 Brown et al., *Missing Voices*, 105.
29 Brown et al., *Missing Voices*, 105; Kedgley, *Mum's the Word*, 202–3.
30 Schnierer, *Making Childhood Happier*, 23.
31 Sister Alice, 'Ensure that Baby Has Enough Sleep', *Weekly Times*, 5 April 1950, 40.
32 Sister Alice, 'Train Your Baby to Sleep Well', *Weekly Times*, 25 August 1954, 55.
33 Kedgley, *Mum's the Word*, 173.
34 Kedgley, *Mum's the Word*, 178.
35 Spock, *Common Sense Book of Baby and Child Care*.

36 Mother M.D. 'Everyday Problems in Mothercraft', *Australian Women's Mirror*, 2 August 1950, 30.
37 Brown et al., *Missing Voices*, 118.
38 Penelope Leach, *Baby and Child* (Harmondsworth: Penguin, 1979).
39 Barnard and Twigg, *Nursing Mums*; Reiger, *Our Bodies, Our Babies*; Thorley, 'Middle-Class Mothers as Activists for Change: The Australian Breastfeeding Association'.
40 Davis, *Let's Have Healthy Children*, 118.
41 Davis, *Let's Have Healthy Children*, 135.
42 Brown et al., *Missing Voices*, 105.
43 Sally Wendkos Olds, '25 Common Questions about Breastfeeding', *Australian Women's Weekly*, 5 November 1980, 41.
44 Robin Barker, *Baby Love* (Chippendale, NSW: Pan Macmillan, 1994), 3–4.
45 Miller, *Making Sense of Motherhood*; Pascoe Leahy, 'The Mother Within'.
46 Kaz Cooke, *Up the Duff: The Real Guide to Pregnancy*, 2nd ed. (Camberwell: Viking, 2009); Heidi Murkoff, *What to Expect When You're Expecting*, 4th ed. (Sydney: Harper Collins, 2009).
47 Tizzie Hall, *Save our Sleep* (Sydney: Pan Macmillan, 2006); Pinky McKay, *Parenting by Heart* (Hawthorn: Viking Australia, 2011).
48 Ruddick, *Maternal Thinking*.
49 Hall, *Save our Sleep*, 19.
50 Hetty Vanderijt and Frans Plooij, *The Wonder Weeks: A Stress Free Guide to Your Baby's Behaviour*, 6th ed. (New York: Norton, 2019), 2–3.
51 May Friedman and Shana L. Calixte, eds., *Mothering and Blogging: The Radical Act of the Mommyblog* (Bradford, Ontario: Demeter Press, 2009).
52 Susan Maushart, *The Mask of Motherhood: How Becoming a Mother Changes Everything and Why We Pretend That It Doesn't* (New York: Penguin, 2000).

# 5

# Mothering the mother: maternal relationships and support

I remember being surprised by how much I wanted her [mother] around ... I was shocked by how powerful that is. Some of it is sort of experiential stuff ... as I moved through mothering S [child], I wanted to ask, 'what was I like at two months of age?' and 'when did I grow my first tooth? Did I make those same kinds of babbly noises?' ... Some of it is that you appreciate your mother for the first, actually truly appreciate – which you can't, fully, until you've occupied the maternal position. It's like, wow, yeah, you've done a lot for me ... But what was manifested most clearly ... was can you be around more at this point in my life? I'd really like to spend time with you, because it's really important to me to be spending time with my mother when I become a mother ...

I had a lovely mother's group ... They were an amazing group of women. I'm fascinated by how quickly you bond with people that are thrown into the same perilous situation as you ... Those women were so important to me ... I think it was shared adversity, probably. I think it goes back to the thing about how difficult it is to describe motherhood, and new motherhood, that it is quite ineffable ... Really going through it is the best way to understand it. To go through it at the same time as another group of people who are feeling equally vulnerable and hopeless and like they've got no idea what's going on I think is incredibly bonding. I think that those groups only work when the children are quite a similar age, because babies change so rapidly ... It's that sense of not knowing exactly what you're doing and ... it was partly troubleshooting that we would do together ... It was also about the ability to whinge, in a group, like collective whinging, that's really powerfully bonding ... We all had slightly different issues and we all had our own approach to parenting, that was quite different, but we somehow navigated it together, and I felt like it was a really supportive group. There was never any judgement ... I really looked forward to that every week, getting together with those women.

Carla Pascoe Leahy

## Introduction

Becoming a mother changes all of a woman's relationships. Her new role as carer of a child shifts her place and status within pre-existing relationships, with her parents, siblings, partner, friends, work colleagues and wider community. Some relationships deepen and acquire new layers. Other relationships show signs of strain and may eventually crumble. Matrescence throws a new light across all the intersubjective dynamics of a woman's life.

Support during this time of transition and strain is critical. New mothers are often physically recovering from childbirth, struggling to learn an array of essential childcare skills and processing intense emotions aroused by their new role. In a time of psychological and cultural transition and an explosion of new work that is unfamiliar and sometimes intimidating, mothers often turn to those around them for support.

This chapter will consider the central relationships and support for the new mother since 1945. The fact that her relationships change, and that trusted support is critical, have remained constant across this seventy-five-year period. But the ways in which relationships have altered and the types of support that are offered and appreciated have shifted, in relation to economic pressures, policy reforms and changing cultural ideas of gender, work, family, community, health and expertise.

## Maternal time

Psychological and psychoanalytic literature has traced the ways in which matrescence changes a woman's role within her social networks. All of her previous relationships are subjected to re-evaluation and her place within her family is redefined.[1] The anticipation and arrival of a first baby 'sends a ripple through all surrounding family and close relationships'.[2] Within their maternographies, women repeatedly spoke of how their relationships with other people in their lives had been modified by first-time motherhood. Recurrent themes included love and estrangement from a partner (that motherhood could deepen or strain a relationship); closeness and distance within extended families (as new mothers negotiated either a rejuvenation of intergenerational relationships or delineated a greater separation); and embeddedness within a matrix of community (experienced as supportive or disconnected).

## Love and estrangement

For women in intimate couple relationships, becoming a mother fundamentally shifts their relationship with their partner, a change that often begins in pregnancy. Reflecting on the ways in which parenthood shifted her relationship with her Scottish-born partner in 2013, Māori mother Avril explained that:

> It brings you closer together but at the same time because you're learning new skills and it's a very new environment, it's easy to fall into arguments about all the little stuff ... But then at the tail end of it it's just a bond that ... I find it hard to explain. But she has brought us together and we will always be in each other's lives because of H [daughter] even if we were to break up or whatever. We'll always have her in common.

As Avril describes, having a child creates a bond between a couple that is inseverable: regardless of whether the romantic relationship ends, the child will always link both parties. But the birth of a child also creates potential for tension and disagreement, because there is wholly new territory to navigate in childrearing and the stakes are higher – a child's future potentially depends upon the ways it is raised by its parents. Avril's reflections also reinforce the ineffability of matrescence: she admits it is 'hard to explain'.

Mary and her husband were born in the Netherlands and as adults moved to Africa then Australia. Their first child was born in 1974. Mary noticed that motherhood strengthened her bond with her husband, which she felt was especially true as migrants far from their established support networks. Their relationship became more caring ... You think a bit more about how you do things, what you do. It's more focused on the family than just being the two of you that can do whatever they like ... Especially we left our home country. You left your family and friends behind. So it was just you, the two of you with the child. So that makes a very strong unit.

Torres Strait Islander mother Somi expressed how her relationship with her partner changed and deepened when they had their first child in 2013. Because creating a family was not central to the reason for the relationship, it did not feel like a source of tension within or pressure upon that relationship. Somi and her partner are also bonded by their joint project of trying to overcome the fighting that they both experienced within their families as children.

> I think we've both been really good at recognising each other's strengths and adjusting our life to those ... We've discovered a huge depth of patience in each other. I've a huge amount of respect for him, that I think is really different from our relationship before. Yes, I don't know how else to explain it ... The life that we have is one that has been hard fought for and that we're really proud of and that it's something that we did together ... I just feel like we're part of a team now and sometimes you want that to be less practical and involve more sex and fun and intimacy. But also, in the periods when it's not those things, it's kind of just lovely and okay for it not to be those things.

Anglo-Australian Molly similarly reflected that she and her partner now have multiple modes of relation. They are not solely providing emotional, practical and sexual support to each other – since 2013, they are also engaged in a joint project of parenting. She stated, 'He's not just my lover [laughs]. He's my partner more now. We're more partners in crime in this escapade'. Like Avril, she has observed an added 'depth' to her relationship as well as 'bigger fights', which she believes are 'because you're stretched, you're burning the candles at both ends and the middle'. The joint project is wholly new, one in which they are both deeply invested, and is carried out under conditions where they feel sleep-deprived and time-poor.

Not only are partners now *more* than lovers – they are sometimes also *no longer* lovers. Many women report a decreased desire for sexual intimacy in the early stages of motherhood.[3] Sometimes, this is a product of birth injuries or trauma. Often, it is a reflection of the fact that the new mother is engaged in a passionate love affair with a new person: the baby. Anglo-Australian Sarah reflected that after her first birth in 2013, she shared so much daily touching and holding with her baby that she did not feel as great a need to be physically intimate with her partner. 'I'm constantly cuddling and kissing J [child]. The bond and that closeness is day in and day out. You don't have that need for touch, probably, that your partner wants. Although, the poor buggers, they've probably still got that same need, because they're working during the day.'

In addition to experiencing a reduced sexual interest, new mothers report a realisation that their once intimate twosome has expanded to admit a third person. After an extended and difficult birth in 2010 which left her exhausted and nauseous, Anglo-Australian Andrea asked her husband to hold their newborn while she recovered. That first moment of touch between infant and father triggered a sudden new awareness for Andrea.

> There was this instant jealousy, so big, and I thought, oh my God, because I was looking at the way he looked at her and I thought he loves her more than me and I have been his number one for nearly ten years and yet I already know that he loves her more than me.

Andrea's narrative reveals the way that everything is in flux at matrescence, including the new mother's relationship with her partner if she has one. She vividly recalls her unexpected feelings of jealousy and displacement after her challenging labour.

Several birthgiving mothers (in heterosexual relationships) spoke about the quotidian miracle of genetics, that they and their partner had created a wholly new human being, one who was equally comprised of both parents. Dutch-Australian Michelle spoke of the bizarre and wonderful experience of seeing herself and her partner reflected in their child after her birth in 2013.

> She started off as a mini me and she's slowly turning into a mini T [partner] which is really strange. I couldn't see any of him in her at first but now it's mini T ... Just to see them giggling together and some of the expressions on her face, it's like that's T.

Having a first child can be the first time that a couple has markedly dissimilar experiences of a major life event. By definition, the partner (either a father or co-mother) cannot experience physiological transformations such as gestation, childbirth and lactation as birthgiving mothers do. This means that the transition into parenthood is a distinct experience for both parents – commencing in pregnancy – which makes it hard for each to empathise with the position of their partner. Anglo-Australian Kira reflected on how matrescence shifted her relationship with her wife, J.

> *Carla*: Did you find that becoming mothers changed your relationship with J?
>
> *Kira*: Yeah, yes. I think – well, there was a few things. She was really nervous when we were pregnant that she would be obsolete, because I was the birthing mother and I was so involved, but we had twins, so it was a bit all hands on deck, and she wasn't as obsolete as she kind of wanted to be, but I think she did still feel a bit like – because she went to work, and I was the one doing everything all day, you know – I thought that I was giving gentle advice, but perhaps it was received a bit more as criticism … so there was that dynamic change, where I was kind of the expert … I was the only one that could tell the babies' cries apart … There were just things that I knew, that she didn't … We parent really similarly, and we both really just wanted to give 100 per cent to them, so that didn't – I suppose, in some ways, that created other tension, where they were kind of one, and we had spent no time just us, so we needed to revisit that, but we didn't have issues with wanting to parent differently, if that makes sense.

Although they were both mothers to their twins, Kira and her wife found that their different forms of maternality – as breastfeeding, birthgiving mother and as breadwinning co-mother – meant that they had different expertise and different roles within their family. But ultimately, both mothers respected each other's roles, and supported and loved each other through the exhausting task of raising twin infants.

For some couples, the arrival of a child creates superficial strain but ultimately deepens their relationship. For other couples, parenting triggers or exacerbates more serious challenges. In relationships where pregnancy was unexpected, or both partners were not equally enthused about becoming parents, differing levels of commitment to parenthood can create serious difficulties.[4] Sarah had been told that she would not become pregnant without assisted reproductive technology (ART) because of a medical condition. When she then experienced an unplanned pregnancy in 2012, her partner's response was challenging.

> I was very surprised and pretty hurt that he was so negative about it ... I tried to only talk to him about the positive experiences and only share with him the positive times ... Throughout the pregnancy, he never really got on board. He's probably only, actually got on board when J [son] hit about the three-month mark, and he became a bit more interactive ... He [partner] still struggles with his new identity, I think, and his new lifestyle, because it's changed a hell of a lot ... Think about what the pregnancy could do for a couple and how close it could bring you, and I feel like we really missed out on that part of it. I feel a bit annoyed at him for tarnishing pregnancy for me and making it not this joyous experience that it could have been.

In Sarah's account, her partner's negativity was due to feeling that he was not prepared for fatherhood and not ready to give up the privileges of their child-free lifestyle. Other mothers spoke about a different kind of strain that parenthood can place on a relationship: where a woman's love for her child exceeds her love for her partner. Anglo-Australian Genevieve had her first child in 1989 in North Fitzroy. She recalled, 'I remember my mother warning me to be very careful that I didn't allow my love for my child to adversely affect my relationship with my husband'.

Anglo-Australian Brenda felt that it was becoming a mother in 1978 that caused her relationship with her husband to slowly fall apart. Partly this was because of the strain of raising three children, but primarily it was because her husband was jealous that:

> My whole person became encompassed in my role as a mother ... Which is probably the main reason why S [partner] and I separated ... He became less significant in my life, and he resented that, and I think was quite jealous of my relationship with my children ... That's where our relationship really started to break down ... Having three children is extremely demanding on a couple ... By the time we had a third child, our relationship was just suddenly so much more complicated than it was when we first met as young lovers.

Brenda remembers her relationship as being stable before she had children. Welsh-Australian Sybil's situation was different. Her marriage was 'already rocky', but she hoped that having children would 'smooth things out'. Instead, the demands of parenting after her first child was born in 1979 accelerated the demise of her relationship. Women like Sybil and Brenda whose relationships ended while parenting reflected tearfully on how much harder it was to raise children as single mothers. By contrast, mothers who were well supported by their partners found that this eased their transition into motherhood.

## Closeness and distance

Just as her relationship with her partner changes, so too does matrescence shift a woman's place within her family. With the arrival of a first child, a whole new generation is born within an extended family. The new mother is a 'generational pivot' between this new generation and the old.[5] Her own parents, now grandparents to her child, will often have a significant emotional investment in the baby. Irish-Australian Penny recalled fondly how excited her father was to meet his first grandchild in 1975. 'My dad was sort of hands-on, and it was interesting that the first visitor I had after N [first child] was born – he would never take time off work, but he did, because he wanted to be the first in the family to see his little granddaughter.' Penny's father died unexpectedly less than twelve months later, lending this recollection an especially poignant quality in her maternography. When she birthed a son several years later, she gave him her father's name, further cementing intergenerational links. Avril also reflected that becoming a mother in 2013 had 'brought us closer together' with her siblings because of a shared 'understanding' of parenting and an ability to 'put aside our differences because it's not about us anymore. It's about H [child] and her cousins'. Both Avril and her brother feel a reinvigorated investment in maintaining close family relationships, for their children.

One of the relationships that shifts most profoundly at matrescence, apart from that between mother and child, is between the new mother and her own mother. Stern asserts that the most important relational triangle in the new mother's life is with her child and her own mother.[6] After having her first child in 2013, Sarah was very aware of a strengthened bond with her mother, based on her renewed appreciation of the quality of maternal love.

I appreciate her so much more. I feel closer with her than ever. Even as an adult, I never really reflected on how much she would have given up for us, and the burden that children are. I think it's made me more appreciative of her, as a mother, and just as a person in general ... It's the most overwhelming feeling ever. People say you won't know until it happens to you, but it's just so true. It's this consuming love and consuming feeling. It's amazing, but so overwhelming ... I said to Mum, 'Do you love me as much as I love J [son]?' She's like, 'Yes' ... It's nice to know that someone loves you as much as you love your little baby.

Several mothers reflected that matrescence offered them a new comprehension of the sacrifices of motherhood, and a lived experience of the ferocity of a mother's feelings about her child.

Matrescence has strong matrilineal inflections, in that becoming a mother forces a woman to re-evaluate her own mother and her experiences of being mothered, whether consciously or unconsciously.[7] Becoming a mother reawakens a woman's early memories of being mothered during her infancy, although some women are more aware of this than others. Reflecting on her renewed matrilineal connections to her mother, narrator Mary, Michelle explained,

I've got a photo of myself when I was a baby and F [her daughter] when she was a baby and we're exactly the same ... I definitely see myself in F and I often asked Mum, 'Did you sleep me on my back or on my front?' I slept on my front. 'Was I breastfed? How long was I breastfed for? What did you feed me?' especially when we started feeding solids to F.

As Michelle's reflections highlight, matrescence triggers a backwards-looking gaze towards the new mother's early life as a child. As an intergenerational link between present and past, the infant activates memories of the mother's own infancy. Through that process, she relates to her baby as the baby she once was, and also relates to her own mother's experience of caring for a vulnerable child. New motherhood shifts a woman's relationship with her own mother, as she is called to accept, adapt or reject the mothering style with which she was raised.[8]

Matrilineal connections were more complex in some families than others. In Chapter 2, we heard Petronela's story of her close relationship with her grandmother, who was her primary carer as a child. Kay explained that her intergenerational links extend through both her adoptive mother and her birthgiving mother. Kay was born to an Aboriginal mother (N) in 1952 and then relinquished. She was adopted by a non-Aboriginal couple and raised on the rural fringes of Melbourne. Kay had a very happy childhood with her adoptive mother and father, and grew up knowing that she was adopted, which was rare at the time. She remembers her adoptive mother, V, as a strong, intelligent and deeply moral person, who bequeathed her a way of contextualising her problems that has fortified Kay throughout her life.

> If I ever had some issues ... it always ended up talking about broader issues, or overarching issues, or issues that were affecting the world ... We developed a code, which was PMA, which was positive mental attitude, which I still use. She's left me that legacy of, you know, catching myself if I turn inward. I think, as a mother, I've used that with my daughters, and it seems such a simple thing, but it's – to be able to approach personal problems, but look out, and then look at that overarching thing, I think that's a gift that she gave me of, you know, being able to consider the world in a bigger picture. And I think that really helped me as I later met my birth mother, which I didn't choose to do.

Growing up, Kay did not know anything about her relinquishing mother or the fact that she was Aboriginal. It was only when she was in her thirties, with two young daughters (born in 1983), that her mother N tried to make contact with her after changes to adoption laws made this easier. Kay recalls feeling 'shocked' and 'gobsmacked'. She remembers that: 'I really didn't want to meet N. I just didn't know – where do you go from here? How do you go and meet your mother after – you know, I was in my thirties – how do you go and meet her?' After exchanging letters and photographs, they eventually organised for N to visit Kay and her young family. Kay described what it felt like to meet N and her family, slowly tracing her (other) maternal line. She discovered that N's fateful decision to relinquish Kay had haunted her for years, and ultimately coloured her relationship with the children she raised. Kay was also able to connect with N's mother, who raised six children of her own as well as raising other people's children. Kay's maternography was a complex and multi-layered story encompassing different places and families, revealing the ways in which family inheritance can echo down many generations. It illuminates the ways in which family is something you make as well as something that you are born into. Kay sits at the nexus of two separate but intertwined family trees. She really had two mothers, and they both influenced her life story and her own mothering in powerful ways.

While some women felt a renewed link to their mothers at matrescence, other women actively sought distance from their mothers, or sought to limit their influence. Others felt that their mothers could only have a limited involvement in their children's lives because of mental illness, ill health or disability. Anglo-Australian, second-wave mother Susan told me that her mother's bipolar disorder meant that she 'wasn't that interested' in both her maternal and grandmaternal roles.

> She'd had four children and she wasn't really that interested. By that time, she already had five other grandchildren. As I said, my mother is bipolar, and she'd been in and out of hospital a few times through my childhood. She was gorgeous, she was a beautiful mother ... but she just wasn't that interested ... I was happy to share it with her but there was no demand on the other side really. She was a bit like, 'Well, up to you now. Your job, not mine, I've done my bit'.

The influence of one's own mother can come in many guises. Some maternographies showed that new mothers can be influenced by events that transpired many years ago, such as Justine's story in Chapter 2 of the ways in which miscarrying her first pregnancy in the early 1990s connected her to her deceased mother's experience of stillbirth in the 1960s. English-born, second-wave mother Joanna was also influenced by her mother's long-ago maternal experiences. Her mother's first child had died as a newborn in the 1940s, and the sadness of losing her sister haunted Joanna's childhood and caused her to long for siblings while growing up as an only child in postwar England. She eventually had six children of her own in the 1970s to spare them the loneliness she suffered.

> I think every kid, actually, is often looking for a sibling, a brother or a sister, and the knowledge that I'd had one and lost it ... I think I used to dream up sisters ... It was really unusual to be an only child, actually, in those postwar years ... It was automatically assumed you'd be spoilt, a spoilt brat.

Her mother's suspicions that she may not have received adequate antenatal care, contributing to the child's death at three days, influenced Joanna's decision to seek private obstetric care for her pregnancies. This was despite the fact that Joanna's mother was half a world away in England when Joanna started her family in Australia, with their only communication through letters.

While some women admitted that they longed for greater emotional closeness and practical support from their families, familial relationships are not always experienced as welcome or helpful, as Macedonian-Australian Miroslava recollected. After the birth of her first child in 1975, her parents-in-law came over from Macedonia to stay with them. Miroslava and her husband were already residing with her parents at this time. Thus, Miroslava had both her parents and her parents-in-law, as well as her husband and her baby, all staying in a compact terrace house in the dense urban neighbourhood of Fitzroy. Miroslava was expected to adhere to Macedonian tradition and stay home for six weeks, only leaving the house to go to maternal child health appointments. This was viewed as being in the best interests of the baby but also the mother. Miroslava's experience contrasts strongly with that of many Anglo-Australian mothers who felt isolated in the home after giving birth. But there were suggestions in her maternography that this atmosphere felt suffocating. For example, when the baby cried during the night, her parents-in-law wondered if they should rush in to help settle him. Consequently, there was not much space or privacy for Miroslava and her husband to make their own decisions about what kind of parents they wanted to be, what kind of family they wanted to create and what kind of values they wished to embody in raising their children.

Family can be a positive influence and support at matrescence, but they can also be experienced as overbearing and interfering. Julia and her Italo-Australian husband co-habited with his mother from their marriage in 1974 until his mother's death decades later in 2011, influenced by Italian cultural traditions of elder care. But Julia could not predict all the ways this would influence her new motherhood. When her first child was born in 1978, Julia felt that her mother-in-law undermined her maternal authority and agency. Her mother-in-law insisted on allowing a steady stream of family and friends to visit after the birth and 'if the baby was asleep, they'd wake the baby up'. When the baby woke during the night, her mother-in-law would rush to the nursery first, until Julia brought the bassinet into her bedroom. There were really two mothers in the house, and as her children aged, Julia's desire for them to learn to do chores or to walk barefoot on hot days were thwarted by her mother-in-law. Though Julia was not able to mother her daughters the way that she wished, she has reclaimed her maternal style with her grandchildren.

> I can do things with M [grandchild] the way Mum did them ... When M's with me, I feel like, yeah, I do, I feel like my old self ... I'll pick up a book from the bookshelf and it'll be a book that Mum has given to my girls ... I feel like my old self again when I'm looking after M because I feel there's this connection with Mum as well.

Now that she is no longer in her mother-in-law's shadow, Julia can regain her maternal inheritance of her own mother's childrearing style.

Tensions with mothers-in-law were apparent in several narratives, and were perhaps heightened for someone like Chen, who experienced new motherhood away from her birth country and her family. Born in 1935, she was raised in a wealthy family in Hong Kong, in which servants did most of the work of caring for children and her mother was a distant figure. Chen migrated to Australia as an adult and met her future husband. Chen believes that her Anglo-Australian mother-in-law never felt she was an appropriate spouse for her son. Her mother-in-law's coldness heightened Chen's feelings of loneliness and lack of support when she became a new mother in 1966, contributing to what she believes was undiagnosed perinatal depression. Chen's narrative also speaks to the difficulties of mothering across cultural differences and with no clear maternal role model as guidance.

Matrescence triggers powerful memories not only for the new mother and her mother, but for others around her too. Polish-Australian Petronela realised that her mother-in-law was transported back to her own past through watching Petronela mother in 2017.

> Watching F [Petronela's partner] and I finding ourselves in the role of new parents was really quite triggering for her ... because it reminded her how shit her own experiences of early motherhood was ... She had three kids in quick succession as her relationship was falling apart, and as her husband was being really not as supportive as F has

been of me. So, to see us, more or less, in this quite happy place, even with all my sleeplessness, reminded her of everything she didn't have or missed out on in her own early motherhood.

While some women could tolerate physical proximity to their parents or parents-in-law during early motherhood, others found that they needed to move away to forge their own path. Anglo-Australian Dorothy reflected that her own parents were too generous and too involved in her life before and just after she had her child in 1956. Eventually, she and her husband and child decided to move from Victoria (the southernmost part of Australia) to Darwin (the northernmost Australian city) to create some geographic, and hence emotional, distance.

## Friendship, community and support

If relationships with family members shift, so too do relationships with friends. New mothers find that motherhood dominates every aspect of their lives, reorienting their centre of gravity. This is such a cataclysmic and yet difficult-to-describe transformation that it can become harder to relate to friends who are not themselves parents, or interested in parenthood. Millennial mother Molly felt that her friendships changed during pregnancy, in anticipation of motherhood.

> I did feel left out, because a lot of my friends weren't pregnant and a lot of them don't have babies. So they didn't know what I was going through and they were doing their own thing. So I kind of felt left out, not invited to things, or invited and I was the designated driver and you know it just felt a bit awkward at the time.

Lebanese-Australian Sally recalls that becoming a mother in 1978 sparked a development in her social life to spending more time with other people who had children. 'There were other friends who had babies and little ones and so we began spending a lot more time with them and so we kind of re-engineered our lives really around people with children because they understood, you know, the circumstances.' Many interviewees related that their friendships changed with matrescence, as they became closer to some peers and more distant from others.

After she became a mother in 2010, Welsh-Australian Ariana felt that her mothers' group in suburban Malvern were a bit like group therapy. They were all experiencing a challenging moment in their lives and honestly sharing their struggles with that.

> I think the best thing was just knowing that you had a group of people who were at exactly the same stage in a certain part of their lives that you were and that part of your life was actually really tricky ... Every week at the same time you got to speak to people who were sitting in exactly the same boat as you. I think that's why it was so good. So we could all say 'oh my God, my baby's been terrible this week' or 'hey, is anyone else's baby doing this?' or 'is anyone else's husband doing this?' and those kinds of things.

Support is critical to new motherhood: whether a woman feels that she is coping with the many demands of matrescence often comes down to the existence of adequate support from those around her.[9] Support is connected to and mediated through relationships, but it is also a separate issue. A new mother may feel that she has positive relationships with certain people but is not necessarily supported by them. Support can be from family. Michelle was conscious that weekly visits from her mother Mary (a lengthy journey from Mary's regional home to Michelle's Fitzroy apartment) to help look after her baby strengthened their matrilineal relationship, as they would 'go out for coffee and just have moments where we just talk about our upbringing and the olden days'. On her way home on the train, Michelle's mother would send her 'encouraging little comments' like 'I had such a lovely day with F [baby] today. It's so nice to see you embrace motherhood'. Michelle was conscious that the regular assistance she received from her mother and mother-in-law helped underpin her sense of coping with motherhood:

> It's just great to have that time that I can trust them to take her out and spend that quality time together. But then give me the freedom to do what I want to do, whether it is going to the gym or catching up on work or just going out and doing some grocery shopping. When I walk to the supermarket without F ... I feel like a different person. It's good. If I didn't have that I could imagine you'd sort of feel a bit trapped I reckon.

For Michelle, the support offered by her baby's grandmothers helps her to feel like she has 'freedom' and is not 'trapped' by her new role. There are suggestions that it connects her to her old, pre-maternal self, as well as situating her meaningfully within reframed relationships which include conversations about the past and encouraging feedback on her new maternal role.

Amanda grew up in Melbourne to English-born parents. As an adult, she moved to Ocean Grove. Amanda became a mother in 1991 and struggled with sleep deprivation and a lack of support. When she asked her mother to visit her (a drive of about an hour and a half), her mother's response was, 'You're the one who chose to move away'. Amanda did not feel that she had much in common with her mothers' group in Ocean Grove, who she believes exaggerated their childrearing successes. Most profoundly, she found her husband to be incompetent and disinterested from the moment she brought their baby home from hospital.

> When I got home … he didn't have the heater on – the house was freezing. To make matters worse, M [baby] … did this almighty poo and it went all the way up the back of the capsule and into her hair, this black poo. Got her home and we were originally planning to put the baby bath on the kitchen sink, so I didn't have to bend over. There was dishes all in the sink – I was just so angry with the whole thing. The homecoming was not a pleasant homecoming.

Although her husband had taken 'a couple of months' of long service leave after the baby's birth, his presence did not lighten Amanda's domestic workload.

> I'd say, 'Can you go and hang out the washing'? And this was … autumn and winter and he might decide to go and do it at three o'clock in the afternoon. I said, 'No, you've got to get it out in the morning, otherwise it doesn't dry'. In the end, I used to go and do it myself.

Years later, Amanda's husband told her, 'He didn't want to come home because I was such a crotchety old bitch'. Amanda believes she suffered undiagnosed perinatal depression partly because a lack of support exacerbated her emotional difficulties in the transition to motherhood.

By contrast, meaningful support can play a powerful role in helping women adjust. Torres Strait Islander mother Somi felt that she received practical and emotional support from her partner, mothers' group, mother and mother-in-law when she had her first child in 2013. Whether support consisted of hand-me-down baby clothes, long conversations or tips from Facebook pages, Somi recalls that it helped her to realise that 'everyone was just having a hard time, no matter what they were going through – it wasn't me'.

Support does not only come from partners and family – those bound by marriage or blood. It can also come from the new mother's community. Several women who received community assistance during their transition to new motherhood were very positive about the difference it made. Community support was particularly palpable in towns or neighbourhoods with strong communal ties. Living in the small regional town of Ocean Grove, Carol felt very supported after each of her six babies were born in the 1970s and 1980s. Other mothers would drop in on their way home from school and offer to do a load of washing or fold her clean laundry. When she was in hospital recovering after the birth of twins, members of the local community set up a cooking roster, with friends from the Nursing Mothers Association bringing meals one week and friends from the Catholic Church bringing them another. Joanna had a similar experience in the same town during the same era. She and her husband were newly arrived English migrants when they started their family in the 1970s. Many of their friends were also without family close by so they supported each other, through Nursing Mothers, the Uniting Church Playgroup, the Neighbourhood Centre and a babysitting club. It was 'full of people who came from somewhere else'. Joanna feels that having family close by can be a double-edged sword: it can provide the benefit of practical assistance, but often accompanied by unsolicited parenting advice from older generations.

As a single mother raising her two children in suburban Malvern in the 1980s, Welsh-Australian Sybil was grateful for the warm community spirit in her street.

> We had a Greek family next door to us who took us in basically and we celebrated all their Greek religious days with them, lamb on the spit and everything. The lady opposite me was Italian ... They both looked after the babies from birth ... She was a lovely lady. M [Sybil's son] learned how to cook cannelloni, the pasta. He learned that from scratch from her ... She taught him many things. She had him under her wing until he was grown up, both of them.

Such meaningful and long-term support from adults beyond the birthgiving mother is akin to the kinds of 'othermothering' described in African-American communities by feminist Patricia Hill Collins or the 'alloparenting' theorised by anthropologist Sarah Blaffer Hrdy as part of the reason for the successful evolution of homo sapiens.[10] These terms broadly refer to the idea that it is not only the biological mother who can play an important caring role in a child's life. Grandparents, extended family, friends, neighbours and other community members can provide alternative forms of care beyond the paradigm of the individual birthgiving mother so normalised in contemporary industrialised societies.[11]

Beyond these specific examples of othermothering and alloparenting, in popular consciousness, there is a dominant collective memory of the so-called 'village': the idea that once, the community gathered around a woman to help guide her though matrescence.[12] It is encapsulated in the adage 'it takes a village to raise a child'. Second-wave mother Genevieve asserted that the reason many women struggle with learning to breastfeed is because 'we're so far away from the village'. Millennial mother Kristen concurred:

> These days, you bring a baby home, and you're not bringing him into a village – it's the proverbial village that it takes to raise a child isn't there for most women of my particular demographic – they don't have their sisters and their friends and their mother around them, sharing that load.

While this nostalgia for an imagined golden age of communal childrearing is seductive and is often juxtaposed to a lack of community support for new mothers in the twenty-first century, it is by no means clear which historical era or culture supposedly enjoyed the benefits of 'the village'. Rather than viewing this concept as a historically or culturally accurate portrayal of a society that once existed, a more useful question is perhaps why this concept has such broad appeal. I would suggest that the notion of 'the village' operates as a critique of the lack of social supports surrounding new motherhood. In other words, these regular references to the mythologised 'village' can provide some clues as to the support mothers desire during matrescence.

There are significant relational continuities across this seventy-five-year period. When a woman becomes a mother, it consistently reorients her relationships with all of those around her. Relationships with partners, family, friends, work colleagues and her broader community shift, with some relationships deepening and some buckling under the pressure. Support remains critically important to how easily women weather the inevitable difficulties of matrescence and are given the space and opportunity to be enriched by the experience.

## Generational time

### Postwar mothers

While much has remained constant in new mothers' experiences of relationships and support, there have been significant changes relating to cultural understandings of gender, work, care and community since 1945. Material circumstances have also fluctuated, with employment rates, wages, living costs and housing costs all influencing the work/care arrangements of Australian families. Postwar mothers often had little adult companionship during their day-to-day lives. Middle-class women who did not work were particularly isolated. Raising children and keeping house were labour-intensive and time-consuming in an era before disposable nappies, washing machines and dishwashers. Many postwar mothers recalled that they did not have a car they could use during the day – either because the family did not own one or because it was driven to work by the father – so moving around with children was difficult. Women who had babies in the 1950s and 1960s remember often not having adults they could talk to during the day, though they did not necessarily recall feeling overwhelmed or lonely.

In an era before organised playgroups, women did not often come together to compare their maternal difficulties and triumphs. There was also a different set of cultural expectations around sharing personal experiences. For English-born Marjorie, remembering her matrescence in 1953, the challenges of mothering were 'private' in a similar way to breastfeeding.

> We spoke because I had a big circle of friends, but we never spoke in front of the fathers ... Nobody had a car. We were all muddling along as best we could. We didn't have playgroups and we didn't sit around and talk. I don't know what it – it was private. It was something that you didn't openly talk about.

If postwar mothers received less explicit support, they also did not necessarily expect it. When Anglo-Australian Eve first became a mother in 1950, she was isolated in a rural setting where she rarely saw other mothers except for monthly church attendance in town. She recalls being 'very, very happy' and does not remember feeling anxious about her limited opportunities to seek advice from others.

Postwar mothers occupied a leading role within the domestic space and felt respected for the authority it gave them. Eve was clear on the gendered division of labour with her marriage.

> I was in charge of bringing up the children and the home and that my husband worked very hard and he provided for them ... I was very respected ... I was the one to make the decisions where the children were concerned ... I made all the decisions for the household.

Marjorie recalls that her husband never did any domestic tasks like bathing the children or cooking meals. She harboured no resentment because that was the dominant gender order of the postwar era. 'R [husband] could knit and sew, because R had been in the Navy ... R was very clever at doing stuff. He just didn't do it because it wasn't the thing. It just wasn't done. I didn't expect it and he didn't do it.' Most postwar mothers felt that their husbands worked hard to provide for their families, and both parents accepted this as the appropriate role for a father.[13] Many women, like Grace, Rachel and Pamela, talked about their husbands working long hours, and the ways that impacted on family life. While parental overwork constricting family time is sometimes portrayed as a twenty-first-century phenomenon – that work–life imbalance is a feature of the neoliberal economy – long paternal working hours seem to have been common in postwar families. Postwar mothers often spoke of this as though their partners had no autonomy in deciding the hours they worked, which differs from the expectations of millennial mothers.

Anglo-Australian Rachel remembers that neither her father nor her husband was highly involved in raising their children, in the

1940s and 1960s, respectively. Both men were real estate agents in suburban Melbourne who worked long hours. Rachel said that they were both good fathers and stressed that her husband was a 'very good provider' – which in her mind seemed to be the most important aspect of his paternal role. Anglo-Australian Pamela recalled a gendered split between paid work and domestic work when she started her family in the late 1960s in Ocean Grove. Her husband worked long hours as an architect. He made the children furniture and toys but did not actively participate in the daily tasks of looking after them. However, not all postwar fathers were alike. Although working full-time, Irish-Australian Jane's husband was highly involved in the everyday tasks of raising their eleven children, including changing nappies, bathing and reading books. Jane asserted that 'J [husband] knows more about mothering than I do'. As they grew older, the elder children assisted, with the eldest boys in particular very good at changing nappies and looking after the smaller children. While the involvement of Jane's husband was unusual in the 1950s and 1960s, larger family sizes could necessitate a more active paternal participation in childrearing (as well as requiring the assistance of older siblings).

New mothers had differing levels of engagement with their own mothers at matrescence. Raising her children on a farm in western Victoria several hours away from her mother and grandmother in Melbourne, Eve nevertheless felt that her maternal style had matrilineal influences of the 'unconditional love' she received as a child. She stayed with her mother for one month after her first child was born and afterwards wrote weekly to her mother and grandmother to stay connected and to seek their advice. By contrast, Anglo-Australian Patsy did not feel supported by her own mother. It is unclear whether this was her mother's maternal style, or whether this lack of connection was influenced by the circumstances of Patsy becoming pregnant as an unwed mother in 1967. Patsy spoke of her disappointment that her own mother had not offered assistance after her children were born. She twice repeated that she felt hurt but 'got over it', as though trying to convince herself of that fact. In her own mothering, Patsy has been almost ostentatiously supportive and caring towards her daughters and her grandchildren, perhaps to make up for the matrilineal support she lacked.

In hindsight, Marjorie can see that cultural norms restricted the matrilineal exchange of emotions and experiences for her generation of postwar mothers. 'You didn't tell your mother how you were feeling. You spoke to friends and had a few giggles, but even then, there was like a barrier that you just held back ... It's like a different planet when I look back.' From her current vantage point in the twenty-first century, Marjorie is now conscious that postwar social expectations governed what kinds of maternal information could be communicated and with whom, and can reflect upon how emotional expressiveness has increased across her lifetime.

## Second-wave mothers

Women who came to motherhood during and immediately after the women's liberation movement did so in an era in which female peer support was more available and there was a greater openness when discussing aspects of motherhood previously considered 'private'. From the 1970s, a range of groups were forming in Australia that gave mothers access to greater peer support and advice. Such groups arose partially in response to the problem of the lonely postwar housewife identified by feminists such as Betty Friedan, trapped and disaffected in her suburban castle.[14] Second-wave mothers began forming and joining groups in their local neighbourhoods such as playgroups, toy libraries, babysitting clubs and breastfeeding support groups like the Nursing Mothers Association of Australia (discussed in Chapter 4). Playgroups served a dual purpose of being a place where preschool children could play with others their age (in an era before the widespread provision of childcare) and mothers could pool their child minding to gain some time for domestic chores. Irish-Australian Penny had her first child in 1975. She remembered that in her suburb of Melbourne:

> They didn't have mothers' groups ... but they had playgroups ... It wasn't in a home; it was usually in a hall ... It was where the mothers could leave the kids and go and do the shopping ... and you took turns at being rostered on. One of the mothers sort of saw the need, and they started a playgroup.

In her town of Ocean Grove, Anglo-Australian Tania recalls flourishing networks like the Nursing Mothers Association, a

Uniting Church playgroup and a babysitting club, which were all new organisations representative of 1970s ideas about building community and mutual support through peer networks in one's local neighbourhood.

> The Nursing Mothers in Ocean Grove were so strong ... They were trained leaders in breastfeeding with a really strong organisation behind them and that was a big part of meeting people. And through playgroup. Playgroup was very strong. It used to meet three days a week at the Uniting Church ... I joined an existing babysitting club ... and it was twenty or so parents together. You didn't pay money, but you joined ... If you wanted a babysitter, you would ring and they would then look down the list ... and they would ring around to find you a babysitter.

Buoyed by the social movements of this era, mothers in the 1970s actively organised themselves to provide community networks to support each other through the challenges and successes of raising children.

Second-wave mothers were on the cusp of significant changes in gender attitudes towards parenting. Indeed, this was one of the explicit demands of the women's liberation movement.[15] When she had her first child in 1970 in Ocean Grove, Anglo-Australian Wendy recalls that she received ample support from a husband who 'knew more about babies' than she did and was 'such a great help'. Lebanese-Australian Sally explained that she and her partner felt that parenting 'was a shared project' and that she never felt 'solely responsible', musing that 'if you don't have a supportive partner, it's going to be extremely difficult'. She explained further that:

> We'd certainly talked through the fact that we thought that we had to agree on how we approach things and then be consistent ... I think I was terribly lucky in that he actually did put in. You know, a lot of men talk about it, but he actually did put in. So I think he's quite unusual still actually when you look at even at grandparenting, I think he puts in more than most ... So that made it easier for me.

Sally's arrangement with her husband was uncommon in that they literally halved work and care tasks when she returned to paid work six months after the birth of their first child in 1978. Sally worked half a day and then cared for the baby for half a day, swapping with her husband at lunchtime. Their employment as teachers (hers in secondary education, his in tertiary education) made this flexibility possible. Most 1970s relationships were less emphatically egalitarian, but many second-wave mothers expected a greater paternal involvement in childrearing than their postwar predecessors.[16] Penny felt that fathers of her second-wave generation were more involved than her parents' postwar generation. She and her husband 'felt it took two of us, and we were building a family'. Her husband was 'very hands-on'. They had a routine that 'I breastfed at night, he then changed the nappies and settled the baby'.

But when questioned more closely, second-wave mothers still usually did the lion's share of the work of keeping house and raising children. Anglo-Australian Susan reflected that her estimation of her husband's contribution to raising their children in the 1970s and 1980s depends on what she is comparing it to. 'He was a lot more involved than my father would have been. That was good enough for me. But when I see what husbands today do for their wives it was very different. We were still old school.' Welsh-Australian Sybil had her first of two children in 1979 before her marriage ended in 1986. Sybil recalls exaggerating her husband's contribution to dinner party preparation in order to meet changing cultural standards of men's domestic involvement.

> I do remember thinking, I shouldn't be saying this but I'm going to say, 'Oh, I [husband] made the beef or whatever' when I know that I cut up every vegetable and put it all there on the bench and he gets all the accolades ... But it never, ever made me feel cross. I just remember thinking, 'I am such a fool for saying it in the first place' because I wanted people to think that our work was pretty well shared. I did more of the work simply because it was more efficient ... But I don't really feel cross about that because I think it was relatively normal and he was better than a lot of people.

She also reflected on how much compensatory work she would do in order that her husband could contribute more to cooking meals or minding children. From a twenty-first-century standpoint, she is more critical of her younger self – but not her ex-husband.

Maternal influences were also evident with this second-wave cohort of mothers. In some ways, this generation was especially required to clarify what they wished to emulate and what they wished to change of their own mothers' lives, because they were experiencing matrescence in the midst of profound social, economic and political change. For some women, like Irish-Australian Brenda, the quality of maternal love they practised was similar to their mother's, but amidst different life circumstances and choices. Brenda had her first of three children in 1978, living in Fitzroy. She began her maternography by talking about her own mother's experience of being trapped in difficult circumstances in the postwar era, which made Brenda determined not to become similarly constrained. Her mother was constantly exhausted from looking after eight children and was living in relative isolation on a farm, imprisoned in an unfulfilling marriage.

> My mother was a very loving, caring, nurturing mother; but ... her life situation was very, very different to mine, because she had so many kids and she was poor, and didn't really have a good relationship with her husband, so she was quite sad, and flat, and depressed. But the most significant thing about her was that she was very loving and caring to all of us; and I guess that's how I have been with my children, and I see my children – the two of my children who have children – being very much like that with their children.

Brenda made conscious decisions in her life to try to be different to her mother and particularly to be financially independent so that she would not feel unable to leave a dissatisfying marriage. But despite these points of clear differentiation, Brenda could perceive an intergenerational transmission of parenting styles that she valued. Her mother was extremely loving towards her offspring and Brenda saw those traits demonstrated in her own maternal style and that of her children.

If there were generational tensions between second-wave mothers and their own parents because of changes to the socio-historical context of women's lives, such tensions were often heightened for the offspring of migrant parents because of cultural differences between the old country and the new.[17] Children of migrants can occupy 'an ambivalent and often liminal space between the world of their parents and the broader Australian society'. This sense of occupying a contradictory middle ground, forced to conduct complex generational negotiations, is particularly evident for girls, who bear a heavy responsibility for maintaining family traditions and 'ethnic morality'.[18] Girls are central to intergenerational negotiations around the transculturation of migrant families, forced to actively accept, revise or reject their parents' values which are of both a different era and a different culture.[19] Miroslava was born in Australia in 1946 to Orthodox, Macedonian-born parents, and she was very conscious of the heightened strictness which governed her mother's parenting practices compared to some of her peers. Miroslava felt particularly frustrated that her mother had different standards for her sons and daughters. While her brothers were allowed relative freedom, Miroslava was not allowed – even as a young adult – to socialise with her work colleagues or go to other social events outside her Macedonian-Australian community. Later in the interview, Miroslava returned to this theme when asked about her own mothering and explained that she consciously gave her daughter (born in 1975) more freedom and responsibility than she had been permitted and insisted that she attend university.

Mary was born in the Netherlands in 1951. Her parents came from different cultural backgrounds: her father's family was German-Dutch while her mother was Indonesian. Mary recalls that when she became a mother in 1974, she valued the advice of her mother because she appreciated the ways she had been raised. Despite this strong identification, Mary was also conscious that there were some aspects of her mother's parenting she did not wish to emulate.

> I always thought I want to be like my mum but there are certain things that I would like to change and will do differently ... My mum was an Indonesian, Asian background, was pretty submissive. So she would often say, 'Well, go and ask Dad', while I wanted her to make the decision. So I've always had that very strong feeling, if the child comes to me and asks Mum, then I'll make a decision on that and if it's something that I feel we need to discuss, then I discuss it with my husband and then we make a joint decision.

While Mary was very positive about most aspects of her mother's maternal style – and transmitted this matrilineal inheritance to her own daughter Michelle, as explained above – there were also aspects that she sought to adapt in her own life, amidst a changing historical and cultural context.

### Millennial mothers

Millennial mothers, like their predecessors, find that relationships are transformed by new motherhood, but within a different economic and social context. While folk wisdom holds that mothers in the past had more support from the communities around them, this is not strictly accurate if measured over the last seventy-five years. Twenty-first-century mothers have more formal support in the form of access to subsidised childcare, maternal child health services (which include the facilitation of new parent groups) and parental leave. Yet this support is arguably more important than ever before, as Australian women are now likely to be juggling several roles simultaneously, particularly in combining paid work with care work.

New family configurations have been enabled by cultural, legal and technological changes. It is now possible to be a single mother by choice, like Greek-Australian Connie, and actively choose to have a child on one's own without a partner. Lesbian couples can legally access ART in order to have children, though as we shall see in the next chapter, same-sex couples do not necessarily contravene breadwinner/homemaker divisions within relationships. Couples like Anglo-Australian Heather and her wife L both confirm and deny traditional gender roles. As the mother who is more career-focused and earns more, L acts as primary breadwinner, while Heather has been the primary carer since their first child was born in 2012. Yet both mothers have acted as birthgiving mothers in the family: Heather has carried two pregnancies while L has carried one. Heather is conscious that they are actively and deliberately fashioning new models of how to 'do' family. In their family with a known sperm donor, the biological father plays a prominent, albeit non-traditional, role. He does not cohabit with the family, but is actively involved in the children's lives, including making parenting decisions and being involved in day-to-day care.

In her heterosexual relationship, Māori mother Avril felt that she and her partner had been bonded in a profound way by having a child in 2013. In an era in which marriage is increasingly seen as optional – or at least not essential when making a long-term commitment to another person – Avril's narrative hints at a sense that perhaps having a child together is seen as a more important commitment to millennial mothers than getting married.

> We both agreed that having a baby was the priority for us. We plan to get married next year but to me it's just like oh yes, whatever. It's changed for me. The wedding is just like, well, let's have a barbie

[barbeque] and it's no big deal because we've had a baby ... I want to get married to G [partner] but when you've gone to that end of the scale, it's hard to come back.

Polish-Australian Petronela found a 'whole new depth of love' for her partner when their child was born in 2017 and says he has been 'excellent at helping me out, sort of pre-empting my needs and he's just excellent with U [child]'. Even in strong relationships like Petronela's which have been relatively egalitarian before parenthood, many millennial families find that they fall back upon caring and breadwinning roles after a baby is born.[20] Partly, this is because work and taxation regimes make it easier to have one person at home and one earning money for the family. Partly, it is also because childrearing expertise is self-perpetuating.

> I had this idealistic notion that I would be in charge of everything that went into the baby and he'd be in charge of everything that came out of the baby. That has, in practice, not really been the case, because I still change way more nappies than he does. In those first five months of U's life, when he was finishing up his degree, he was very hands-on ... In the very first weeks, he was really good at offering to do night-time feeds with expressed breastmilk, but, in practice – look, this apartment is so tiny that when she woke up, I woke up ... Sometimes he showers with her and sometimes I do. He sings little songs and plays with her, he takes her in the carrier grocery shopping. We're still, I guess, figuring out how proactive he is.

Petronela is conscious of a dissonance between her pre-maternal image of an egalitarian division of labour and the reality of caring for a small child, when the greater experience of the primary carer breeds greater expertise.[21]

> Again, as a feminist, on one hand I expect and I want him to take initiative in initiating baby-related tasks. On the other hand, I am the expert because I've been doing these things more often ... It's a challenge for me to figure out how to leave the room and give him enough space to figure out his own ways of changing the baby or dressing her or whatever, but, still, making sure it gets done.

Like previous generations, millennial mothers found that matrescence reignited their own matrilineal relationships. Some, like Dutch-Australian Michelle, found a newfound closeness with their mothers, in tacit approval of the way they were raised. Others, like Connie, felt more ambivalent. Generational tensions between herself and her parents were heightened by their upbringing in different cultural contexts: Greece and Australia. She feels that her Greek-born parents were very strict and did not allow her many choices, which resulted in periods of rebellion and depression in their daughter. This led Connie to assume that effective parenting must be very difficult, and for a long time, she wasn't sure that she wanted to attempt it. Connie's mother died before Connie experienced matrescence in 2014, and so her narrative of new motherhood is tinged with a sadness that they cannot share the transition. 'At the beginning, I would have asked her [Connie's mother] how to wash him, how to hold him, how to stop him crying, how to feed him. Then she could have looked after me too.' Connie feels that she has a better appreciation of her mother now that she occupies a maternal position herself. She wishes her mother were present so that she could ask her advice and be mothered a little herself through matrescence.

If relationships with mothers changed, or took on a new light, many millennial mothers have also found that connections to friends and peers have shifted. As more contemporary women decide not to have children (currently between one-third and one-quarter of Australian women will never become mothers[22]), millennial mothers are more likely to feel a dissonance in their relationships with childless friends. Avril felt that shift commence during pregnancy and has noticed that fellow mothers have an ability to communicate despite their 'interrupted subjectivity'[23] – but friends without children find this challenging.

> It's brought me closer to certain friends ... and it's simply because they share motherhood and I've grown apart from the friends that don't have children ... I think it's a natural drift unless you make a concerted effort to stop it ... I don't expect them to understand but you try and we invite them over for dinner and we put H [child] down to bed and she won't go down to bed. Mums can have conversations while children are making noise and stop and start a conversation. It's a skill that mothers have. But if you've not had a child, it's really disruptive.

Anglo-Australian Sarah felt conscious that some of her friends perceived her differently, and felt that she was less fun or interesting when she became a mother in 2013. Perhaps this aspect of matrescence has shifted as mothers have had children at a later age (on average now over thirty-one).[24] Contemporary women have had longer periods of childlessness than their predecessors to develop friendships in which they are readily available to each other. Together, they have developed adult personalities, activities and relationships that centre upon lifestyles without children.

> Some of my friends, I think, definitely see me differently. My closest friends don't. My soul mate friends, the relationship hasn't changed at all. But some of the friends where the only social situations you would have would be when you were going out or going on holidays together or something, I think, they definitely see me in a different way ... They've certainly dwindled off since becoming pregnant.

As motherhood changes every aspect of a woman's life, friends who have not experienced matrescence may struggle to comprehend why so much has changed. For the new mother, too, it can become harder to relate to her childless friends because they have no personal experience of one of the most significant influences shaping the new mother's life. Sarah reflected that this could lead to 'consciously censoring yourself, in a way, around some of these people because you don't want to be boring them with what to you is the most interesting thing ... I don't want to be around people that think my baby is boring'.

Participation in a new parents' group (commonly called a 'mothers' group') is a distinguishing characteristic of millennial motherhood. Experiences of mothers' groups are mixed. For those who feel an affinity with the other members of their group, this can be a fundamental support network, even if members would not otherwise have much in common. After she had her first child in 1989, Anglo-Australian Genevieve did not initially feel that the members of her North Fitzroy mothers' group were 'kindred spirits', but they became her 'lifeline'.

> When M [child] was three months old ... I remember walking around the house thinking, oh my God – there's only so much Terry Lane I can listen to on 3LO [radio]. The new mothers' group formed at the local childcare centre ... and I thought, none of these women are really kindred spirits. But they did become my lifeline, and they filled the gap. And apart from anything, they made me feel like everything's normal. Baby crying, all that stuff ... suddenly I knew there were

other people who were going through the same thing. So that was incredibly reassuring, and some of them have been friends ever since.

As communications technologies have permeated twenty-first-century life, mothers' groups often now communicate online as well as in person, meaning that millennial mothers potentially have access to a network of peer support that is available anywhere, any time. First Nations mother Somi felt that advice, support and camaraderie from maternal peers were critical to surviving her matresence in 2013. It helped her to appreciate that there is a wide diversity of maternal experiences and that experiencing difficulties did not mean she was failing as a mother.

> I had one friend whose son was born sort of six months ahead. The best piece of advice she gave me was that actually, six months is a really long time in those years so you need to use your mothers' group. I'm here but you're just in a different stage. ... The woman that I'm still friends with in the mothers' group, she also had a son who didn't sleep. So I had someone else whose child was six weeks apart from my own who absolutely knew what I was going through. So there was no advice being given, there was just a kind of solidarity. Without that ... I don't know what would have happened to us. While all the other babies were having their naps, you know, she and I would be outside.

Apart from the solidarity she shared in person with a mother suffering similar challenges to her own, Somi found solace in online Facebook groups which gave her 'a really good sense of just how diverse people's experiences were', which helped her to avoid 'self-judgement' or 'a sense of failure'.

Other women found their mothers' groups less helpful, either because they felt they had nothing in common with the other mothers, because they felt their parenting standards were different, or because they felt their child was different. Irish-Australian Caitlyn felt out of sync with her early 1990s mothers' group in Ocean Grove because her perception was that the other women smoked cigarettes, swore constantly and bottle-fed their infants: 'I got sort of allocated to this group and I went down the first day and it was horrendous and I never went back again ... I was like, I've got nothing in common with these people'. By contrast, Anglo-Australian Andrea struggled to relate to the women in her Ocean

Grove mothers' group in 2010 because her first baby's hip dysplasia made her feel like her mothering challenges were not something the other mothers could relate to.

In recognition of this, more specialised groups and services have also developed to speak to distinctive maternal needs. As the mother of a baby born prematurely in 2013, Tessa feels that they were lucky to be supported by friends and family in Ocean Grove, but she did not feel other people around her could relate to her experience or provide relevant advice. When she'd try to speak of her anxieties about her daughter's delayed development to her mother or mother-in-law, they'd say, 'She'll be fine' or 'What do you mean, she's delayed?', and so she stopped sharing her concerns with them. Tessa discovered that other mothers of premature babies were the most effective source of support for her because their experiences resonated more strongly. She connected with them through services such as not-for-profit Life's Little Treasures and the lactation group for mothers of premature babies.

## Conclusion

New mothers commonly discover that their pre-existing relationships are stretched or strained when they have their first child. Matrescence inevitably shifts a woman's embeddedness in family, peer groups, community and work relations. The matrilineal implications of new motherhood have remained profound across the last seventy-five years, though rapid cultural and material changes across generations have perhaps deepened the sense of contradiction between a new mother's experiences and those of her own mother. An increasing belief in the superiority of 'expert' parenting advice has lessened the seeming relevance of older women's childrearing perspectives.[25] As more women have engaged in paid employment, the contrasts between mothers' and daughters' workforce experiences have grown.[26] For women in relationships, expectations of their partner's involvement in childrearing have risen, with the critical issue remaining whether a partner is meeting those expectations. Changes to gender norms and work patterns have certainly amplified cultural expectations of fathers in contributing to the care of children or the domestic work of maintaining a home. Nevertheless, despite high expectations, most new mothers encounter a regression to a more gendered division of household labour after the birth of a first child.[27] Support has remained critically important to the new mother's adaptation to her maternal role. Yet the assertion that community support for new mothers has waned is largely a myth, albeit a powerful one. Contributions of partners, extended family, friends and health professionals have in many respects expanded since 1945. Technological developments have made it possible for women to access formal and informal online support.[28] There has been a growth in organised or facilitated peer support (such as playgroups and mothers' groups), at the same time as rising numbers of childless women perhaps intensify the contrasting life experiences of women with children and those without. Despite increasing supports, the key challenge is that a mother's need for support has risen across this period, as her overall burden of combined paid and unpaid workloads has expanded dramatically.

## Notes

1 Stern and Bruschweiler-Stern, *The Birth of a Mother*, 5.
2 Thomson et al., *Making Modern Mothers*, 91.
3 Stern also notes that reduced sexual desire and activity is a common experience of early motherhood: Stern and Bruschweiler-Stern, *The Birth of a Mother*, 8–9.
4 Imogene Smith et al., '"You Are Not Alone": A Big Data and Qualitative Analysis of Men's Unintended Fatherhood', *SSM – Qualitative Research in Health* 2 (2022): 100085, https://doi.org/10.1016/j.ssmqr.2022.100085.
5 Hollway, *Knowing Mothers*.
6 Stern and Bruschweiler-Stern, *The Birth of a Mother*, 9.
7 Stone, *Feminism, Psychoanalysis, and Maternal Subjectivity*; Paola Mariotti, ed., *The Maternal Lineage: Identification, Desire and Transgenerational Issues* (London and New York: Routledge, 2012); Pascoe Leahy, 'The Mother Within'.
8 Pascoe Leahy, 'The Mother Within'.
9 Heidi Hoffmann et al., 'New Mothers and Social Support: A Mixed-Method Study of Young Mothers in Australia', *Journal of Sociology* 57, no. 4 (2021): 950–68.

10 Patricia Hill Collins, *Black Feminist Thought: Knowledge, Consciousness, and the Politics of Empowerment* (New York: Routledge, 1990); Sarah Blaffer Hrdy, *Mother Nature: A History of Mothers, Infants, and Natural Selection* (New York: Pantheon Books, 1999); Sarah Blaffer Hrdy, *Mothers and Others: The Evolutionary Origins of Mutual Understanding* (Cambridge, Mass.: Belknap Press of Harvard University Press, 2009).

11 Knott, 'Theorizing and Historicizing Mothering's Many Labours'.

12 Kate Johnston-Ataata, 'Reflecting on the Past: The Role of Biographical, Familial and Social Memory in New Mothers' Interpretations of Emotional Experiences of Early Parenthood', in *Australian Mothering: Historical and Sociological Perspectives*, eds. Carla Pascoe Leahy and Petra Bueskens (Cham, Switzerland: Palgrave Macmillan, 2019), 297–316.

13 John Murphy, 'Work in a Time of Plenty: Narratives of Men's Work in Post-War Australia', *Labour History: A Journal of Labour and Social History* 88 (2005); John Murphy, 'Breadwinning: Accounts of Work and Family Life in the 1950s', *Labour & Industry* 12, no. 3 (2002): 59–75.

14 Friedan, *The Feminine Mystique*. See also Beverley Kingston, *My Wife, My Daughter, and Poor Mary Ann: Women and Work in Australia* (Melbourne: Nelson, 1975), 137–8.

15 Barrett Meyering, *Feminism and the Making of a Child Rights Revolution, 1969–1979*; Isobelle Barrett Meyering, ' "There Must Be a Better Way": Motherhood and the Dilemmas of Feminist Lifestyle Change', *Outskirts* 28 (2013).

16 Alistair Thomson, 'New Wave Fathers? Oral Histories with Australian Fathers from the 1970s to the 1990s', in *Australian Mothering: Historical and Sociological Perspectives*, eds. Carla Pascoe Leahy and Petra Bueskens (Cham, Switzerland: Palgrave Macmillan, 2019), 219–35.

17 A. James Hammerton and Alistair Thomson, *Ten Pound Poms: Australia's Invisible Migrants* (Manchester; New York: Manchester University Press), 243–7.

18 Francesco Ricatti, *Italians in Australia: History, Memory, Identity* (Cham, Switzerland: Palgrave, 2018) 75–89.

19 Loretta Baldassar, 'Marias and Marriage: Ethnicity, Gender and Sexuality among Italo-Australian Youth in Perth', *Journal of Sociology* 35, no. 1 (1999): 1–22.

20 Alistair Thomson, 'Gender Culture or Gender System? Family Gender Arrangements and Stay-At-Home Fathers in Late-Twentieth-Century

Australia', *Gender & History* 34, no. 2 (2022): 534–53, https://doi.org/10.1111/1468-0424.12563.
21 Miller, *Making Sense of Motherhood*; Tina Miller, *Making Sense of Fatherhood: Gender, Caring and Work* (Cambridge: Cambridge University Press, 2011).
22 Australian Bureau of Statistics, 'Family Formation: Trends in Childlessness' (4102.0 – Australian Social Trends, 2002), www.abs.gov.au/AUSSTATS/abs@.nsf/bb8db737e2af84b8ca2571780015701e/1e8c8e4887c33955ca2570ec000a9fe5.
23 Baraitser, *Maternal Encounters*.
24 Lixia Qu, *Families Then & Now: Having Children* (Australian Institute of Family Studies, 2020), https://aifs.gov.au/publications/having-children.
25 Pascoe Leahy, 'The Mother Within'.
26 Pascoe Leahy, 'Little Wife to the Supermom?'
27 Craig, *Contemporary Motherhood*.
28 Lorin Basden Arnold and BettyAnn Martin, eds., *Taking the Village Online: Mothers, Motherhood, and Social Media* (Bradford, Ontario: Demeter Press, 2016); Nathanson and Tuley, *Mother Knows Best*; Friedman and Calixte, *Mothering and Blogging*.

# 6

# Motherload: maternal work

I must have been uncertain, because I said to my boss at the time that I didn't know when I wanted to come back to work ... I said to him, 'Look, I've never done this before – is it okay with you if we keep it flexible? I might want to come back after six months, I might not be ready until twelve months' ... I think the thing about the earlier date was about what if I don't really enjoy this and I'm actually really wanting to go back? The thing about the later date was, what if I can't bear to leave her? ...

I would definitely say that my strength of feeling towards my children surprised me ... In the twenty-first century, we don't talk about women's longing to have children or be with children much, publicly. It seems a bit embarrassing, a bit overly emotional, a bit messy and a bit like nineteenth century, a bit old school. So I do think there's something cultural about that, but there probably is something personal for me as well. I was surprised by my strength of feeling to be with my children and how hard I found it to leave them, even for short periods. I was not prepared for that ...

It's like this ongoing debate in feminism around whether society puts all of the burden of motherhood on women, or whether women actually won't relinquish that 'burden', in inverted commas ... For all that I talk about the ideal of sharing it equally, could I? I don't know ... I could now that they're older, but in the early days, no, definitely not in the first year of life. No, I wanted the intensity of that mother–child relationship all to myself. Well, not all to myself, but primarily to myself ... It's not just the burden, it's also the privilege. I don't want to share the privilege of motherhood.

Carla Pascoe Leahy

## Introduction

Motherhood changes a woman's relationship to her work, both in terms of how she feels about and performs her work, and in terms of how others view her as a worker. Often, those changes commence in pregnancy for birthgiving mothers, as we saw in Chapter 2. But what counts as work, and the ways in which work is balanced with other aspects of maternal lives, has shifted over the past seventy-five years. This dynamism is perhaps more true of work than any other aspect of becoming a mother.

Since the mid-twentieth century, how we understand and define work has expanded. The women's liberation movement successfully fought for domestic work and childcare to be recognised as 'real' work, and as work that other sections of the economy depend on. The Wages for Housework campaign led by second-wave feminists like Sylvia Federici argued that under capitalism, the productive labour that keeps economies moving is underpinned and made possible by the reproductive labour that often takes place in the home and family.[1] In journalist Annabel Crabb's formulation, most male workers need a 'wife', in the sense that male workers engaged in paid employment in the public sphere are usually supported by the unpaid labour of wives in the home.[2] But as economist Marilyn Waring has shown, women's unpaid work still often 'counts for nothing': it is neither valued nor remunerated.[3]

Feminist scholars have argued that we need to expand our understanding of work to include the myriad of tasks that mothers perform. These include the organisational labour of managing households,[4] the emotional labour of attending to the psychological health of children and partners[5] as well as the domestic labour of cooking, cleaning and laundry.[6] As our understandings of 'work' have changed, so too have our understandings of 'care'. Care is a contested term – sometimes categorised as work and sometimes in opposition to, or needing to be balanced with, work. The increased outsourcing of many types of care work – care of children, the elderly and people living with disabilities, for example – has led to a greater recognition that there is labour involved in caring for others. These lesser-paying and lower-status roles within the economy tend to be dominated by and associated with women. Despite these debates and historical shifts in the labour market, in everyday parlance, the word 'work' still tends to refer to paid employment, often outside the home, rather than the housekeeping and care-related tasks that mothers routinely perform in the home for no remuneration.

Across the last seventy-five years, the locus of female identity has broadly shifted from mothering to career, notwithstanding the fact that some mothers in the past have always worked[7] and some mothers today do not.[8] More mothers are engaged in paid employment and more women grow up expecting to have a 'career'. But whether mothers should work has remained a contested issue that is subject to moral condemnation from others.[9] Where mothers once felt judged for working, they now feel judged if they stay at home.[10] Regardless of a mother's preference, economic changes in wages, housing costs, employment rates and more have often dictated employment decisions as much as personal choice. It remains difficult for mothers to freely choose their desired balance of caring for children and paid employment. Despite legislative changes designed to protect working mothers from discrimination, women still find that they suffer both explicit and implicit workplace discrimination when they are pregnant, breastfeeding or caring for children.[11] Although we see glimpses in these maternographies that women may actually find that their workforce capabilities are enhanced by mothering, the view that mothers are a liability or a burden upon employers persists.

But while more and more Australian mothers have taken on greater roles in the workforce since 1945, some continuities persist. Mothers still desire to be with their children, and many feel ambivalent about leaving them to perform paid work. Most find that the complex logistics of juggling transport, movement, schedules, feeding and caring – the management of time, spaces and bodies – is a job in itself. Despite increases in their paid workloads, mothers still shoulder the bulk of domestic, unpaid work. Fathers' domestic roles have enlarged slightly, but gendered divisions of labour remain stubbornly entrenched overall.[12] This chapter explores the changing balance of maternal work and care over the past seventy-five years. It examines the extent to which women wish to engage in work outside of mothering and whether they feel socially judged or supported in their personal choices.

## Maternal time

Much has changed in the ways in which Australian mothers think about, engage with and perform paid employment. But certain themes have remained constant. Unpaid work – usually women's work – is not always recognised as a form of labour. Motherhood changes a woman's relationship to her work, and this change often commences in pregnancy. Women's relationships to work are influenced by other people in their lives, including their parents, partners, friends, children and broader society.

### *Misrecognition*

In many of the maternographies created for this research, women told me that they or their mothers did not work. Apart from the ways in which this obscured the cleaning, cooking and childcare regularly performed by these women within the home, it also became apparent that this hid many other forms of out-of-home labour conducted by women that would have been classed as 'work' if they were paid. For example, Welsh-Australian Sybil initially told me that her mother did not work during the parts of her postwar childhood that were spent in Queensland. Reflecting on the ways in which her naive father would entrust money to people who betrayed him, she then corrected herself.

> My father had too much trust. So my mother, I think, took on a big burden with trying to be the financial bearer of the family as well and the hardworking mother of little children. Actually, I said when she lived in Queensland that she didn't work. She didn't work for money probably. She had a market garden with another man ... and they worked very hard in that garden. They sold those veggies, beans and tomatoes, I remember. She had a great green thumb, my mother. She knew how to garden ... I loved my father unconditionally and never saw anything bad in him, if you like. But I now see that my mother worked very hard to look after him as well.

Anglo-Australian Eve similarly characterised herself as 'a mother and as a housekeeper', omitting her years spent working alongside her Lebanese-Australian husband in the newsagency they managed together in the 1980s after their children were adults. In talking about the working lives of her Macedonian-born parents in the 1950s and 1960s, Miroslava described her father as a 'café proprietor' and her mother's profession as 'home duties', despite the fact that her mother cleaned the café at night after the customers had left. Women similarly tended not to count their volunteer, community or activist roles as 'work' – a pervasive devaluation of the critical roles that women often perform as the glue that binds families and communities together.

## Transition and tension

Another consistent theme that emerged in these maternographies is that becoming a mother has always changed women's relationships with work. For many women, that shift begins in pregnancy, both in terms of their own feelings and the ways that colleagues perceive them. Women struggling with fertility issues may find their feelings about work shifting even before conception. American-born Katerina described to me how she came to the difficult decision to leave her 'demanding' job in government to become pregnant in 2012. Due to infertility challenges, Katerina and her partner knew that they would only be able to conceive via IVF. She found the treatment process of recurrent medications, scans, procedures and surgery 'incredibly unpredictable and gruelling' and realised 'there's no way I could have done both at the same time and remain sane'. Although she had no regrets, the decision was 'very weighty' and 'hard for me to make'. When we constructed her maternography, Katerina's child was nine months old and she was considering whether to return to paid employment before trying to have a second child, which would involve another lengthy, difficult and expensive IVF process.

> So yeah, but now, you know, you think okay now I've got this happy, healthy child, and, you know, it's very fulfilling. But I still need to do something, you know, for myself, and I think even as a parent I want my son seeing that my world doesn't only just revolve around him. I have things that I'm contributing to community and to society. I think that's important for him to see that. So it's kind of like, well, how do I transition back into work and what will that look like? How can you do that when you're a mum, and you don't have support? Or if you want to go back and even try for a second,

you know that's a whole different process, than I've got a job, and oh, I've fallen pregnant again two years later, four years later – it has to be quite deliberate and, you know, it's different for us, and we acknowledge that. So you know we're trying to figure out those things as well. Because then, you know, if we did go through IVF and managed to have a second, then that probably means I'm out of the workforce for a total of like seven years, and then you're like, how do you transition back? Or, you know, do you start up your own business and do something more entrepreneurial? Which is in a way a lot more work, but you have some flexibility. So you know, you have all these questions immediately and you only have a child that's nine months old [laughs].

Although Katerina felt affirmed in her decision to leave work to focus on IVF, she now faces difficult decisions about when she should recommence paid employment and whether she should return to the same job or try something new. Many women feel that motherhood rearranges their priorities in ways that force them to reconsider their working lives.

Once pregnant, many women find that their gestating bodies intrude on their working lives in multiple ways. For women in physically demanding jobs, this is very evident, with their growing baby bump a constant reminder of their altered physical state. Dutch-born Mary was working as a nurse in a role that involved a lot of lifting when she became pregnant in 1974, and she found that her changing physiology impacted upon what she was capable of at work.

> I mean, the bump is there all the time. You're just reminded of it any minute of the day ... My work was very good at giving me options to either stop early or not but if you feel good, you go and keep doing it and I worked at that stage ... with handicapped people sitting in wheelchairs. So there was a lot of lifting involved in it. So at one stage, I got to the point that it was getting too difficult and maybe also that focus on having everything ready at home ... That focus was going to shift from work, from a total concentration on work to a little bit more on yourself and it was nice to have that little bit of time beforehand to arrange everything.

Mary's narrative hints at the ways in which her priorities were changing too, partially in terms of preparatory tasks in anticipation of the baby's arrival, but also in terms of turning her gaze inwards. Many women feel an affective shift while pregnant and recall changes in their emotional relationship with the world.

Despite her expectations that she might feel more emotionally volatile during her 2013 pregnancy, particularly in the stressful world of advertising in which she worked, Māori mother Avril found that she felt a heightened sense of calm which may partially have been reflective of a reordering of her priorities 'to move away from work'.

> I was surprised actually because you hear about hormones and pregnancy and losing it a bit. I had never been so calm and so – it's a very stressful industry that we work in and it was really just water off a duck's back – just nothing fazed me. So I was really kind of consistently calm … I think I must have emotionally been starting to check out, to move away from work. So yes, I definitely think that shift had something to do with it. But even so, I think normally I'm still quite an emotional person and I've just never been calmer … I think it does put everything into perspective.

Avril wondered whether her deliberate shifts in diet and exercise, to optimise the health of her foetus, may have contributed to her calm. Polish-Australian Petronela also noticed changes during her pregnancy in 2017, but characterised the shift she felt during late pregnancy as a lack of 'mental energy and focus'.

> Second trimester I felt full of life; end of third trimester I just had no focus. I couldn't string a sentence together. It's just incredible that I even finished doing this work. I don't know how that happened and then funnily enough after I gave birth, I kind of regained that sort of energy again, like mental energy and focus even though I was obviously a lot more tired on account of lack of sleep. That was a much more manageable tiredness in a way, it's just sleeplessness, than just the lack of life force that I had in those last weeks of pregnancy.

Some women feel accepting of such changes, such as Avril's appreciation of how calm she felt during her pregnancy. Others, like English-born Helen, felt 'resentful' of the ways in which pregnancy and then motherhood disrupt their connections to their work, particularly if they felt passionately committed to their job.

> I felt very resentful at first … It was really hard to miss that, because I love what I do … The hormones I think of breastfeeding and of childrearing, and the exhaustion of all of that, I think just means

that my mentality or my mental focus is just not where it is ... It also recreates the word 'job', in a way, because this motherhood ... it isn't even a job, it's a role. It's a lifestyle. How does work fit into that and earning money fit into that? Like a jigsaw puzzle with missing pieces, with missing corners, big pieces ... Work doesn't have a place in my life, and my identity is no longer related to what I do through work the way it was before I had a son.

As an artist who usually practises and teaches her craft, Helen had to give up some aspects of her work entirely when she had her first child in 2013, while she feels that she can't perform as well as she'd like in others. She struggled to put into words how hard it is to 'balance' – or even weigh up – two incommensurable things such as work and mothering. At the point of this interview, six months after having her first child, she could not fathom how she would eventually make all the pieces of this puzzle fit together.

While all of these narratives challenge the simplistic stereotype that motherhood inhibits women's capacities or availability in the workplace, many maternographies struggle to articulate the ways in which motherhood might actually enhance their work potential. Perhaps because of her creative background, Anglo-Australian Heather was able to enunciate this perspective.

I found instantly that I was at a disadvantage career-wise in the workplace because my kids would always take priority and I was the primary carer ... But I quickly discovered that actually I gained a whole lot by becoming a mother in the workplace, like that I was much more efficient ... It also gave me a different kind of wisdom – I felt a patience. Just a sense of kindness and care and things that I'd always had but ... it was bigger and I listened more ... I sort of found myself watching and listening a lot. I feel like that came from that early motherhood of like learning to kind of listen to cues. I actually found early motherhood, I remember feeling like it was a really big creative act. As in all of the principles that I sort of engaged in artistically and creatively in my work came to the fore so much, so much about instinct and the unconscious. And all of those things really.

In this passage, Heather beautifully articulates how her matrescence in 2012 has changed her as a person, and therefore changed her relationship to her work. Her description of how careful watching and listening develops particular qualities of patience, wisdom and empathy is reminiscent of Sara Ruddick's formulation of how maternal thinking develops through the day-to-day practice of caring for a vulnerable being whose needs are constantly changing and whose demands of the mother are therefore always evolving too.[13] Heather's experience reminds us that the skills and qualities of maternal thinking can be an asset as much as a hindrance in the workforce.

## Matrilinearity

Mothers were influenced by many factors in redefining their relationships to work after matrescence. In particular, it was evident that mothers were influenced by other people around them, including their mothers, fathers, partners, friends and broader society. We have seen in previous chapters that a woman is heavily influenced at matrescence by her own mother and her maternal style. This was evident in relation to work, though this was also where some of the sharpest matrilineal conflicts and contrasts arose.

Anglo-Australian Genevieve described her mother as a woman who put mothering at the centre of her life in the 1950s. She explained that this was why she decided to do the same, even though she came to motherhood in 1989 in a very different era, when expectations around maternal work were changing and many people expected women to go back to work after having children. In speaking of her parents, Genevieve explained that:

> it was of primary importance that the love they showered on their children was extraordinary. They didn't care about wealth; didn't care about status ... So I just anticipated that this would just round out my life. This is what I was meant to do. And because I was a little bit older, I didn't want to quickly have children and pop them in an institution before they were going to be popped in the institution anyway by law, at five, when they went to school.

For Genevieve, inheritance of her parents' values around parenthood enabled her to prioritise mothering, even when it felt to her like she was going against the grain of her generation. This was not a purely regressive or conservative definition of 'good' motherhood. Later in her maternography, Genevieve spoke very affectionately of the way her mother did not care much for cooking and cleaning and might, for example, feed the family tomatoes on toast for dinner, but nevertheless took great joy from having and raising children.

When Lebanese-Australian Sally experienced matrescence in 1978, her mother Eve played an influential role in Sally's decision-making around care and work, though it was her mother's encouragement rather than example that influenced her. Sally recalls feeling torn about whether she should go back to work while her first child was still a baby, despite her ideological commitment to the feminist principles of the women's liberation movement. It was incredibly reassuring to her that her mother assured her that her baby would not be indelibly harmed by such a decision.

> I remember my mother, God bless her, saying to me – and this is a woman who had eight children and was home full-time the whole time – she said to me when I was going back to work and feeling really bad about it, she said, 'This child is a blank slate and the only expectations the child will have are the ones you build into her so if you feel guilty she'll pick it up. So you're doing the best you can and you're doing what you think is right in your circumstances and don't feel guilty about it'. It was kind of the best advice I had at the time and I think for her era and given her own background, I thought that was enlightened actually. The other thing she did at one stage, I feel emotional even thinking about it, but she actually said to me a couple of times, 'I think you're a good mother', and I remember how important that was, you know, that my mother thought I was a good mother.

Sally articulates this more explicitly than most, but an implicit theme underlying many maternographies was the desire to receive approval from their own mother. When women have different experiences or understandings of work to that of their own mothers, this can set up a tension that is painful for both. Torres Strait Islander mother Somi explained that there was a tension in her relationship with her mother after she had her first child in 2013, some of which was sparked by differing views of whether Somi should be working.

> I sort of felt like my mum was not very helpful. That's partly distance I think, but I think that's also – I guess I can appreciate that me becoming a mother raised a whole lot of things for her. I think she sort of thought that my life was much easier, not particularly sympathetic to the things that were hard about it. We had a huge falling out actually at L's [first child's] second birthday because she felt very

much that I should have been with L at home ... I think that her words at the time were 'L needs you and you're not there for him', so that cut pretty deep.

Somi told me of the ways she has tried to explain to her mother that their material experiences are not comparable because of their different socio-historical contexts. Many millennial mothers find themselves, like Somi, trying to perform 'both roles' of provider and caregiver, and to explain this difficult juggling act to their own mother.

> She really struggles to understand the ways in which my experience has been different ... I sort of said to her about a year ago when I was trying to explain how, you know, she talks a lot about how hard it was when Dad was doing his PhD and she was home with the kids and she wasn't able to work. My father has had a very challenging career and I said to her, I said, 'what you need to see is that I'm doing both those parts'. She kind of didn't really click and then the next day she came to me, she's like, 'oh, I just understood what you meant when you said that you were doing both bits' and I'm like, 'yes, it's a lot'.

Somi's maternography is an interesting representation of a tension inherent in many maternal lives. Their own mothers exercised a powerful affective influence over the circumstances of new mothers' lives, including the combinations of work and care that they tried to manage. New mothers sometimes felt that their own mothers did not fully appreciate that they were making decisions under very different socio-historical circumstances particular to their generation. In other words, during periods of rapid cultural change across the second half of the twentieth century, a conflict could arise between generations in a family that were a product of socio-historical generational shifts.

For many women, motherhood evokes changes in their selves, their relationships and their priorities that force a re-evaluation of their relation to paid employment. Some mothers continue doing the same kinds of work, though they may change their hours or their level of responsibility. Some women I spoke to clung desperately to their pre-maternal work as a kind of anchor through the many and varied changes of matrescence. For other women, the changing priorities in their lives occasioned by motherhood became a prompt for deeper questions about their careers. Particularly for millennial mothers, matrescence often triggered a shift in thinking about the role of work in their lives and the type of work they performed. It was as though in upending their relationships to their bodies, to other people and to their sense of self, women reassessed what they valued most in their lives and where their contributions could best be made. However, the eventual outcome of that reassessment was strongly influenced by the historical context in which motherhood was unfolding.

### Generational time

Of all the aspects of matrescence considered in this book, maternal relationships to work have perhaps undergone the greatest historical changes over the past seventy-five years. Shifting cultural understandings of gender, work, care and subjectivity have encouraged maternal participation in paid work. Such cultural shifts have been intertwined with changes to government policies and economic structures to enable maternal workforce participation. In particular, government support for childcare increased from the 1980s, allowing women to take up greater paid employment. Parental leave has expanded, with the introduction of unpaid parental leave in 1990 and government provision of paid parental leave from 2011. Reflecting on the experiences of her mother (born in 1930), herself (born in 1952), her daughter (born in 1978) and her granddaughters (born from 2007 to 2014), Sally offered her understanding of these generational changes:

> For my mother [Eve], she planned to be a full-time mother, she was a full-time mother. I think she was enormously fulfilled by that and that was her generational expectation. I was in the generation that was at the forefront of changing expectations and I probably was one of the kind of the change-ready people but in a relationship where that was possible. So I think for our generation, it was a contested space and there were, you know, mixed expectations. We lived in progressive circles and we mixed in progressive circles so it was for us pretty easy. But I watch my daughter and granddaughters and I feel enormously pleased for them that they can choose to spend longer at home with their children and it not impact on lives as dramatically. So, for example, there are childcare opportunities that weren't there when I was there. There are, you know, parental leave schemes,

there are government benefits, there are a whole range of things that actually mean that women can take an interruption to their career to be parents and it doesn't have to have a dramatic impact on their professional lives and I think that's absolutely fantastic. You would hope that for, you know, my granddaughters that it would be even easier for them.

Despite Sally's optimistic assessment of generational change as perceived through the lives of female generations in her family, paternal participation in raising children still lags behind maternal involvement. It is the state – and private childcare providers – that have largely moved in to fill the breach created when mothers engage more in paid employment. While fathers are now more likely to engage in childrearing tasks outside of work – like changing nappies or picking kids up from school – the raw statistics on their participation have not shifted dramatically. Only one in twenty Australian fathers takes primary parental leave.[14] In 2014, 85 per cent of fathers and partners still took less than four weeks leave at the birth of a child.[15] Time use studies show that women's time is much more dramatically impacted upon the birth of a child than men.[16] In other words, there has been a revolution in the ways in which mothers engage in paid work and care work, but fathers still lag behind.

## Postwar mothers

This study begins after World War Two, when maternal workforce participation was relatively low: in 1954, 15 per cent of married women were in the labour force.[17] Our cultural memory of the postwar era is that mothers did not work but were rather full-time housewives and stay-at-home mothers.[18] This picture is partly true, but the reality is somewhat more complicated.[19] Working-class and migrant women often worked throughout their lives, compelled by financial pressures. In the inner-city, working-class areas of Melbourne such as Fitzroy, where Anglo-Australian Daphne lived, many women like her always combined work and mothering.[20] Daphne (born in 1930) worked as a factory worker, waitress and shopkeeper. In the days before widespread provision of paid childcare, her children were usually minded by relatives or neighbours. Living in Fitzroy in the same period, Miroslava's

Macedonian-born mother also worked alongside mothering, fitting it in around the other parts of her life. Miroslava (born in 1946) remembered that two nights per week her mother cleaned the café that her parents owned. Her mother would wake the children at 11 pm, to take them with her to the café for a couple of hours so she could clean. They would then walk home together in the middle of the night. Interestingly, this wasn't counted as 'work' by Miroslava, who listed her mother's profession as 'home duties'.

A common pattern for many middle-class women in the 1950s and 1960s was to commence paid work when they finished school but to stop working when they married or became pregnant. Sometimes, this decision was a personal one; sometimes, it was forced upon them by discriminatory laws. Anglo-Australian Maggie was forced to leave the Commonwealth public service when she married in the mid-1960s because in those days, married women were barred from working in the public service. She felt annoyed that her career had been cut short and did not return to work until her third child started primary school. Interestingly, Maggie observed that her sense of identity shifted from work to mothering when her first child was born, and that she felt 'depressed' when her youngest child started school because she was 'a bit lost', having restructured her life and identity around mothering.

Sometimes, middle-class women engaged in further paid work when their children were older. Anglo-Australian Rachel had her first of three children in 1964, raising them in Glen Iris (a Melbourne suburb adjacent to Malvern). She helped her sister-in-law run a catering business in the 1970s by cooking from her home. While Rachel did not need to pay for childcare because her work was occurring in the home, it was a form of paid employment. However, Rachel did not really enjoy the catering work. When I asked her whether she performed it for financial reasons or for other reasons, she rushed to reassure me that her husband was 'a very good provider'. We see a glimpse here of one of the many reasons why postwar mothers may not have characterised their work *as* work – to admit that a married mother was working may have implied that her husband was not an adequate breadwinner, within a cultural milieu in which this was an essential part of the paternal, masculine role.[21] Relatedly, to concede that a mother was working may have implied to contemporaries that she was not adequately performing her maternal, feminised role and that her children may have been suffering the consequences of maternal deprivation.

Some mothers found ingenious methods to combine paid work with motherhood, depending on carefully balanced care and living arrangements. Before becoming a mother in 1953, English-born Marjorie had owned her own hairdressing salon from the age of nineteen. She worked until she was six months pregnant, eventually stopping because she found it too tiring being on her feet all day. When her two daughters were three and five years of age, she returned to paid work, opening another salon. Her husband was a travelling salesman who was often away for a few days at a time, so they hired a local nanny who would take the girls to and from school and kindergarten. On the days that Marjorie worked late, the nanny would get the children ready for bed. Marjorie explained that the decision to return to work was financial rather than driven by her own personal ambition or preferences.

> We needed the money. You couldn't live on one wage with two children. And so, we bought a little salon. I'd had one before when I was single, and we lived upstairs and behind the shop. It was a nice life. So I actually was never far away from them, because even when they came home – [the nanny] would bring them home from school and kinder and they were sort of in the back – in the dwelling we used to call it – a dwelling, and I was in the front of the shop so they could come in and say, 'Mum', you know, whatever – 'can I have something?', and I'd say, 'yes, ask [the nanny]'.

The co-location of her home and her workplace made it easier for Marjorie to facilitate her return to paid employment. But the need to hire a nanny was also because postwar fathers rarely performed the daily tasks of raising children.

> Men didn't do anything ... R [husband] was lovely, he loved L [child] and she was crazy about him. She probably loved him more than she loved me, but he didn't do anything. He didn't bath the baby or – or change the baby, but I don't know, it was just a different dynamic. The mother did for the child. The father went out to work ... It suited me, and it suited me that R did all the finances and R made all the decisions ... I had a business, and I was like a very determined modern woman, but I didn't mind being the little wife.

Maternographies suggest that such attitudes to parental responsibly for raising children were commonplace in the postwar era. Men did very little child minding or domestic work and this gendered division of labour was accepted by the overwhelming majority. Women felt respected for their housekeeping role and men for their breadwinning role.[22]

Some postwar mothers did, however, express frustration at their sense of life opportunities curtailed by fathers or husbands. When Anglo-Australian Pauline (born 1937) wanted to stay at school past Year 11, and continue on to study at university, her father would not allow her. She later married and became a mother in 1963, and when she wanted to go back to paid work after having children – in order to 'use her brain' – her husband told her that he preferred that she stayed home with the children. Pauline told me that on balance, she was glad she had not returned to work, because there is an important moment when children first come home from school and want to share stories from their day, an opportunity which is missed once the moment passes. But although Pauline felt she had done the right thing in staying home with her children, there was a wistfulness in her response – a subtle thread of missed opportunities or curiosity about what she might have made of her life if she had been born into a different generation.

Some postwar mothers were very fulfilled by their paid work and did not see it as conflicting with their maternal role. Jane had her eleven children between 1954 and 1969, eventually returning to work when the children were at school (emergency teaching at a nearby school). She went back to work both because she enjoyed teaching and to help financially support her large family. Jane explained that although it was expensive raising so many children, as people who had grown up during the 1930s depression, she and her husband were content to live a simple life without many luxuries. For postwar mothers who had their children in the period between 1945 and 1969, work was a smaller part of their lives and less central to their sense of identity. Nevertheless, work remained an insistent presence that surfaced regularly across these maternographies, suggesting that our collective memory of the postwar housewife is an oversimplified, and culturally limiting, construct.[23]

## Second-wave mothers

Structural, social, economic and political changes transformed the ways in which second-wave mothers engaged in care and work during the 1970s and 1980s. Many of these changes were key demands of the women's liberation movement, including equal pay, equal education and access to childcare. The progressive Whitlam Labor Government was elected in 1972 and introduced a raft of changes that benefited women including no-fault divorce laws, gender pay equity in the public service and a single parent's benefit. During the 1980s, the Hawke Labor Government passed the Sex Discrimination Act and the Affirmative Action (Equal Opportunity in Employment) Act, as well as overseeing a massive expansion of childcare.[24] While feminists had pushed for community-based childcare in the 1970s,[25] government-provided or supported childcare became more common from the 1980s, as political leaders realised that increased maternal workforce participation relied upon accessible and affordable childcare.[26] (Australian childcare later underwent another shift in the 1990s towards more private provision of childcare.)

Inner-city areas like Fitzroy in Melbourne were at the vanguard of childcare changes. During the early and mid-twentieth century, these once-working-class areas were unusual in having access to childcare so that working-class mothers could work.[27] Anglo-Australian Regina was living in Fitzroy from the late 1960s and 1970s and recalls that there were several childcare centres operating. They provided important care options for working mothers but tended to be underpinned by paternalist philosophies. Regina explained that: 'That one was very much built around the idea that Fitzroy was a poor area and you could assume that most people were not looking after their children properly and it was a very top-down sort of childcare centre there'. In the 1970s and 1980s, as more students and academics moved into inner-urban neighbourhoods, innovative new childcare models sometimes emerged. As an academic, Regina was also involved in establishing a childcare centre at her university.

Despite such changes, the extent to which mothers should engage in paid work and the impacts of childcare upon children remained contested. Lebanese-Australian Sally recalls enormous social and personal ambivalence about these issues before and after she had her first child in 1978.

> It was highly contested. There was real conflict like you could go to, you know, dinner parties or whatever and, and shackles [sic] would rise ... They were competing narratives so one was the woman's place is full-time mothering in the home. The baby will be scarred for life and that's what you should do and then there was the feminist movement which was, you know, women can do it all ... Structures should be redesigned so that they can have children in childcare. Childcare's good for children and that the woman doesn't then, you know, lose part of her life to parenting ... There was a level of unreality about both of them.

Despite the fact that attitudes and structures were changing in the 1970s, Sally's arrangement with her partner – where they split care and work equally – was unusual. As more mothers engaged in paid employment, childcare services were more likely than fathers to take up the care of children. But a continuing ambivalence about childcare persisted, as suggested by the fact that second-wave mothers were more likely to take their children out of childcare if they did not enjoy it than millennial mothers would be today. Irish-Australian Brenda had her first child in 1978. She tried returning to her job as a midwife when her first child was young but postponed her return to work when the child did not adjust well to childcare.

> I went to work at the Royal Women's Hospital, I think when E [child] was about three. Two and a half ... So [husband] looked after her, and ... she went to a local childcare centre in Fitzroy, and when she first went to childcare, she found it really difficult, and cried a lot. And so I took her out because I didn't want my baby to cry. And then I waited for about ... another year – before I put her into childcare – when she was older and more able to handle the separation.

Many second-wave mothers stayed at home until their children were in school and then returned to part-time work. Dutch-Australian Mary was a full-time mother for more than ten years after the first of her two children was born in 1974. In 1988, she started studying to become a kindergarten teacher. She vividly recalls the 'conflict' that she felt between her roles at that point.

> My focus changed. I was doing something that I as a child always wanted to do. I wanted to become a kinder teacher. Now I had the

chance and I threw myself in for 110 per cent. I just loved it to death. So it was sometimes a bit difficult because when M [first child] was getting to HSC [end of secondary schooling] and he needed a little bit more help with his work, I felt really bad that I sometimes had to say sorry but I have to have this assignment and I need to have it finished by today. So there was a conflict between being a mother and I must have sometimes chosen for the thing that I should not have chosen for maybe but I loved it so much, but they didn't suffer. I don't think so ... You want to do it all. I didn't want to give it up. I had a part-time job. I had part-time study ... So the family had to sort of sometimes work around me and I had to work around family and my husband had to do a little bit more. So there was sometimes a bit of conflict that happened and it makes you feel bad as a mother.

Mary eventually gave up some of her study because she was concerned about the impact it was having on her family. In reflecting on the reasons that she chose her mothering over study, Mary mused that a father would always prioritise his employment, and possibly mothers in her daughter Michelle's millennial generation would now say, 'I don't have to be at the last spot all the time'.

Second-wave mothers were less likely to find their lives rigorously controlled by their fathers than postwar mothers like Pauline above, but the influence of parents is still apparent, especially in migrant families. When she finished school in the late 1960s, Macedonian-Australian Miroslava recalled that she wanted to be a teacher but her father didn't think that was an appropriate choice so he organised a job for her in a bank. There were other instances in Miroslava's maternography where her working-class, migrant father's wishes over-rode his daughter's preferences. For example, when an Anglo-Australian colleague asked her out on a date, she had to decline, knowing that her parents would not allow her to date a non-Macedonian-Australian. Miroslava reflected briefly, but poignantly, that her life may have taken a different course if she were allowed to form her own relationships.

Other second-wave mothers described the ways in which their employment choices were constrained by family pressures or broader cultural ideals. Feminised professions associated with care, like nursing and teaching, were considered appropriate options for women in that generation. Sally recalls her mother assuming that her daughters would engage in work alongside mothering but advising them to choose employment that would complement their maternal roles.

> My mother ... had said to all the girls that we should do teaching because we could go to school with our children and come home with our children ... She clearly felt quite strongly about it and interestingly for the boys it was complete open slather ... So that was interesting in that she hadn't worked herself [but] assumed that we would have a profession and assumed that we would combine work and motherhood.

Anglo-Australian Wanda recalled that she chose nursing as her profession in the late 1960s because she thought it would help her to travel. She remembers feeling that she had to quit her job when she became pregnant in 1978, because it would have been frowned upon to be pregnant, and she would not have received maternity leave anyway. While many educated women of her generation chose to stay at home until their children were in school, Wanda chose to return to part-time work in the early 1980s when her third child was about eighteen months old. She felt comfortable with this decision because they had a close friend who could assist with child minding. When their children were young, she felt that her husband was very involved in their upbringing. But when reflecting upon his role in hindsight, she perceives that it involved rather minimal tasks of bathing or reading to the children before bed. Wanda had primary responsibility for caring for their children and managing the house, and her husband did not reduce his full-time work hours when they became parents.

Second-wave mothers, having internalised the demands of the women's liberation movement, were more likely to choose to combine work and motherhood than their mothers. Many felt, like Welsh-Australian Sybil, that mothering was deeply important to them but it was also important to be more than 'just' a mother. In their preschool years, Sybil cared for her children during the day and taught in the evenings (before returning to primary school teaching in the mid-1980s when her children were at school). When I asked if motherhood had changed her, Sybil said, 'I think I was very proud to be a mum but I was also at the same time aware that if you're a mother at home and that's all you do, then I might not have liked that'. At the same time, she felt that, 'I loved being a mother at home and I loved that opportunity and I'm grateful that I had that because I was at home a lot with them and I think that if you're not, you can lose some aspects of them growing up'.

Women who did engage in paid work alongside mothering in the 1970s and 1980s were often less professionally ambitious, or focused upon career progression, than millennial mothers would be today. It was important to Sybil that she remained in contact with her 'craft' and 'profession', but she was satisfied to stay at the same level as a teacher. By contrast, her daughter, Ariana, who Suzanne may be thinking of when she speaks of 'mothers now', feels the weight of both financial pressure and career ambitions. Reflecting on generational change, Sybil muses that,

> I think it's a little bit hard for young mothers now because they've got to go back to work, because they've got to keep paying the mortgage, because they've got to keep everything running, keep their profession going because if they lose too much time out of it, they don't get the promotions. I think that's tough. I remember feeling pleased that I was able to be a teacher and not lose the momentum of going ahead with teaching.

Second-wave mothers were at the forefront of changing social attitudes around where women's worth lay – the home or the workplace. As pathbreakers, they often felt conscious of the judgement of others.

## *Millennial mothers*

Millennial mothers feel deeply conflicted about what the appropriate balance of paid work and care work should be in their lives. They have grown up during and after the women's liberation movement, assuming that part of their identity will be based upon their chosen career, that motherhood is a choice rather than compulsory and that if they decide to mother they will do so in combination with paid employment. Sociologist Tina Miller's interviews with British women in the early 2000s found that in an era in which women are accustomed to feeling a sense of agency at work, many find transitioning into the less controllable realm of motherhood difficult. Miller discovered that her interviewees spent a lot of time thinking and talking about their plans to return to work after having a baby, as a way of returning to a sphere where they felt in control.[28] Simultaneously, her interviewees' narratives showed evidence of an internalised intensive mothering ideology, and many women felt torn between a need to be 'good' mothers *and* 'good' workers.[29]

Millennial mothers in 1990s Australia were in many ways living through a crossover decade. Sociologist Belinda Probert identified this decade as a time in which the gender culture was in flux and Australian attitudes as to mothers' roles were split.[30] Women were still wondering whether they could be both mothers and workers and whether they wanted to take on these dual responsibilities. Rising costs of living (particularly housing) were increasing budgetary pressures on Australian families, making it financially difficult for a woman to mother full-time. Working mothers struggled within an inconsistent policy environment which sent mixed messages. The conservative Howard Government (1996–2006) created disincentives for (partnered) working mothers through the tax-benefit system and a refusal to introduce paid parental leave, though unpaid parental leave became a legal right in 1990.[31] Government expenditures on childcare increased, resulting in a greater number of available places in paid childcare and a shift from a nonprofit to a corporate model of childcare provision.[32] Female labour force participation continued to grow. In 1985, only 46 per cent of mothers with dependent children were in paid employment, climbing to more than 60 per cent by 2004.[33]

Class and locational variations were very apparent in the maternographies of women who became mothers in the transitional decade of the 1990s. Irish-Australian Caitlyn lived in the regional town of Ocean Grove when she had her first child in 1990. Caitlyn was ambitious and career-focused, and determined to maintain connection to her work. She felt that it was unusual to be a working mother in her regional town in the 1990s and felt judged for her decisions because 'childcare was a dirty word'. By contrast, some urban women felt judged if they did *not* return to work soon after having children. Raising her children in the middle-class suburb of Malvern in the 1990s, Anglo-Australian Justine recalled that the majority of her contemporary mothers went back to work, most of them part-time. Of her mother's group, only two decided to stay home with their children. Justine felt that her prioritisation of her maternal role distinguished her from other mothers in her area.

Anglo-Australian Genevieve similarly felt out of touch with her urban milieu. Living in the inner-city area of Fitzroy when she had her first child in 1989, Genevieve felt like she was on the cusp of a new generation in the 1990s in which most women did return to work after having children. 'In a social situation, someone would ask me, 'And what do you do?' And invariably, if I said, 'I'm a mother at home' they would just turn and talk to somebody else. I became totally invisible.' Genevieve believed that the thoughtful, considered care of children provided all the stimulation and socialisation that they, and she, needed. She recalls that many mothers in her local area went back to work quickly after having children but she was fortunate to have a small group of friends who shared her views.

> We all considered that we were doing a job that deserved respect, and equal status – if not a superior status, actually ... We didn't feel like we were drudges at home ... So in that way, I felt that I was being a strong feminist, because I was pursuing what I wanted to do, and what I thought was important to do.

She recalls feeling 'incredibly happy' raising her young children and took 'an educational perspective to my mothering' by socialising her children at local shops, borrowing plenty of books from the local library and becoming politically involved in a community campaign to save the library from closure.

While Genevieve's overarching memory is that she did not work while her children were young, and it is important to her narrative construction of her remembered mothering that she prioritised her children, there were inconsistencies in her interview. As she was talking, she recalled that she did some 'tutoring young children how to read' 'when M [first child] was a baby'. She also remembered that she did bookkeeping one day per week for some 'pocket money', but she distinguished these roles from 'real' work that she returned to later.

> I didn't actually go back to work, per se, until M [second child] was doing two days – full days – of kindergarten. M [first child] was at school by then – and that's when my friend P and I developed our own business – a writing business. And even then ... we worked around school hours. Incredibly bloody minded about it. The only institutional care our children got were in the traditional school system.

It was important to Genevieve that any work she took on was flexible and could fit around school and kindergarten hours, or was at a time when a family member could mind her children. This is partly because she wanted to emulate her mother's maternal style, and partly because she was sceptical of the supposed benefits of institutional childcare. While postwar mothers felt social judgement if they utilised out-of-home care for their children, by the 1990s, some mothers like Genevieve felt a pressure to use it.

> I just hated that idea of dropping a little thing off at a childcare centre and not picking them up until six o'clock at night ... That harping of, 'Children love it! They're so stimulated! They'd be bored at home! They've got all those toys, and they're socialising with the other children, and it's just fabulous'. I'd had this for years and years, so when ... M [first child] was in kinder, so to go to that one day a week work, I put M [second child] in the local crèche. And he hated it. He would beg me not to leave him there.

Despite her resistance to institutional childcare, Genevieve's perspective has mellowed with the passage of time.

> All the people I know whose children are in care, they're not really suffering – it's not as if they've grown up to be frail, disaffected children – but at the time, I didn't think it was the right thing to do. But I think maybe I just wanted to replicate the way my mother brought me up.

In hindsight, Genevieve feels less adamant that childcare is negative for children. But she is self-reflexive enough to perceive that perhaps some of her resistance was a desire to imitate her own mother's maternal style.

Many millennial mothers found that their expectations of work and mothering did not match their reality. Anglo-Australian Sophia had her first child in 1997 in Fitzroy and planned to return to work four days per week when the child was ten months old. But when the time came, Sophia visited the childcare centre and found that she could not bear the idea. She instead negotiated to return to work on a smaller fraction. Like many mothers, Sophia felt torn between feeling guilty about leaving her baby in the care of others, and feeling that she needed some time away from her child for her own sanity. Despite the challenges posed by second-wave feminism to traditional gender roles, in the millennial era, most fathers were still expected to be primary breadwinners and performed less care work than mothers. Sophia said that her husband was very involved in the care of their children. But, when asked, she admitted that there had never been any discussion about whether he would take time away from work to care for their children. As in many families, it was simply assumed that as primary earner, he would continue to work full-time and she would take time off work to be primary carer.

For millennial mothers who had their first child in the 2010s, the challenges thrown up by first-time motherhood were even more acute. Anglo-Australian Molly found her new maternal role 'really hard' in the first three months after her child was born in 2013, because:

> I wasn't doing something that I felt was constructive. My way of being constructive was to work and to engage corporate sector, or be in meetings, or have my phone. I'm busy, I must be busy, I'm on my phone the whole time type thing. Then I had to stop and slow down also the way of doing things.

She explained that her identity has expanded so that she's not only '[Molly] the corporate relations manager, it's [Molly] the mum'. She anticipated that when she returned to work, she would have to find balance 'between the two roles, because I can't just be one person – it wouldn't be fair to R [child] and it wouldn't be fair to me too.' Molly's solution to resolving that existential dilemma of being two people simultaneously was through complex scheduling.

> I've always got a plan. I'll probably go to work at 6:00, 7:00, be there at 7:00 in the morning, and then get H [husband] to drop R off to childcare – she's going to be there three days a week hopefully if we get a place, fingers crossed. Then I'll finish work at 3:00 on the dot, and then I'll go and pick her up from childcare, take her home, play with her, do that sort of thing. Then I'll start to do dinner, blah, blah, blah.

Molly anticipated doing some more work from home in the evenings after her child was in bed, but was adamant that her mothering would come first.

> I'm only going to have one child, and I don't have a child just to be a part-time handbag type thing. So I have to work for money, but I also want to make sure her years as a baby, I interact with her as

much as possible. Because I've worked in early childhood care and development, and the first three, five, years of any child's life are the most important. So to waste that and not invest in that I think would be sad.

In her maternography, Molly gestured to the ways in which her work industry had shaped her thoughts about childrearing and mothering. Dutch-Australian Michelle similarly felt that her industry had shaped her perspectives on mothering, but in a different way. She admits that both she and her male employer used to think that mothers strategically used their children to make excuses for being less than fully productive. She believed that 'mothers used it as an excuse and look they may not have but I always thought negatively about that'. Her boss similarly would express 'old-fashioned' views such as, 'oh pregnant again – that costs me money'. But with Michelle's pregnancy in 2012 – and the introduction of government-funded parental leave in 2011 – both started to 'think differently' and be 'more open minded'. She reflected that 'with parental paid leave and a lot of views changing a lot over the past few years about keeping your workers is harder than replacing them – replacing someone's harder than keeping a good worker'.

Michelle possibly found the transition to her maternal role easier than some because she never fully left her paid employment, so her sense of an identity shift was less profound. From the earliest days of her first child's life, she continued doing the accounts for her employer, which took about two or three days per month 'so I can do it a couple of hours here and a couple of hours there and at night-time as well when I put her down'. Michelle also stayed in touch with her workplace, which was very close to her Fitzroy apartment, by 'popping in' every week or so. She reflected that 'I haven't been disconnected from work at all since the pregnancy'. But both Molly and Michelle found their formal return to work was more ambivalent than expected. Michelle had planned to return full-time when her child was three months old, but ended up delaying her return until six months at two days per week. Both Michelle and Molly's narratives also reveal the enormity of the organisational planning that underpins maternal working lives. Such finely tuned schedules require significant energy, mental labour and emotional investment.[34] Part of the explanation of how much time and effort goes into this planning is that on some level, mothers are conscious of feeling torn between two worlds with a foot in each sphere. They want to be effective and engaged in the world of work, yet they also want to feel reassured that their children's care and wellbeing is not compromised.

Millennial mothers also found that sometimes their expectations had to be altered in the face of ill health, disability or simply different characteristics of the mother or child than was anticipated. Anglo-Australian Tessa never expected that she would give birth to a premature child of twenty-eight weeks' gestation in 2013. While she was fortunate to receive one year of maternity leave at half pay from her employer, the fact that her premature daughter was more vulnerable to contracting illness meant that Tessa did not feel comfortable with her starting childcare too young. When her daughter was eighteen months old, Tessa did some casual work that could be completed at odd hours when her partner was home. When their daughter was two, she started childcare. Tessa has not generally felt torn between work and mothering. She feels that because she was an older mother who had progressed in her career before having a baby, it was easier for her to pick up well-paid, flexible and satisfying work. But she is careful to make work choices that don't leave her feeling compromised as a mother. The only times that Tessa has felt really conflicted were when her daughter has been too sick to go to childcare but Tessa had important commitments at work.

Many millennial mothers describe finding it difficult to resist the pressures of the household economy and the neoliberal job market to work more. In the twenty-first century, many millennial mothers recommence paid employment after twelve months of maternity leave, returning to work part-time. The care of their children is usually through formal (paid) or informal childcare, often performed by grandparents. In 2005, 44.8 per cent of families with young children relied on grandparents to facilitate maternal employment while in 2011, this figure was 39.2 per cent.[35] Yet the working hours of Australian fathers have not reduced as the working hours of mothers have increased in the twenty-first century, with Australian fathers still working among the longest hours in the OECD.[36]

Welsh-Australian Ariana became a mother in 2010. She spoke passionately about what her three children mean to her, but simultaneously she is committed to her marketing career. After each child, she took twelve months of maternity leave before returning to work four days a week. Her children have spent two days a week in paid care and two days a week with their grandmother, Ariana's mother Sybil. There seemed to be undercurrents of conflicted emotions in Ariana's maternography, but she does not generally allow herself to focus on her ambivalence. She feels that she has no choice financially if she and her partner are to continue paying their mortgage (in an era in which housing has never been less affordable) and to offer their children a private school education. Yet she also told me sad stories of her children not wanting to go to childcare. One of her sons constantly tells her, 'I don't want to go today Mum – I just want to stay home with you'. Ariana told me that she tries not to let herself feel guilty about this, because she feels she has no choice. She yearns for more time in her days, time for herself and time for her children. Listening to Ariana's maternography encapsulated all of the pressure and conflict of twenty-first-century motherhood.

In recent decades, news media has consistently highlighted the figure of the 'mumtrepreneur' as a kind of collective fantasy of the twenty-first century – the idea that by choosing flexible and self-directed work, women can 'have it all' and be available to both their families and their careers. Some millennial mothers spoke of trying to pursue the elusive ideal of the mumtrepeneur, the mother and small business owner who finds the solution to the irreconcilable demands of twenty-first-century motherhood by choosing or creating a type of work that can be done from home, fitting flexibly around her caring. Genevieve tried to do this through a writing consultancy in the 1990s. Amanda did some sales work, launching what she believes was an early example of an online business in the early 2000s, selling sewing supplies over the internet. When I interviewed Anglo-Australian Kristen in 2017, she was in the process of setting up an online business selling clothing and working from home, after spending eight years as a full-time mother to her three children. Kristen was unusual in that she decided before her children were born that she did not want her children in childcare before two years of age, partly on the basis of study she had competed in child psychology. This left her feeling estranged from other mothers of her generation in her middle-class suburb of Malvern, who all returned to work by the time their first child was twelve months old, and who Kristen did not feel she could discuss her decision with. Kristen describes work as the 'new religion' among contemporary mothers: it is heretical to state that one may want to stay home and experience a slower pace of time 'down among the children', in Anne Manne's redolent phrase.[37]

Some other mothers were unsure, but found the attempt to return to work too difficult, for multiple reasons. Anglo-Australian Andrea attempted to return to casual nursing when her first child was eight months old in 2010. Her husband was uncomfortable with the concept of placing their children in childcare, so offered to take time off his work as a handyman whenever Andrea was offered a shift. But there were several occasions when a shift was cancelled with only a couple of hours' notice, and her husband had already taken the day off work, resulting in lost income for the family. On top of that, Andrea felt 'heart-wrenched' leaving her child. She and her partner were not under financial pressure for her to work; it was only that Andrea did not want to lose her nursing skills. By that time, the couple were trying to get pregnant again (they eventually had three children all eighteen months apart). Eventually, Andrea decided not to return to paid employment. She spent four and a half years either pregnant or breastfeeding, before going back to part-time nursing when her oldest child was five. Women like Andrea, or Alison, who took twelve years away from paid work to raise four children, demonstrate that not all millennial mothers have a sense of self deeply rooted in their career. Particularly for women who are not tertiary-educated, and who live in regional areas, identity is not necessarily strongly associated with paid employment.

Polish-Australian Petronela was able to stay home for a year after her first child was born in 2017, to enjoy deep immersion in baby time, partly because having just completed her PhD before having a child, she did not have a job to hurry back to. (She did, however, have intellectual stimulation from the time her baby was six months old, as she was transforming her thesis into a book in spare hours.) As a feminist and tertiary-educated women, Petronela told me she intellectually admires countries like Sweden where fathers are encouraged to adopt more responsibility for the care of children through expansive parental leave policies. One minute later during her maternography, she told me how difficult it was when she spent one day away when her baby was four months old. Petronela flew to Canberra for a conference and left her partner with bottles of expressed milk. She recalls, as soon as I'd landed, he's calling me kind of going, 'where are the baby clothes?' and I'm like, 'Dude look at our apartment, there's not that many places you can hide baby clothes and also, you've seen me dressing our baby every day – where do I normally get the clothes from?' He figured that out. It was both heart-wrenching for me to leave her and it was also fantastic for me to leave her with him partly again because it's nice that he had a day of bonding, also because he got to see how tricky it actually is.

Petronela's memory of this day apart from her daughter vividly evokes the ways in which intimate care of a baby develops specialised expertise in the primary carer – usually the mother – that is often not fully appreciated until it is absent. This expertise is also grounded in a deep emotional bond – an intimate knowing of mother to child, child to mother – that can be both enriching and painful for the mother, as her heart and her body yearn for the child when they are separated.

On the flight ... there was this other new mother on the flight sitting next to me. A beautiful woman, nicely done up, wearing a little suit and she also had a three-/four-month baby with her and I thought, who has choreographed this – why are they putting me on the seat next to this woman with a baby, my own baby's age? As she started to breastfeed as the flight was taking off, my breasts were just bursting and in pain from just watching this because it was triggering whatever hormone in me.

Petronela's experience of being separated from her young baby demonstrates the ways in which the visceral connection of mother to child is not severed with the umbilical cord. Petronela found that her yearning for her daughter took on a physical form that made her reflect anew on 'the pain of motherhood and these constant little jabs of emotional pain and physical pain once they start chomping down on your boobs'.

Cultural discourses concerning parent–child relationships tend to focus on the separation anxiety that children can feel when separated from their mother. It is rarer to acknowledge the wrench that mothers also feel when that bond is stretched or severed. With the lack of cultural discussion of what Andrea and Petronela called feeling 'heart-wrenched', it is easy for millennial mothers to feel that that they are just being silly or soppy when they miss their child, or that they need to 'get over it', rather than recognising such emotions as the sign of a deep emotional attachment that is nourishing for both members of the relationship.

## Conclusion

Maternal participation in different types of work has shifted significantly over the past seventy-five years. In broad terms, changing understandings of work, care and gender have resulted in women doing more paid work – and men performing more care work. Shifting economic pressures and structural supports have also underpinned rising maternal workforce participation. But although many contemporary heterosexual couples enter parenthood assuming they will perform an equal distribution of care, most couples regress to a breadwinner/caregiver model. Time use data reveals that unpaid domestic work increases substantially at parenthood, but the enlarged domestic load still falls much more heavily upon women.[38] This is partly because of financial pressures and partly because of the intractability of gender norms. Despite an increasing expectation that mothers will combine work and care – in the form of government encouragement, social pressures and individual aspirations – women are often surprised to find that they feel conflicted separating from their children to re-enter the workforce. Although they feel that they have changed and grown with maternity, the workforce rarely values their new maternal skill set.

Finding that motherhood is inadequately supported and insufficiently recognised by society, many women feel disappointed and betrayed. They long to feel a sense of agency and worth in the world but instead find that they are undervalued as mothers. Despite formal anti-discrimination legislation, mothers often still suffer from maternal prejudices in the workforce, where children are seen as a burden and a limit on productivity and potential. There is little public discussion of what some mothers tentatively tried to explain to me: that motherhood feels enriching, an opportunity for personal development that actually expands and enhances their potential in other domains. The next, and final, chapter will explore the ways in which becoming a mother transforms women, and the ways in which the new centrality of motherhood in their lives can feel challenging for women who have based their identities around their careers.

## Notes

1 Silvia Federici, *Caliban and the Witch: Women, the Body and Primitive Accumulation* (New York: Autonomedia, 2004); Silvia Federici, *Revolution at Point Zero: Housework, Reproduction, and Feminist Struggle* (Oakland, CA: PM Press, 2012).
2 Annabel Crabb, *The Wife Drought* (Melbourne: Ebury Australia, 2015); Annabel Crabb, 'Men at Work: Australia's Parenthood Trap', *Quarterly Essay* 75 (2019): 1–73.
3 Marilyn Waring, *Still Counting: Wellbeing, Women's Work and Policy-Making* (Wellington: Bridget Williams Books, 2019).
4 Eve Worth and Laura Paterson, '"How Is She Going to Manage with the Children?" Organizational Labour, Working and Mothering in Britain, c. 1960–1990', *Past and Present* Supplement 15 (2020): 318–43.
5 Helen McCarthy, 'Career, Family and Emotional Work: Graduate Mothers in 1960s Britain', *Past & Present* Supplement 15 (2020): 295–317.
6 Ann Oakley, *Housewife* (Middlesex, England: Penguin, 1974).
7 John Murphy and Belinda Probert, 'Never Done: The Working Mothers of the 1950s', in *Double Shift: Working Mothers and Social Change in Australia*, eds. Patricia Grimshaw, John Murphy and Belinda Probert (Beaconsfield, Vic.: Melbourne Publishing Group/Circa, 2005), 133–52.
8 Elizabeth Reid Boyd and Gayle Letherby, eds., *Stay-at-Home Mothers: Dialogues and Debates* (Bradford, Ontario: Demeter Press, 2014).
9 Harper and Richards, *Mothers and Working Mothers*.
10 Pascoe Leahy, 'Little Wife to the Supermom?'
11 Australian Human Rights Commission, *Supporting Working Parents: Pregnancy and Return to Work National Review*.
12 Jennifer Baxter, 'Fathers and Work: A Statistical Overview', Australian Institute of Family Studies Research Summary, May 2019, https://aifs.gov.au/aifs-conference/fathers-and-work. See also Alistair Thomson, 'Gender Culture or Gender System?'.
13 Ruddick, *Maternal Thinking*.
14 Walsh, 'Fathers and Parental Leave'.
15 Australian Human Rights Commission, *Supporting Working Parents: Pregnancy and Return to Work National Review*.
16 Craig, *Contemporary Motherhood*.
17 Murphy and Probert, 'Never Done', 134.

18 Carla Pascoe, 'Home Is Where Mother Is: Ideals and Realities in Australian Family Houses of the 1950s', *Journal of Australian Studies* 41, no. 2 (2017): 184–206; Murphy and Probert, 'Anything for the House'.
19 Murphy and Probert, 'Never Done'.
20 Janet McCalman, *Struggletown: Public and Private Life in Richmond 1900–1965* (Carlton, Vic.: Melbourne University Press, 1984).
21 Murphy, 'Work in a Time of Plenty: Narratives of Men's Work in Post-War Australia'; Murphy, 'Breadwinning'.
22 Murphy and Probert, 'Anything for the House'.
23 Stephanie Coontz, *The Way We Never Were: American Families and the Nostalgia Trap* (New York: Basic Books, 1992).
24 Patricia Grimshaw, 'Mothers and Waged Work Following Equal Opportunity Legislation in Australia, 1986–2006', in *Australian Mothering: Historical and Sociological Perspectives*, eds. Carla Pascoe Leahy and Petra Bueskens (London: Palgrave Macmillan, 2020), 359–80.
25 Winsome McCaughey and Pat Sebastian, *Community Child Care: Resource Book for Parents and Those Planning Children's Services* (Carlton, Vic.: Greenhouse Publications, 1977).
26 Deborah Brennan, *The Politics of Australian Child Care: From Philanthropy to Feminism* (Cambridge; Melbourne; New York: Cambridge University Press, 1994).
27 Brennan, *The Politics of Australian Child Care*.
28 Miller, *Making Sense of Motherhood*, 83–4.
29 Miller, *Making Sense of Motherhood*, 85.
30 Belinda Probert, '"Grateful Slaves" or "Self-Made Women": A Matter of Choice or Policy?', *Australian Feminist Studies* 17, no. 37 (2002): 7–17.
31 The Federated Miscellaneous Workers Union of Australia v. Angus Nugent and Son Pty. Ltd. and Others (Paternity Leave Case 1990).
32 Deborah Brennan, 'Babies, Budgets, and Birthrates: Work/Family Policy in Australia 1996–2006', *Social Politics: International Studies in Gender, State and Society* 14, no. 1 (2007): 32.
33 Iain Campbell and Sara Charlesworth, *Background Report: Key Work and Family Trends in Australia*, prepared for ACTU Work and Family Test Case (Melbourne: Centre for Applied Social Research, RMIT University, 2004).
34 Grimshaw, 'Mothers and Waged Work'; Worth and Paterson, '"How Is She Going to Manage with the Children?"'

35 Jennifer Baxter, *Child Care Participation and Maternal Employment Trends in Australia*, Research Report No. 26 (Melbourne: Australian Institute of Family Studies, 2013), https://aifs.gov.au/publications/child-care-participation-and-maternal-employment-trends-australia.
36 Brennan, 'Babies, Budgets, and Birthrates', 36.
37 Manne, *Motherhood: How Should We Care for Our Children?*
38 Craig, *Contemporary Motherhood*.

# 7

# The maternalisation of the self: mothering and identity

I am really interested in ... the extent to which a person changes irrevocably, when they become a mother ... It's a certain way of relating to the world, and I would have to use adjectives like nurturing, caring, caring for – there's a quality that's almost ineffable, that I think mothers have, that I think they gain through the practice of caring for children. I don't think you sort of, like, flick a switch when you have a baby ... It's selflessness, as well, but I was trying to think of a word that I could use, apart from that, because I think we sit a bit uncomfortably with ideas about sacrifice and selflessness. It's partly because the whole point of feminism was supposed to be about women putting themselves first, and that we've put other people first for centuries, and I appreciate that history, but I think – life is a bit empty when you only ever put yourself first ... For me, I've never been happier than when I – happy is not the right word – more satisfied, than when I've had to learn to put other people first. Not just generic other people, people I love more than I love life itself.

I'm not saying that ... putting a child first is always so great and I love it. It's much more complicated than that, but I do feel like it's enriched me, and I feel like this sense of serving someone else, and someone else for whom my feelings are really uncomplicated ... For me, the love that I feel for my children has never been in doubt. It consumes my entire being, and I've never had to put any question mark around whether they are worthy of it ... They don't have to prove any worthiness. So, the sense of making sacrifices for someone in that category actually feels way more profound than all of the putting myself first that I've done.

Carla Pascoe Leahy

We have seen throughout this volume that motherhood changes every domain of a woman's life: emotional, physical and social. Psychologists have analysed the significant change in identity that accompanies maternality.[1] Anthropologists interpret matrescence as a rite of passage, accompanied by cultural rituals which signify a shift in social position.[2] Yet my narrators gave a range of answers when I asked them whether becoming a mother changed their sense of identity, with postwar mothers less likely than millennial mothers to say it had. Many women described matrescence as simultaneously the most challenging and the most enriching period of their lives, with these opposing extremes linked within their narratives.

Psychosocial researcher Wendy Hollway argues that individual identity changes are not fully transparent to the person going through them.[3] We can never be totally clear-sighted in describing ourselves and our identities, particularly when that identity is undergoing a transition. There is doubtless much truth in her argument. But I also wanted to accord my narrators the agency of inviting them to respond to this question, and to take their opinions seriously in trying to understand why there are generational differences in interpreting whether matrescence entails an identity transformation. Bringing together all of the threads followed throughout these pages, this final chapter confronts two central questions. What impacts do becoming a mother have upon a woman? And has matrescence become more challenging for new mothers across the last three-quarters of a century?

## Maternal time

The maternographies created through this research eloquently expressed an array of stunning emotional responses to matrescence. Many conveyed a sense that becoming a mother is inherently, inescapably transformative – and that part of the challenge of matrescence lies in that enormity. Maternality shifts relationships with self, others, work, body, objects and spaces through a transitional process that is variously described as taking place at pregnancy, birth or childrearing. Listening closely to these maternographies, there were a range of themes that surfaced repeatedly: of intensity, responsibility, mindfulness, intersubjectivity and corporeality.

## Intensity

Helen was born in the UK, raised in the US and moved to Australia as an adult. She found that the birth of her first child in 2013 rearranged every aspect of her pre-maternal experience, particularly her emotional and social worlds.

> There's just such a change that comes and a sacrifice of self and a shift of energy that has to happen, it has to ... I think the act of having a child does change who you are. Even if from the little things. I have a newfound respect for life in a way ... Things I never knew I'd be afraid of. Responsibility I never thought I'd feel. A connection with other parents that I just didn't even know was possible and connection with another life. It's all so new. It's taking the parameters of what I thought life was and just extending it. Even if it's by a millimetre, it's incredible how much harder I found things and how much sadder I was, how much more stressed I was and how much more elated I have been since then. How much warmer I felt. Absolutely, I think it changes you and I think it changes your place in the community as well.

Here, Helen articulates the powerful feelings sparked by matrescence that range across a whole spectrum of emotional intensity: they cannot be simplistically categorised as 'good' or 'bad'.

Katerina was raised in Ecuador and the US and had her first child in 2013. Her maternography echoed this theme of emotional extremes:

> Of all the difficult challenges that one might have had before parenthood, being responsible for someone's life as a parent on all those levels is unbelievably challenging. It's yeah, like physically, emotionally, it is an incredible marathon, but a joyous one. I mean at the end of the day ... you love them, and it's so fulfilling, and people kind of go from one extreme to the other ... They're like, oh my God, it's the hardest thing you'll ever do in your life, you know, or ... it's the most amazing thing you can ever imagine. Probably overall, the truth is like generally somewhere in-between. Like you have probably the lowest points you could ever feel ... and then the highest points you could ever imagine. I think especially in the first couple of months ... But you know, you can't imagine life without them. If I think about when he starts growing up and leaving the house already, I'm like I'm not ready for that. Just the thought of it is just too much to me – I'm that attached to him already.

## The maternalisation of the self

Katerina evokes the sense of intensity that characterises the early months of mothering, expressing the ways in which matrescence is both 'the hardest thing' and 'the most amazing thing' she has experienced and can imagine. In fact, these extremes are linked in her narrative, implying that the satisfaction and joy of mothering stem from mastering – or at least surviving – its difficulties. Her narrative also hints at how mothers can endure the bits that are 'unbelievably challenging' – through an all-consuming love which means they 'can't imagine life without them'.

### Responsibility

Katerina's words also express the idea that maternal love requires sacrifice and pain, a theme that is taken up in Hazel's maternography. For Anglo-Australian Hazel, her matrescence in 1989 evoked both vulnerability and strength. She found that maternal love aroused a fierce protectiveness towards her children, but simultaneously rendered her exposed in an unprecedented fashion, for she discovered that anything that harmed her child wounded her also.

> I think it changes you profoundly. It opens up areas of vulnerability, and of course joy, but with that comes a real vulnerability with your children. I was very surprised by things I've not felt before like the extremely protective feeling when the child's born or even when they're in their twenties as mine are ... This very basic feeling of wanting to protect, look after, look out for your child ... For me, it's been without question the very best thing I've done with my life and the source of both sometimes intense worry, but also great joy.

Just as Hazel described the emotional intensity of motherhood – the 'intense worry' and 'great joy' – some narrators were visibly emotional as they talked about the transformation of matrescence. Anglo-Australian Susan had tears in her eyes as she described how becoming a mother in 1976 fulfilled something she did not know she needed, lending her life a new meaning. Susan became deaf when she was two years old. Because of this hearing impairment, her mother was worried about how Susan would cope with raising a child, whether she would 'come down like a ton of bricks'. But Susan found that 'having the first baby made my whole life worth living'. She explained that having her first child (narrator Kristen),

> made me who I am today ... But I didn't know I needed K [first child]. It's the most beautiful thing that could happen to anyone. Especially she gave me something to turn me into a more normal person. Because at the time I grew up, I should have been put in an institute but having a wonderful crazy mother that helped me to do what I wanted to do. I wanted to go to a normal school so she made sure I did. So, my whole life was like being normal ... I think having a baby just gave me a confidence because it was something that I was born to do. It fulfilled my dreams and satisfied me. Right from the beginning. And I just felt so content. I thought I was a contented person – anyway, I didn't know I wasn't until I had this baby. I thought, wow, this is it, seriously.

In Susan's narrative, becoming a mother felt natural, giving her a confidence she did not realise she lacked. As a person with a hearing impairment, Susan always wanted to be 'normal' and not singled out as different. In becoming a mother, she took on a role that felt natural to her and thus helped her feel 'contented' and 'satisfied'.

## Re-evaluation and clarification

Some women (particularly millennial mothers) describe matrescence as a form of biographical disruption, similar to how sociologist Michael Bury theorised chronic illness as having the potential to radically transform a person's life.[4] Anglo-Australian Andrea feels that she changed 'totally' after becoming a mother in 2010. She became a different person – more confident in her body, beliefs and values. She felt proud of herself, that she had achieved something important. She felt that her priorities became clearer and she no longer worried about little things. Likewise, after becoming a mother in 2013, Māori mother Avril explained her theory that having children forces a re-evaluation and reprioritisation of what is important in one's life.

> They're really good actually – because you're taking the focus off you – really good at just cutting away all the stuff and the things you don't need and relationships you don't need or whatever. Just really getting back to basics and keeping it really simple. I think kids are really good at doing that. They force you to do that.

Similarly, Anglo-Australian Lily explained that her pre-maternal life before 2012 had been less considered and deliberate, as she

## The maternalisation of the self 221

became swept up in 'the rat race' without stopping to make conscious decisions. Mothering forced her to 'step back' and 'slow down', forcing a re-evaluation of her life. She speaks of a different ethical position – a 'greater appreciation for life and how precious life is' – which is similar to Helen's reflections above.

> I just have different priorities in life, so like being more present and mindful, trying not to get hung up on things that don't matter ... now I'm more focused on what's important to me. So I feel like I'm living more the life that I want, that is more true to me – how I want to live. I think inherently happier ... Taking the step back, having [her first child] did slow my life down. And so now I'm just loving life. Because it's more the life that I want.

Lily's response here also explains that she is 'more present and mindful' as well as 'slowing down'. This suggestion that matrescence can trigger a different relationship to temporality – a sense of living in the present moment – surfaces in other maternographies also. We saw in Chapter 4 that Heather felt that becoming a mother in 2012 made her more mindful and observant, as well as changing her relationships with temporal phases like the seasons and with space and distance. Like many mothers, her life became essentially perambulatory, constantly seeking to leave the house and creating journeys through the streets of her local neighbourhood and watching the ways in which changing seasons and weather affected her local environments. 'I would kind of do the same walk every single day and I would notice particular things that were different on the walk and yeah, I suppose it was sort of like a much more attention to detail that I had never experienced before.' Critically, Heather was aware that mothering meant that 'everything slowed down', enough to pay attention to these quotidian elements of her surroundings, creating a more intimate connection to her immediate places and phases. She explained, 'I really enjoyed that sort of neighbourhood vibe' of visiting local shops and parks and connecting with other people when they would comment on her baby. As we saw in Chapter 6, Heather was aware that motherhood taught her new qualities of watching and listening, becoming more attuned to the emotional states of those around her through quiet, patient observation.

## Intersubjectivity

Matrescence is not a purely individual or internalised change. Rather, it is a shift born of an intense intersubjectivity, stimulated by the mother's relationship of unprecedented intimacy with the child (see Figure 5). Anglo-Australian Justine described the changes of maternality as two-way, triggered by her interactions with her children. She also explained that the births of her son and daughter in 1996 and 1998 changed her in distinct ways, as the different genders of her children brought forth and taught her different things as a mother.

> It's a very rich experience being a mother because ... if you have a male child, you get an insight into the male psyche that you've never had ... Obviously, because I did have my first-born that I – that died as a boy, and then my beautiful eldest son, L, is a boy I've got a very special bond with him ... I've learnt more from him than anybody in my entire life ... When E was born and I realised I was going to have a daughter ... knowing that you're going to have a female in your life was very special because obviously I'd lost my mum ... I do associate very strongly my mother/daughter relationship with E with

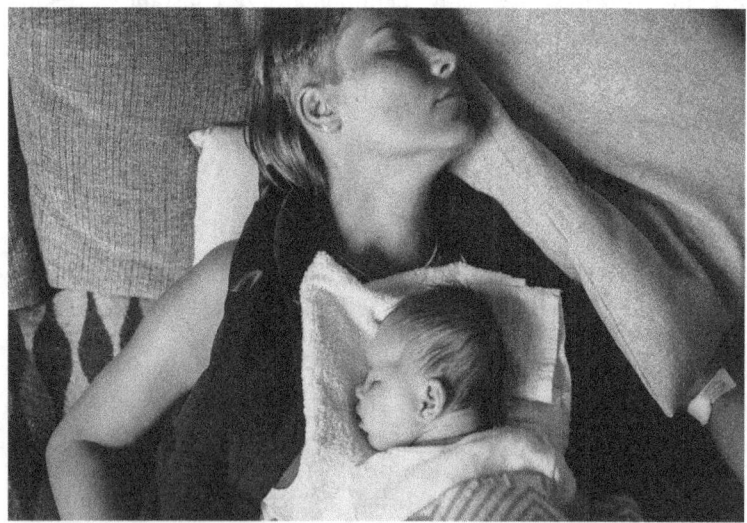

**Figure 5** Millennial mother with first child, inner Melbourne, 2013 (private collection)

> my mother. Because it's a very close kind of female relationship so from the minute I saw that she was a girl, I have thought that all the way through that I was very lucky to have a girl because of losing my mum.

Here, Justine shares her perspective on the different psychic registers of having a son or daughter. For a mother, a son connects her to male psychology with an intimacy she has never previously experienced. A daughter is a connection to a mother's own daughterhood, and a reignition of the matrilineal relationship once shared with her own mother. Sons and daughters are both powerfully affective for the mother, but for different reasons.

We saw in Chapter 4 Dutch-Australian Katherine's description of how her prenatal ambivalence about her unplanned pregnancy transformed into a sense of rightness and acceptance after her first birth in 1993. Before having children, Katherine felt she was 'drifting' with 'unrealised potential'.

> Then having children just gave me this incredible sense of purpose and groundedness. Even though it was really tough in many ways. I do sort of feel like I actually got my career together because of having kids because I (a) I had to financially do something, and (b) because I wanted to do something that I would feel proud of and therefore my kids – I wouldn't resent my kids about, if that makes sense. I think it totally made me as a person.

Matrescence gave Katherine's life a new sense of purpose in multiple respects. In particular, her feelings about her career crystallised when viewed through the lens of her relationship with her children.

Some mothers also told me that matrescence engendered a turning inwards – through the self-abnegation of motherhood they gained a new level of self-insight. In Anglo-Australian Sophia's experience, the transformation of motherhood in 1997 was irresistible.

> I don't think you can help but be different ... It's deepened my own understanding of me, and in some ways, learning to be a better person, because you have to – they come first ... I don't know whether I'm a different person, but, I think, it's an experience that can't help but change you, and it's just given me so much joy and insight, that I would never have experienced had I not had children, I think.

Just as Justine found that having a daughter connected her to her own mother, Sophia also found that the mothermorphosis was necessarily matrilineal, provoking a new comprehension of her own mother's role from a position of affinity.

> I think it certainly made me understand, for the first time, I have much more in common with my own mother and understanding that … It deepened my appreciation and my understanding of her, and doing what I did, but, she had to do it all on her own really, with no help at all.

New mothers describe feeling a new type of love that is different to what they've felt before, that enables them to occupy a position of radical self-sacrifice. But that does not mean that it is easy. Anglo-Australian Kira spoke of how this willingness to do anything for one's children 'changes you' and 'humbles you', but that mothers still need to be looked after themselves. Her twins were born in 2015. In the early months of their lives, Kira had to undergo two major surgeries: a hysterectomy related to her endometriosis and bowel surgery to remove cancer. These personal health challenges, and the fact that she was raising twins with her wife as a first-time mother, meant that Kira sometimes gave too much and pushed herself too hard.

> There were days between the diagnosis, between the hysterectomy and the surgery … that I just had to prop myself up against a wall to be upright, because I was in so much pain and no one could kind of tell me why, so that was quite scary, but I think what it showed me is … I literally am willing to do anything for them, but also, on the other side of it … I just literally spent twenty months giving everything I had, and for however long, kind of lost my identity, just being A and R's mum. So, it's taught me, also, about the fact that you can't just give and give and give and give and give, and you do have to refill that cup, and it's really important for everybody that you do that.

As a childhood victim of family abuse, Kira was determined to give her children an upbringing completely different to what she experienced. But while her personal history sometimes made matrescence 'confronting', it was also 'healing' to see herself as a child through her daughters.

> It's been really healing, really confronting, because it has brought up, from very tiny babies, brought up traumatic memories that I hadn't thought about, but also really healing … I think I can be quite hard on myself, and I think I had seen a lot of it through adult's eyes, and

## The maternalisation of the self

now I see what – now, I get to see that I was a child, because I can see through them, and their innocence of who they are ... I've had such a horrible childhood, in retrospect ... It took a lot of my early twenties, and even late twenties, to kind of heal from that. I kind of feel like part of becoming a mother is also becoming who I am, and healing from that, and being just me now, just getting to me, and be A and R's mum, and not be so impacted by all of those things that happened to me.

The transformation of matrescence, for Kira, also liberates her from her traumatic past by opening a wholly new chapter in her life.

Torres Strait Islander Somi explained that becoming a mother in 2013 gave her a heightened level of self-insight and a greater degree of self-acceptance and self-compassion.

I see a lot more consistency over who I am and how I engage with the world that I didn't have any kind of serious sense of, before becoming a mother. So I guess there's a kind of level of self-insight that motherhood has given me. Yes, there are things that have changed. I think I'm much kinder to myself than I've ever been in my life. I think I'm much more patient than I have been, which is not to say that I'm still not a little bit of an impatient person. But I think I am more, just a little bit more trusting of the future ... Because ... I have learned that you can love people unconditionally ... Recognising that, I think, has allowed me to be a little bit more accepting of that for myself ... I'm more forgiving of myself I think.

Through experiencing the unconditional love that she felt for her child, Somi realised that she too was loved that way by her parents, that someone has always loved her that much her entire life. In changing her in the present, maternality has changed her relationship to her past and future – she understands that she has always been loved unconditionally by her own parents and she is 'more trusting of the future'.

### Corporeality

If motherhood changes a woman's inner spaces, it also changes her outer spaces, transforming her body. In Chapter 2, we discussed the many physical changes wrought by pregnancy. But when the foetus is released from the womb, a mother's body does not revert to a pre-maternal state. Rather, her body is permanently marked by motherhood. She often bears scars of birth, whether the incision of a caesarean or the tearing of a vaginal birth. Many women who have given birth will experience a prolapsed uterus, though sometimes not for years afterwards. Pregnancy often leaves a lingering imprint in the form of stretch marks, varicose veins or pelvic floor dysfunction. If she breastfeeds, a mother's breasts and nipples adapt to encompass the demands of daily feeding, and she may experience initial pain followed by sensory pleasure as mother and child adapt to lactation.

In effecting a transformation of the shape and function of a mother's body, new motherhood also commonly shifts a woman's sexuality. When asked if her identity had been changed by her matrescence in 2013, Anglo-Australian Sarah responded that 'The only part of myself that's died is the sexy side. That's gone. And, how I see myself sexually is very different'. Parts of a woman's body she regarded primarily as erotic become more associated with reproduction and with the functional tasks of birthing and breastfeeding a child. Describing her breasts and vagina, Sarah regretted that

> Their ornamental qualities are not what they once were. Obviously, my vagina has stayed the same because I had a caesarean birth, although I've got a great whopping scar down there now. That part of things is normal. Although, mine was very numb for months afterwards, so, that was a bit of a bummer. But, my boobs, Jesus Christ, they're a shadow of their former self, in terms of appearance. It's not just the physicality though, it's the way you feel about your body. It's the energy levels too.

Speaking six months after the birth of her first child, Sarah explained that her desire for sexual intercourse was much reduced and she thought about her body primarily as a system for growing, birthing and feeding babies.

Some women have more individualised physiological responses to motherhood. Anglo-Australian Dorothy lost so much blood when her uterus ruptured during her 1956 birth that she nearly died. She required a hysterectomy, meaning that she was not able to biologically bear another child and experienced an early menopause. Welsh-Australian Ariana found that after each of her pregnancies in 2010, 2013 and 2016, she would become very unwell and develop styes in her eyes, hives on her skin, swelling in her joints and lose most of her hair. Anglo-Australian Lily suffered a prolapse after

## The maternalisation of the self

her first birth in 2012 which meant she had to radically change her active pre-maternal lifestyle which once involved running, netball and going to the gym. 'When I found out I had the prolapse and I saw a physiotherapist and when she said you should never run again, I remember just crying there and feeling silly, because that's not the worst thing in the world; but now ... it's opened up other avenues of different things.' Motherhood can impact a woman's body with considerable intensity. Despite advances in medicine, many women still endure strong physiological responses to pregnancy, birth or breastfeeding, finding that their sense of inner transformation is mirrored in outer, physical changes. Motherhood is an embodied as well as an affective experience.

### Generational time

These examples suggest that maternality is in many ways a total transformation of body and mind. It is perhaps not surprising that some women would find this transition challenging. For some, this results in a diagnosis of perinatal depression or anxiety. It is now estimated that one in five mothers and one in ten fathers will experience perinatal depression or anxiety.[5] In the maternographies created for this research, it was evident that while most younger women report difficulties with the transition to maternity, fewer older women remembered challenges. In this section, I will chart historical shifts in women's descriptions of matrescence and discuss whether becoming a mother has become more challenging over the last seventy-five years.

#### Postwar mothers

Postwar mothers were often dismissive when I asked whether mothering had changed them, though a small number agreed that it had. Anglo-Australian Jane felt that becoming a mother in 1954 definitely changed her, describing the awe-inspiring sense of responsibility she felt when she had children. 'Oh, I think so because there was somebody totally reliant upon me for everything. I just think it makes you plan your life quite differently. You have different priorities. I suppose it's a maturing experience.' English-born Marjorie felt that after having a child in 1953, 'You're not the same and your body's not the same. Your mind is not the same'. But she also told a story that suggested that the transition is not affected immediately – there is a period in which a new mother's sense of identity is still in flux, and she can experience moments of cognitive regression where she momentarily forgets that she has crossed over into another world.

> I remember walking up the street the first time with the baby in the pram and feeling such pride ... I remember the first time I ever went shopping. I went to the butcher shop and left the pram outside because it was a very big pram and a tiny little butcher's shop ... and I walked out of the butcher's shop and I forgot I had a kid [laugh]. And I walked out and I thought, oh, I've got a baby, and I walked back. I mean, I only went about four yards, but I can remember, like, forgetting that I had a child.

Anglo-Australian Eve felt that she was growing rather than fundamentally changing. But she also implies that this is not the kind of question she would have reflected upon at the time of her matrescence in 1950 – and perhaps this kind of self-analysis developed slowly across the second half of the twentieth century, with the popularisation of core psychological concepts and in an increasingly autobiographical age.

> I think I felt it was an extension of myself and that I was growing, and it was another experience ... another phase of my life and I didn't feel any different at all, except that I was broadening maybe ... I don't know that I thought about myself very much at all or – or analysed myself very much at all ... Apart from the fact that ... there were a lot more skills that I was, you know, as a housewife, as a mother, as a wife ... I just felt that I was the same person but growing in skills and growing in what I did; if I thought about it. And I doubt that I did.

Anglo-Australian Pauline explained that she did not feel that her identity shifted markedly when she had her first child in 1963, linking that to the fact that she had always assumed she would become a mother. She implied that any sense of significant transition or adaptation was lessened by that pre-maternal assumption.

> When I became a mother, yes, it was very different; but I was prepared to take that step, because that's what I expected of my life, that one

day I hoped to marry, and I hoped to have children. And so I guess in my head, I prepared for it.

This raises an interesting question: does the transition to maternality potentially begin in childhood, for girls who plan and desire to become mothers? Does their identity develop in line with that expectation so that they carry a fledgling pre-maternal psychological constellation before they even become pregnant or assume responsibility for a child?[6] Pauline seemed to imply that perhaps maternality comes as a greater shock or disruption for millennial mothers, who have grown up in the aftermath of women's liberation not necessarily assuming that they will have children.

Another generational difference evident in the maternographies of postwar mothers was a different lexicon for emotional expressiveness, with a pervasive stoicism often evident. This was a generation who lived through major global crises like the Great Depression and World War Two, and tended to downplay the comparatively minor inconvenience of difficult emotions. Many postwar mothers offered pragmatic accounts of matrescence that were often broad brush rather than fine-grained. They were more likely to describe daily rituals of washing nappies or buying groceries than the emotional or relational components of their early maternal lives. It is not always clear whether this difference in timbre is due to the passage of time diluting the vividness of memories, or whether this is evidence of a generational shift in the willingness to recall and share feelings. Anglo-Australian Dorothy, for example, described her 1956 pregnancy with the words, 'I listened to people ringing in [on the radio] and moaning and groaning but to me it was just the normal sort of thing to do. There was no fuss made about it'. Like many postwar mothers, she felt that motherhood 'was inbred. It wasn't a big deal. You just got on with your business'. Yet there were also tantalising allusions within her story, such as when she mentioned that she considered adopting a second child and decided against it, partly because she nearly had a 'breakdown' raising her first child. But this was expressed flippantly and without further explanation.

Anglo-Australian Regina similarly rejected the suggestion that becoming a mother in 1967 might have changed her identity and avoided offering emotional responses to my questions. She conceded that, 'certainly, it does mean change, obviously. But I think I was fairly prepared and knew what to expect. It didn't come to me as a great shock'. It is often unclear the extent to which memory can no longer recall the rich texture of emotions felt more than half a century ago, or whether postwar mothers are revealing something of the affective milieu of their childbearing years. These were decades in which public expressions of emotion were relatively rare and cultural discourse was not permeated by psychological concepts such as 'identity' and 'ego' in the way they are in the early twenty-first century.

There were, however, some postwar mothers who recalled struggling with the transition to motherhood, despite the lack of a contemporaneous language to describe their difficulties. Anglo-Australian Grace adopted her first child in 1962. She struggled after the adoption of her second child in 1963. As the boys were only eighteen months apart in age, Grace was essentially looking after two babies. She felt socially isolated because she did not know many neighbours and most of her friends had had their children at a younger age, so she lacked a cohort of maternal peers. In hindsight, Grace believes she suffered a form of perinatal depression (technically post-adoptive depression for adoptive mothers). It persisted for about two years and was only really alleviated when her elder child started kindergarten, improving markedly when both sons were in school and kinder and she returned to paid work.

> Managing two babies, and being isolated all day with nobody but the babies ... In those very early years, it was terribly difficult, and I remember being seriously depressed ... I remember the time when I thought I might put my head in the gas oven, but then I remember deciding not to ... Anyway, we staggered through that period; I got some help to come in and help in the house, and I did, but I was home for six years. Again, that's what you did in those days.

Examples like Grace raise thorny and complex questions of historical analysis. Does a person require a cultural milieu which contains language, concepts and permission to express them in order to feel, name and express that they are struggling with a mental illness? Did perinatal depression exist before we had the words and tools to diagnose and treat it? Certainly, some women in the 1950s and 1960s struggled with their mental health during and after becoming mothers. Their ability to express and to explain those difficulties has changed over time. In his book *Moving Stories*, oral historian

Alistair Thomson creates detailed accounts of the lives of four women who migrate from the UK to Australia, through memory sources crafted at different points in time such as letters, photos, memoirs and interviews. One woman, Dorothy Wright, believes in hindsight that she suffered perinatal depression though she did not understand it as such at the time. By creating an oral history interview decades later, during a period when perinatal depression has entered the domain of popular culture and women are encouraged to speak about maternal difficulties, Dorothy has the opportunity to reinterpret her experiences through a different lens.[7] Thomson offers an illuminating account of how experiences can be understood differently in hindsight, as new concepts and language emerges.

## Second-wave mothers

Second-wave mothers entered matrescence during a changing cultural era. This was a time in which there was greater, and growing, discussion of psychology and emotion. The women's liberation movement explicitly encouraged women to express themselves more and the children's rights movement resulted in more expressive and empathetic modes of parenting.[8] Feminism influenced the rise of women writing and speaking about their personal experiences through a self-reflexive mode, including experiences of mothering.[9]

Many second-wave mothers felt that they were changed by matrescence, such as Susan and Hazel quoted above. Dutch-Australian Mary felt that it was the inherent responsibility for another life that most changed her. This sense that being for and being with another is at the heart of early motherhood was reflected in many narratives quoted earlier. Mary's maternography also expressed the way in which a mother is partially created through reflections: when a woman assumes responsibility for a child, she realises that others perceive and interact with her differently. She has assumed a different status in their eyes – and therefore in her own, as well.

> That responsibility, that weighs a bit on you I think, and that changes you completely and ... I think that people see you in a different way too. They react differently ... For instance, you go with your baby and you go to the shops and people look into the pram and they start

talking to you and that sort of contact. All of a sudden, you're not a person that just comes in a shop and gets something and goes home but you have a lot more contact and I liked it.

When I asked Mary to clarify how and why she felt her life changed in 1974 with motherhood, she explained:

> In all ways. You change as a person in that responsibility is there all the time. That's a bit difficult to put in words. Everything changes. Absolutely everything around you changes. Maybe it's not so much how you look at it but how the outside looks at you as well. I don't know why it is. Maybe it's the motherly feeling. All of a sudden, you've got that child that you have probably dreamt of because I remember as a girl, I always wanted to be a mother.

Mary's narrative also echoes Pauline's postwar maternography, in that she is clear that she always dreamt of being a mother from the time she was a girl. Unlike millennial mothers, who were less likely to report childhood fantasies of maternity, Mary grew up imagining an adult future in which mothering would be central.

But few second-wave mothers reported serious emotional difficulties with matrescence. Irish-Australian Penny wondered if part of the reason she was not enormously challenged by the transition was that she had already experienced the satisfaction of living autonomously as an adult. On average, second-wave mothers had their children at a slightly later age than postwar mothers, with the average age of primigravida rising to twenty-five by 1971.[10] Penny was slightly older than average when she became a mother in 1975 at the age of thirty-two.

> I did teacher training and became a primary school teacher. I can't remember how many years I taught for, but then went overseas and travelled and worked for about three years. So had a good life … which meant I was happy to settle down. Yes, didn't always wish I'd done this, done that.

Second-wave mothers are often more emotionally expressive about their memories of matrescence than their postwar predecessors. Lebanese-Australian Sally described herself as an 'incurable optimist' but nevertheless found her initial experience of mothering in 1978 very challenging. When she and the baby suffered health issues, she found her confidence dinted, as she wondered whether her actions had contributed to the problems they experienced.

> There's no doubt the first six weeks were pretty close to hell on earth. They were such a shock to the system in every way like my own health because I've always been a healthy person and then the baby having these series of illnesses and somehow each time you think, well, did I contribute to that? ... Was there something I did wrong? ... But once we got into the groove, we really loved parenting.

Relatively few women in my sample were diagnosed with perinatal mental illness before the 1990s. Musing on why that might have been, Anglo-Australian, second-wave mother Carol wonders whether her generation may have entered matrescence with more realistic expectations.

> Is it that the expectations of motherhood have changed? ... Like our generation ... we were very much get up and get on with it. Not that there wasn't sympathy, but you were meant to cope regardless of the circumstances ... Whereas, I wonder sometimes these days is there this image that motherhood is easy and you have this wonderful little baby and it's a bit of a Hollywood saccharin version of motherhood. Whereas I think we were the school of harsh reality ... I'm sure expectations are important, and I'm sure our expectations weren't that it was going to be all easy and sweet little baby.

Contrasting the experience of her daughter's (Andrea's) generation to her own, Carol suggests that second-wave mothers had more prior life experiences of responsibility and sacrifice to prepare them for motherhood.

> You have to be very self-abnegating as a mother initially, don't you, and that can be hard ... If you've had a fairly easy time growing up as a young person and you've been travelling and seeing the world and having a rip-roaring time then ... stopping of all that and putting this little crying bundle first can be, it's a really tall order isn't it?

For second-wave women who did struggle emotionally with becoming a mother, there was less popular understanding and awareness of perinatal depression, and its causes and treatments, than there is today. Macedonian-Australian Miroslava had a twin sister, M, who experienced difficulties with her transition to maternity in the 1970s, which Miroslava explains as a product of living with a controlling mother-in-law who usurped responsibility for raising the children. Her husband and parents-in-law were unwilling to concede the seriousness of M's condition and her need for support.

> She lived with her in-laws, as all good Macedonian girls did, and unfortunately, her mother-in-law ... wasn't a really nice lady and she kept on telling her that it's nothing. You know, you're all right. You're being silly. Because they looked at it as a mental problem and no daughter-in-law of ours was going to be diagnosed with a mental issue and that – even made her husband the same way. My sister-in-law and myself would beg her to let us take her to the hospital and we did secretly. She would have to come here without her family knowing so we could take her to the Women's [hospital] and they diagnosed her and they wanted to keep her in and they kept her in and then when the husband found out, he went to the hospital and dragged her out of there and said, 'My wife's not a mental case'.

Miroslava explained to me that her sister died soon after in mysterious circumstances, possibly linked to her poor mental health at the time. In her maternography, M's death figured as a cautionary tale to explain why Miroslava always asks new mothers how they are feeling and coping. From a longer-term historical perspective, it highlights the tragic incomprehension that many people had towards maternal difficulties, in an era in which perinatal depression was not widely diagnosed or understood.

### Millennial mothers

Many millennial mothers were conscious of feeling that their identity had changed with matrescence and were more able to express difficulties adjusting to mothering than their predecessors. Māori mother Avril could feel herself beginning to change during her pregnancy in 2013 and that she was 'developing another side of me'. It was partly due to a 'very big shift in lifestyle' but one that she was 'completely ready for' rather than feeling that she had lost something. She characterised matrescence as a form of radical self-abnegation:

> I think it's just the capacity to care wholeheartedly with everything that you've got. So a friend of mine kind of put it in context for me originally when ... I was talking about it and kind of trying to play it down a bit and she's like, 'No, no. You have to understand you are keeping a human being alive. Without you, this human being would

die'... I think it's the ability to selflessly give yourself to another human being that I have never done before because I've never had to.

This maternal ethic of self-sacrifice can come as a rude shock to twenty-first-century women, who are inheritors of the second-wave feminist demand that women be freed from domestic servitude, and have grown up in a cultural climate that asserts that happiness stems from self-exploration and prioritising one's own needs, wants and desires.[11]

The emotional expressiveness of women's maternographies has shifted not just because cultural discourses around emotion have changed, but also discourses concerning motherhood. Polish-Australian Petronela expressed this eloquently in her maternography. She feels that it has become 'heretical' in the twenty-first century for a new mother to express positive experiences of birth and breastfeeding. (Interestingly, in staking her desire to contradict dominant discourses, she drew upon religious language in a manner similar to Kristen's characterisation of the 'new religion' of working motherhood that we saw in Chapter 6.)

> With some of the other women in our mother's group, it's almost like it would be heretical to say that I had a positive birth experience and that I not only find breastfeeding easy, I really like it. I feel that's boastful to say those two things. When we talk about experiences of childbirth and early motherhood and breastfeeding, we are supposed to only complain about how traumatic and difficult it all is.

There is a seeming contradiction here between women claiming that they were only offered a sentimentalised version of motherhood before having a baby and Petronela's contention that mothers never talk about the enjoyable aspects of childrearing. Perhaps one way of explaining this paradox is that different communities of communicative honesty surround the new mother. On the one hand, some mothers feel that they were not really told how difficult life would be with a new baby. This implies that there is a community of knowing mothers who have already passed through and are unwilling to scare or warn those on the other side – the becoming-mothers – how trying some aspects of their new lives will be. This is a form of censorship which sentimentalises the view of motherhood from the outside. But Petronela's experience was that, once inside, new mothers tend to focus on maternal difficulties because of their shock at how unexpected and profound these struggles are, which often has the effect of silencing positive experiences of mothering. A kind of black humour can often be found among online parenting groups, where new mothers jest among themselves about the difficulty and desperation of their new role.

First Nations mother Somi felt that matrescence is the unmaking of the illusion of control over one's life. New mothers discover that there is much they cannot control about motherhood. No matter how hard they strive, how much reading they do, how careful they are, which kinds of childrearing props they buy, there is still an element that eludes the mother's agency.

> I think I was still stubborn and wilful and determined that I was going to shape my life. I was going to be one of those amazing women who worked through endless sleep deprivation and produced great things and my child was going to be perfectly well adjusted. I think I was pretty stubborn more or less right until my second [child] arrived, I think. I don't think I really started to see myself and that kind of wilfulness to make everyone fit into my plan. Not my plan but my vision of what a good harmonious functional working family life was going to look like. That took a really long time for me, when I think back to that first year, I think very much like a battle of wills between my son and myself.

Somi grew up in the post-second-wave era in which the vision of the working mother who can effortlessly balance workplace competency with maternal prowess has been a powerful cultural ideal, and it took some time for her to realise the damage wreaked by unrealistic expectations.

As we saw in Chapter 2, Greek-Australian Connie decided to become a single mother by choice in her early forties, when she realised that her reproductive window was closing and she had not met a partner with whom she wished to have children. Although she planned carefully for motherhood, including saving enough money that she would not need to return to work for some time, she could not anticipate how challenging her 2014 matrescence would be on her own. She felt exhausted and lonely during pregnancy, followed by a disappointing experience of birth which left her feeling alienated from her son.

> I was there for five days in hospital. I was very emotional then and continued to be for weeks later. A lot of crying. He took a while to

settle in actually. My last night there when I was alone and probably my first night back home, he just cried a lot and I was beside myself. I didn't know what to do. When I was in hospital that night, I called the nurse and I felt awful. I didn't feel she helped me. He was crying, I didn't know what to do and instead she just said, 'Well, you're going to go home tomorrow – what do you think you're going to do then?' I just sunk and I just felt like a little child and I started crying and I said, 'I'll ask for help'. After that, I don't remember much. She left and I didn't call her again. He cried and I didn't know what to do.

Connie's situation did not improve when she returned home from hospital and her sense of desperation grew.

I came home that morning. I was driven by my brother and my cousin came. We came into the house. I'd been starting to cry in the car silently. When I came into the house I just – I left, who had the baby? I don't know – I went straight to my room and just cried and cried and cried. I cried for hours later. I had to go out and get bottles and a bit of formula and dummies and I was in the chemist and I was crying. I couldn't control it. I did go to see the doctor – the GP – that day. I don't remember now – maybe they just tried to calm me. They made me make an appointment the next day with the baby, maybe just to ease my mind that everything was okay. And everything was okay. I don't quite remember. A lot of the painful moments I don't remember very well.

Connie never had a night of uninterrupted sleep during her son's first year of life. She found the physical exhaustion difficult to bear on her own. She thinks she had 'a couple of breakdowns last year, where I couldn't function anymore. I was so exhausted from lack of sleep that I couldn't respond properly'. Eventually she was prescribed antidepressants and they helped her feel 'a bit more even ... just don't fall in a heap'. Although she was reluctant to characterise herself as suffering perinatal depression, Connie's maternography is in many ways a tale of the toll that a lack of physical and emotional support during matrescence can take on a new mother. She feels that 'the whole experience of being a mother – like the pregnancy – it has been really lonely and the solitude I felt is ongoing'. Her despair is a proportionate response to the almost intolerably difficult situation in which she finds herself.

## Making sense of generational shifts

So what broad conclusions can we draw from these memories of seventy-five years of mothering? The answers are not simple, but we can track some overarching patterns in how women describe matrescence. There is a clear shift from the stoic and pragmatic accounts of postwar mothers to the more personal and emotionally expressive accounts of millennial mothers. There is also an accompanying rise in the numbers of women expressing difficulties adjusting to new motherhood. A number of factors can help to explain these shifts.

Partly, it is to do with the fluid nature of memory and its relationship to identity. For millennial mothers, memories of early motherhood are more vivid, and identity shifts easier to remember. For postwar mothers, matrescence occurred at least fifty years previously, rending early maternal memories less vibrant than for younger women. The difficult – but short-term – challenges of pregnancy, birth and caring for a baby have likely been superseded by the profound role their child has played in their lives. Twelve hours of intense childbirth pain or twelve months of sleep deprivation feel nearly unbearable when one is living through it, but well justified when viewed from the vantage point of a decades-long mother–child relationship. Moreover, the identity transformation experienced at matrescence may still be raw and unfamiliar for a millennial mother, but so well integrated for a postwar mother that it is difficult to genuinely inhabit the feeling state of her pre-maternal being.

Changing cultural norms have also restructured the parameters within which individual lives are lived. Second-wave feminism created a cultural environment in which women were permitted, even encouraged, to critique the ways in which older gender roles had constrained the possibilities of their lives. The rise of an expressive society, and a confessional culture, means that we have a greater collective willingness to reflect upon and share emotional experiences.[12] This has been linked to a popularisation of psychology, meaning that mental health issues are discussed and diagnosed at far higher levels than in the past. Such shifts have broadly heightened the levels of emotional honesty that interviewees feel able to express within an oral history interview.[13]

Mothers now inhabit a cultural environment in which there is an incitation to discourse. From the resounding silence which surrounded women's experience of the reproductive life cycle in the mid-twentieth century (including menstruation, sex, pregnancy, birth and motherhood), we have shifted to a generalised encouragement to voice these personal experiences. We have also created the cultural and technological circumstances where it is possible to exercise an unprecedented degree of choice over one's willingness to participate in these phases. Access to birth control, sex education and termination procedures permit a high degree of autonomy over whether and when one chooses to become a mother. Assisted reproductive technology (ART) has expanded the possibilities of parenthood beyond biological and birthgiving mothers. Perhaps most critically, women born during and after the women's liberation movement have grown up with the awareness that motherhood is a choice – and with choice comes doubt, uncertainty and questioning. This is by contrast to postwar mothers like Anglo-Australian Pauline, who always assumed that they would become mothers and hence integrated a kind of pre-maternity into their identity from childhood.

These 'post-patriarchal' or 'autonomous' mothers are also having fewer children and entering maternality at a later age.[14] While some mothers, like second-wave mother Penny, felt that having children at a later age made matrescence easier, these maternographies suggest that older women today find the profound identity shift of matrescence more challenging. They are coming from a more concretised sense of their selves, having often studied, travelled and engaged in multiple jobs and relationships before having children. Most millennial mothers have also imbibed a sense that a woman's identity is closely connected to her work, which makes the massive disruptions of mothering more difficult to endure. Some scholars assert that the fact that women are having fewer children means they are more determined to have a perfect birth, and characterise their childrearing style as 'intensive mothering', with the implied criticism that this is an overinvestment in a smaller number of 'products'.[15] But this is a rather paternalistic and dismissive view of maternal perspectives, which could equally be understood as the desire for a satisfactory, non-traumatising experience of birth and the opportunity to lovingly invest their time and energy in their offspring.

Feminism has unwittingly contributed to creating a set of competing demands that women can never fully satisfy. The shift of the last half-century to encourage women to pursue self-actualisation through focusing on their own needs has likely created conditions that make it harder for women to accomplish the self-sacrifice that accompanies motherhood. There is a sense of righteous injustice in many personal accounts that claim, 'I wasn't adequately prepared', when perhaps the true implication of this statement is not that parenting advice manuals do not warn of the specifics, but rather: I was raised to believe that women should prioritise their personal needs in the quest for self-fulfilment and the selflessness of motherhood feels like the opposite of that.

Central to that quest for self-actualisation has been the message that career is a core part of one's identity. Careers advice throughout Australian schooling implies that choosing a career that complements one's identity leads to happiness and self-fulfilment. Motherhood is portrayed as a minor inconvenience in this quest, it's disruptiveness largely erased through affirmative action and anti-discrimination policies. And yet, when women who have based their identities around work first become mothers, they often feel inordinately challenged. Not only are there not enough hours in the day to do both work and mothering well, but maternal desire also disrupts a pre-maternal identity that centred upon career, and it takes some time to achieve a satisfactory reconciliation of the two.

A common claim is that the explanation for difficulties in adjusting to maternality lies in the removal of the 'village' that it takes to adequately support a new mother. However, this relatively ahistorical and culturally non-specific account is more a form of collective nostalgia for a past that never existed, as far as this research can discern.[16] Judged from the perspective of the last three-quarters of a century, millennial mothers have *more* support than their postwar equivalents. They have access to a range of technological innovations that have lightened the physical workload of mothering, they are more likely to have meaningful practical assistance from partners and they can potentially seek support from doulas, midwives, obstetricians, lactation consultants, maternal child health nurses, infant sleep experts, psychologists, playgroups, new parent groups, paid childcare and more. Yet this expanded support has been sufficient to keep up with the demands of matrescence.

Some argue that one of the key reasons that contemporary women struggle with motherhood is that the gap between expectation and reality has increased, and more women come to motherhood without hands-on experience.[17] Many maternographies voiced this theme that they did not feel fully prepared. We saw in Chapter 3 that millennial mothers Veronica and Ariana both felt that there was a deliberate silencing of the reality of how difficult birth is, which left Veronica feeling 'betrayed'. Welsh-Australian Ariana recalls running into her a former employer after her first birth in 2010, 'and she said, "It's a massive conspiracy", and I said, "What is?" She said, "How terrible motherhood is in that first year", and I was like, "Oh yes, it is, it's terrible". She said, "Yes nobody tells you ... But just be aware everyone feels it".'

Anglo-Australian Amanda felt similarly unprepared for the reality of her matrescence in 1991, explaining that her childbirth education detailed pregnancy and labour, but not childrearing. 'You're so focused on the pregnancy and the birth, no one tells you what happens afterwards ... You're given so much information beforehand, but afterwards you're not told anything.'

Yet an irony of this contention that there is a conspiracy to silence the truth of matresence is that millennial mothers inhabit an era in which there is more expert advice available than ever before, and less cultural restrictions around discussing these topics with family and friends. This begs the question: if we live in an epoch in which there has been an explosion of discourse around motherhood, but no one feels that they were adequately prepared for it, does this mean that the information is of the wrong sort, or is it possible that matrescence is ineffable? In other words, are we not talking about motherhood in the right ways, or are there some experiences for which it is impossible to truly prepare or anticipate?

I think perhaps both are true. We heard Helen's perspective on the changes wrought by mothering near the beginning of this chapter. Let's circle back to her story again – which we can now place within this wider historical context. Reflecting on her matresence six months after her first child was born in 2013, Helen mused:

> What's more upsetting, I think afterwards, was realising how many people did say that it was hard … They all had said it was hard, and everyone did, but it wasn't until M [first child] was born that I just found myself calling people and saying, 'I had no idea, and even when you said it was hard, I didn't realise how hard it was' … I feel like people did say, but it wasn't until I walked in their shoes that I really understood.

Later in her interview, Helen tried to describe the challenges she faced with early motherhood.

> I can't even begin to list how difficult it was or what exactly it was, because I think it was so many things. And most of all, that you were doing it in the dark, suffocating under a pillow, in the fog, on thin ice, going uphill. Add everything to it, it felt so hard in every sense. I don't think I'll ever forget that feeling of just sheer vulnerability. Complete fear, but I also don't know if I can ever fully remember it again, and I don't think I ever will. I don't think I'll ever find anything as challenging again. Because maybe at least in every other sense I can rationalise it or reason my way through it. Like I couldn't, when he was born.

In this passage, Helen tries out and rejects every metaphor she can think of to express her difficulties. Finally, she admits that she may never be able to adequately describe or remember early motherhood – that the intensity of those emotions resists rational explanation. Perhaps one reason that so many women feel inadequately prepared for motherhood is because matresence is an experience that *almost* defies human language.

This brings us back to the insights of maternal scholars like Wendy Hollway and Lisa Baraitser who contend that it is impossible to truly describe a phenomenon as rich and complex as matresence. At some level, the experience escapes language. And memory cannot completely retain what cannot be fully captured in words. Despite this difficulty, I argue that we need to at least

# The maternalisation of the self

*try* to approximate what it feels like, because the consequences of not speaking honestly about first-time motherhood are serious. So many childrearing advice books and childbirth education classes do not even attempt to explain what is surely one of the most significant aspects of matrescence: that it is an emotionally intense rite of passage that literally transforms the new mother, both inside and out.

## Conclusion

What, then, are the consequences of my findings for Australian women becoming mothers today? There are two related arguments that I wish to make here: one relates to our framing of perinatal depression and the other to how we prepare women for motherhood. Since the 1990s, we have witnessed increased public awareness that many mothers suffer perinatal depression and anxiety, and this normalisation of maternal struggle is in many ways welcome if it makes it easier to voice difficulties. But by framing mothers' challenges as an individual pathology rather than a lack of social supports, we implicitly state that the cause and the treatment reside solely within the individual, when enhanced support would ease matrescence in many instances. It is very clear in these maternographies that for women who struggle, external factors play a role, including: difficult or traumatic births; challenges with infant care such as sleep and breastfeeding; lack of support from family, friends, community and health professionals; and the strain of returning to paid work when the new mother is still emotionally and physically exhausted. While individual treatment is assuredly part of the answer to alleviating perinatal depression and anxiety, ignoring the provision of improved supports for new mothers avoids our collective responsibility for mothers in distress. There is a real and urgent policy challenge for governments to contemplate: if we more effectively supported new mothers through pregnancy, birth and early motherhood, would we have lower rates of perinatal mental illness?

My second argument relates to the preparation offered for new motherhood – including commercially produced books and websites, advice from healthcare professionals and informal information from family and friends. These sources of preparation generally do not discuss matrescence as a psychological transformation or a cultural transition point. Thus, we neglect to prepare new mothers for what is arguably the most profound shift of new motherhood. This inadequate preparation exacerbates the fear and confusion of matrescence, further increasing the numbers of women who find it challenging. We can do much better at helping new mothers anticipate the enormity – and profundity – of what lies before them. The stakes are high, I would argue. More and more women are choosing not to mother in the twenty-first century. I suspect that one factor influencing women who decide against motherhood is that it looks inescapably and inevitably difficult. In this context, we need to urgently expand our shared conversations about what motherhood can be by listening to a diversity of maternal voices.

Motherhood itself is not the problem. It has the potential to be the most enriching and self-actualising experience in a woman's life – but the preparation and supports we provide to new mothers require dramatic improvement. Motherhood can assuredly be challenging – and perinatal depression is a real and serious condition. But when we use only the language of illness or crisis, we strip the profundity from matrescence. The joys and the challenges of first-time motherhood are inextricably linked. It is only by breaking open the mother's old self that a new identity can be called forth by maternality.

Normal matrescence is characterised by an intensity of emotions likely never before experienced. This is hardly surprisingly if we keep in mind that two births are taking place: that of the infant and of the mother. This research is my attempt to enrich our understanding of what mothers experience, and how they can be more effectively supported, through one of the most cataclysmic – and rewarding – experiences of their lives: the maternal metamorphosis.

## Notes

1 Stern, *The Motherhood Constellation*; Stern and Bruschweiler-Stern, *The Birth of a Mother*.
2 Raphael, 'Matresence'.
3 Hollway, *Knowing Mothers*.

4  Michael Bury, 'Chronic Illness as Biographical Disruption', *Sociology of Health and Illness* 4 (1982): 167–82.
5  PricewaterhouseCoopers, *The Cost of Perinatal Depression and Anxiety in Australia* (Gidget Foundation Australia, 2019), https://gidgetfoundation.org.au/wp-content/uploads/2019/11/Cost-of-PNDA-in-Australia_-Final-Report.pdf.
6  Raphael, 'Matresence'; Mariotti, *The Maternal Lineage*.
7  Alistair Thomson, *Moving Stories: An Intimate History of Four Women across Two Countries* (Sydney: UNSW Press, 2011).
8  Abrams, 'Heroes of Their Own Life Stories'; Barrett Meyering, 'Liberating Children: The Australian Women's Liberation Movement and Children's Rights in the 1970s'.
9  Petra Bueskens and Carla Pascoe Leahy, 'Defining Maternal Studies in Australia: The Birth of a Field', in *Australian Mothering: Historical and Sociological Perspectives*, eds. Carla Pascoe Leahy and Petra Bueskens (London: Palgrave Macmillan, 2020).
10  Australian Institute of Health and Welfare, 'Australia's Mothers and Babies', 15 December 2021, www.aihw.gov.au/reports/mothers-babies/australias-mothers-babies.
11  Manne, *Motherhood: How Should We Care for Our Children?*
12  Lynn Abrams, 'Liberating the Female Self: Epiphanies, Conflict and Coherence in the Life Stories of Post-War British Women', *Social History* 39, no. 1 (2014): 14–35; Abrams, 'Heroes of Their Own Life Stories'.
13  Katie Holmes, 'Does It Matter If She Cried? Recording Emotion and the Australian Generations Oral History Project', *Oral History Review* 44, no. 1 (2017): 56–76.
14  Petra Bueskens, 'From Containing to Creating: Maternal Subjectivity', in *Dangerous Ideas about Mothers*, eds. Camilla Nelson and Rachel Robertson (Crawley, WA: University of Western Australia Publishing, 2018), 197–210.
15  Crouch and Manderson, *New Motherhood*; Hays, *The Cultural Contradictions of Motherhood*.
16  Coontz, *The Way We Never Were: American Families and the Nostalgia Trap*.
17  Maushart, *Mask of Motherhood*.

# Epilogue

*Now that we've come to the end. Why this, why did you craft your [research] around this?*

Partly, I felt really pissed off that it had been so ignored ... No one really talks about how motherhood tosses you around and spits you out really different ... I'd heard it talked about in much more pragmatic terms. It was partly that I felt pissed off that historians had ignored it, when I started looking into it and nothing had been written on it, but it really was fundamentally that this is such a peak experience, and that it carries all these paradoxes, that it's both the best thing and the worst thing that's ever happened to me, you know? It's both the most sublimely satisfying and crazily challenging thing that I've ever had to do. I've never had anything push me to my limits and extend my limits the way that motherhood has. That, to me, was something that I felt really needed more teasing out, and it needed teasing out through the words and experiences of mothers themselves.

It was a lot to do with the sense that public discourse is so impoverished that we just talk about we need more childcare, or mothers have so much postnatal depression, and there's no discussion of the intricacies and the profundities. You know, on a really fundamental level, unless you felt called to, why would you become a mother, in this day and age? If you were basing your decision upon what you saw around you, in our cultural sphere, I can't see any logical reasons for becoming a mother. It just looks shit – it looks like everyone that becomes a mother is depressed, women are financially disadvantaged for the rest of their careers ... and childcare is crap and you can't even access it ... That's all we talk about, is how crap it is.

> For women like me, women who are feminists and ambitious, I could have easily missed out on motherhood. If I had only made those logical decisions, or if N [niece] hadn't have been born and I hadn't had that kind of guttural response to seeing my genetic material in the form of an infant, I might have not chosen motherhood, because I wouldn't have seen any powerful arguments for why I should do it. I just think that's incredibly impoverished ... That's really one of the challenges for me ... It's like that tricky balance between talking about how amazing it is without missing the point of how difficult it is. To ignore how difficult it is would be to undermine the sort of everyday heroism of mothers, because I think the fact that mothers keep doing what they do, every day, is nothing short of astounding, and the only thing that sustains us is that love. It's an incredibly challenging quest to try to capture the paradoxes of motherhood in a format that people will understand. That's my challenge and my ambition.
>
> Carla Pascoe Leahy

This is the end of this book. And yet it is not the end of the story, of course.

Motherhood continues, and continues changing, throughout a woman's life. Maternal time persists beyond matrescence. As narrator Pamela taught me – as a grandmother instructing a relatively new mother – though the identity change of motherhood is felt most strongly at matrescence, the unconditional love and responsibility felt towards a child never ceases. I asked her whether she felt like a different person when she became a mother in 1967.

> The responsibility, whoa! Huge! I mean, it's just there, they're just there, they never go away. And until you've had a baby, it doesn't resonate, does it? Did you realise they never go away? And I hate to tell you but you're going to be a mother forever. It doesn't matter how old you are, you will always be that mother. I think that's a hugely kept secret ... When they're little, they have problems and issues and stuff and you can nearly always fix it or make it better or whatever. When they get bigger, the problems get bigger and you often – well, you can't fix it and neither can they often. And but you've still got that attachment that makes it painful for you ... So, the realisation doesn't dawn on you for a very long time that you will be a mother until you die. Most of the time, you wouldn't swap it for the world. But gee, there are painful times when you wish you could

dodge the pain a bit, but no. But that's the way it is, isn't it? You can't have the love without the consequences.

Although this book focuses on matrescence, motherhood never ends. All the mothers in these pages continued on their mothering journeys after the initial intensity of matrescence, and their maternality kept shifting across their lifetimes. Stern theorises that the motherhood constellation, once integrated into a woman's psychology, never leaves. It will not always be uppermost, in the way it is at 'the birth of the mother'. But it is a permanent shift. Katherine, who had her first child in 1993, tried to put into words what this feels like.

> You're never not a mother. I spend a lot of time still thinking about my children ... You just never lose it. I know people who've got kids that are forty, and they're still involved ... You're just always bound up with them, and thinking about them. It's not all-encompassing as it is when they're a baby, but it continues to be encompassing ... You don't think that they get to school and then it's like, I can relax and be myself ... Then they're kind of bigger people, bigger in their personalities and in their impact on you and then they reflect on you, and reflect back at you ... When they're little, it's all about you bestowing your caringness upon them. When they get older ... their conception of you is really sometimes you have to bat it back and go hang on ... there is vast amounts of me that you cannot conceive ... It doesn't stop. It changes, but it doesn't stop.

Just as a woman's embeddedness in maternal time keeps changing, so too does her generational time. Shifting cultural attitudes and medical possibilities are sprouting different expressions of mothering, fathering and parenting in the twenty-first century, including single mothers by choice, surrogate mothers, lesbian mothers and transgender parents. In this book, I have chosen to hold on to the word 'mother', both because it is how my narrators describe themselves and because bearing and raising children has still taken distinctively gendered forms in the second half of the twentieth century. The more gender-neutral term 'parent' erases the many ways in which embodied care and social penalties persist, differentiating the experiences of mothers and fathers across this period. But although mothers still overwhelmingly tend to be the primary carers of children in Australia, fathers in heterosexual couples are increasingly – if slowly – taking on a larger share of the practical and emotional tasks of childrearing. Looking to the future, it is possible that the care of children could escape its feminine and heteronormative associations this century.

Future-gazing has always been implied in fertility decisions. The choice to have children assumes that a potential parent predicts a viable and satisfactory future for their children. Yet this often taken-for-granted faith in futurity is increasingly undermined in this third millennium. Rising numbers of women are choosing not to mother, some for personal reasons and some because they perceive the lack of social supports that bedevils new mothers. Women have an unprecedented level of control over their fertility. Through the availability of sex education, birth control, abortion and ART, more women can decide whether to have children, when to have children and how to have children. It is perhaps unsurprising that increasing numbers of women are rejecting motherhood by choice or accident.

One contributor to declining fertility are the anxious historical times in which we live. The COVID-19 pandemic has swept across the globe with terrifying ferocity, affecting every corner of the world. In addition to the immediate impacts of the coronavirus, in the form of illness, death, social isolation and economic deprivation, more concerning is what it communicates of the many and dangerous effects of environmental degradation. Just as this pandemic is a product of human encroachment into once-wild places, so too are increasing disasters, warming weather and ecosystem damage all a product of our unsustainable relationships with nature. In recent years, Australians have lived through the most devastating bushfires our country has ever seen, followed immediately by the destruction of coronavirus. In these apocalyptic times, it is little wonder that rising numbers of women are choosing not to have children, that environmental change is impacting upon maternal futures. Some women are choosing not to mother in an era of climate collapse, some choosing to have only one child and others changing how they raise their children in an epoch of environmental disasters and destruction. In the age of the Anthropocene, the greatest influence on the present and future of families is environmental. For Australian women becoming mothers since late 2019, pandemic, bushfires and floods are shaping maternal experiences more powerfully than any other force. We are entering a new era in the history of the family. As I complete this research, I discern a new generational cohort rising: Anthropocenic mothers.

Another major contributor to fertility decline is the inadequacy of social policies concerning mothers. When young women learn that they will suffer financial disadvantage across their lifetimes as a result of choosing motherhood – through the gender pay gap and reduced superannuation – they legitimately question whether the benefit of having children is worth the cost. They see the ways in which career progression is permanently impacted by time out of the workforce to have children. They read stories of birth trauma and disappointment, and escalating levels of perinatal depression and anxiety, and they wonder: why mother if it brings such anguish and difficulty? We are still not seeing these issues of maternal disadvantage treated with the urgency and seriousness they deserve.

And there is another contributor to reproductive refusal. Our cultural scripts about mothering are impoverished and superficial. News media highlight perinatal mental illness and problems with the cost and availability of childcare, giving the impression that mothering is an unpleasant burden and mothers are desperate to secure time away from their children. Social media and commercial channels depict mothering as an induction into a new world of consumer goods – a dizzying, confusing and expensive descent into a realm of infant care paraphernalia. Very few depictions in popular culture encapsulate the enriching, transformative aspects of maternality. It is rare to see public admission that mothering is the single most significant and meaningful role that most women will ever perform. Yet behind closed doors, in private conversations, women told me this time and again when given the space and permission to do so.

\* \* \*

I opened this book with some reflections on the ways in which my personal experiences of mothering shaped the research and writing of this work. I have also shared excerpts from my own maternography in introducing each chapter. The inner worlds of researchers are always present in our scholarship, whether acknowledged or submerged.

Oral historians understand that people take elements of their lives that may otherwise appear messy, meaningless or contradictory and work them into narratives. This process of narrativizing, of creating patterns from the random elements of life, helps to give form and meaning to human experience. It is how we make sense of, and come to terms with, our lives and our world. But the ways we can describe, relate and interpret our personal experiences are influenced by the cultural scripts available to us in our socio-historical moment.

This project was born from my conviction that our contemporary and historical accounts of motherhood are impoverished and inadequate. I felt that nothing in the cultural context of my childhood or adulthood had prepared me for the immense profundity of matrescence. Motherhood smashed through my life like a wrecking ball. The extremes of experience and emotion I experienced quite literally stunned me. It was like a spiritual awakening, a divine revelation. And I knew that nothing would ever be the same again.

I began this research as a way of making sense of contemporary motherhood and its living memory, for myself and for other Australian mothers. I wanted to diversify the maternal myths circulating in popular culture, which imply that mothering is limiting and burdensome, and that postwar mothers were naively accepting of such restrictions and millennial mothers were bravely fighting off the shackles of their children. Mothering is one thousand times more complex than this simplified portrayal. Matrescence takes women to the limits of what they can endure, and rewards them with a love more potent than they hitherto imagined. Mothering transforms every facet of a woman's existence, and beckons her into a world of which she was not previously aware.

Motherhood is not inherently depressing or anxiety-provoking. But when we scrub the language of profundity from public discourse, individual women largely lose the capacity to craft narratives of mothering that truly express what they experience at matrescence. By offering women a chance to tell their maternographies, they are given an opportunity to craft a version of their maternal experiences that they can live with. Indeed, an essential part of the emotional labour of matrescence is this intense psychic activity of processing the multiple, heightened emotions and the many novel sensations that are stirred by the unique experiences of becoming a mother.

We can also create the opportunity to pluralise the mother stories that circulate in our cultural sphere, opening up some discursive space in which women can express the full spectrum of intense emotions and experiences that accompany motherhood. Perhaps recognition that ambivalence, joy, despair, elation, frustration are all normal responses to a transition that reframes a woman's identity, lifestyle and priorities can help to alleviate the existential terror and loneliness that some new mothers feel during this rite of passage.

Currently, there are very few contemporary sources that attempt to communicate the miraculous, enhancing and profound nature of matrescence. This book is my small contribution to diversifying and complicating our collective understandings and discussions of mothering. I sincerely thank the Australian women who entrusted me with the co-creation of their maternographies. I hope that this book adequately rewards the gift they offered me, in sharing their intimate experiences of maternality. And I hope that it contributes to enlivening and regenerating our cultural conversations about what motherhood is ... and what it could be.

# Appendix: Narrator biographies

### Postwar mothers

Adriana was born in 1924 and grew up in a Presbyterian, Anglo-Australian family in Queensland. As an adult, she married and had three children, one of them born with an intellectual disability. When her husband abandoned the family, she raised her children as a single mother in inner-urban Melbourne.

Chen was born in 1935 and raised in a wealthy Chinese family in Hong Kong. As an adult, she came to Australia, became a teacher and married. She had the first of three children in 1966, raising them in Carlton.

Daphne was born in 1930 and raised near Ocean Grove and in Fitzroy in a working-class, Anglo-Australian, Anglican family. As an adult, she married and gave birth in 1954, raising her son in Fitzroy. She unofficially adopted another son. Daphne worked as a factory worker, waitress and shopkeeper.

Dora was born in 1921 in Camperdown and grew up on a farm in an Anglo-Australian, Anglican family. She worked as a store assistant before becoming a mother. She married in 1959 and had the first of two children in 1960, raising them in Ocean Grove.

Dorothy was born in 1924 and grew up in an Anglo-Australian, Anglican family in regional Victoria. She married and became a nurse as an adult. She had her only child in 1956 and raised him in Ocean Grove and Darwin.

Eve was born in Geelong in 1930 and spent most of her childhood in Melbourne. She married a Lebanese-born man at the age of eighteen and moved to regional Victoria. She had the first of eight children in 1950. Eve was a housekeeper and mother throughout her life and her husband was a bulldozing contractor.

Grace was born in Sydney in 1932 and raised in Melbourne in a Methodist, Anglo-Australian family. She married, became an academic and adopted two sons born in 1962 and 1963.

Jane was born in 1931 and raised in suburban Melbourne in a Catholic, Irish-Australian family. As an adult, she married, became a teacher and had eleven children between 1954 and 1969. She raised them in Malvern.

June was born in 1923 in Germany. She met and married her husband and they had their first child in Germany in 1947. She migrated to Australia in 1952 and settled in Ocean Grove, giving birth to her second child in 1953.

Maggie was born in 1938 and raised in rural Victoria in a Christian, Anglo-Australian family. As an adult, she married and worked as a psychologist and careers counsellor. She had the first of three children in 1966 and raised them in North Fitzroy.

Marjorie was born in London in 1931. She grew up on in a Jewish, working-class family with an Eastern European background. Her family moved in Australia in 1949. She married in 1951 and had her first of two children in 1953. Marjorie worked as a hairdresser and raised her children in suburban Melbourne.

Pamela was born in 1944 and raised in regional Victoria in a Presbyterian, Anglo-Australian family. As an adult, she married and worked as a secretary then later as a disability integration aide. She had the first of four children in 1967 and struggled with her first child's life-threatening illness. She raised her children in Ocean Grove.

Patsy was born in 1948 and raised in Brisbane, in a working-class, Catholic family. She had her first of three children in 1967 (spending her pregnancy in a mother and babies' home). She married and raised her children in Ocean Grove.

Pauline was born in 1937 into a middle-class, Church of England family and raised in Melbourne, Geelong and Adelaide. As an adult, she married and worked as a bank clerk. She had the first of three children in 1963 and raised them in Melbourne.

Rachel was born in 1940 in Melbourne and raised in an Anglo-Australian, middle-class family. She married and had her first of three children in 1964. She raised her children in suburban Glen Iris, near Malvern.

Regina was born in 1939 and raised in Victoria and Tasmania. She married and had her first of three children in 1967 in the US, before returning to Melbourne and raising her family in Fitzroy. Regina worked as an academic and her husband was a religious minister and a politician.

## Second-wave mothers

Brenda was born in 1953 and raised in a Catholic farming family in rural Victoria. As an adult, she became a nurse, married and had the first of three children in 1978 while living in Fitzroy. She later divorced and raised her children as a single mother.

Carol was born in 1945 and raised in a Catholic, Irish-Australian family in Bentleigh (suburban Melbourne). As an adult, she became a teacher, married and had the first of six children in 1974. She raised her children (including narrator Andrea) in Ocean Grove.

Genevieve was born in 1954 and raised in the eastern suburbs of Melbourne in a Catholic family. She became a writer and had the first of two children in 1989, living in North Fitzroy.

Hazel was born in 1955 in Belgium. She spent most of her childhood in Melbourne, raised in an Anglo-Australian, Catholic family. As an adult, she married, became an academic and had the first of two children in Fitzroy in 1989. She raised her children in Melbourne, Adelaide and Canberra.

Joanna was born in 1947 in England. As an adult, she became a nurse and married. She and her husband migrated to Australia in their mid-twenties and had the first of five children in 1973. They raised their children in Ocean Grove.

Julia was born in 1950 and raised in Tasmania. As an adult, she worked as a legal secretary and married an Italo-Australian man. She had the first of three children in 1978 and raised them in Malvern.

Kay was born to an Aboriginal mother in 1952. She was adopted by a non-Aboriginal couple and raised on the rural fringes of Melbourne. As an adult, she worked as a teacher. She married and had twins in 1983, raising them in Ocean Grove.

Mary was born in 1951 in the Netherlands to parents of Indonesian and Dutch-German descent. She had her first of two children in 1974 (her second child was narrator Michelle). As an adult, she worked as a nurse and kindergarten teacher. She moved to Australia with her family in 1980.

Miroslava was born in 1946 to Orthodox, Macedonian-Australian parents. She was raised in Fitzroy. She became a bank clerk, married and had the first of two children in 1975, raising them in Fitzroy also. She suffered from a debilitating health condition from the late 1970s.

Penny was born in 1943 in Melbourne. She grew up in a Catholic, working-class, Irish-Australian family. As an adult, she became a teacher then married and had the first of three children in 1975, raising them in Ocean Grove.

Sally was born in 1952 and grew up in regional Victoria. Her father was Lebanese-born and her mother (narrator Eve) of Swedish and Scottish backgrounds. As an adult, she became a teacher and married. She had her first of two children in 1978, raising them in Malvern and adjacent suburbs.

Susan was born in 1951 and raised in Melbourne. As an adult, she became a ceramicist and married. She had the first of four children (narrator Kristen) in 1976, raising them in the UK, the US and finally suburban Melbourne. Sandra has been deaf since the age of two.

Sybil was born in 1947 into a Welsh-Australian family and raised in rural locations in Victoria and Queensland. As an adult, she became a teacher. She had the first of two children (narrator Ariana) in 1979 and raised them in Malvern. She was married to a Welsh man until 1986 then raised her children as a single mother.

Valerie was born into a British working-class family in 1949. She moved to Australia in 1961, living in the western suburbs of Melbourne. She worked as a teacher and married her husband in 1981, before having her only child in 1984. She raised her in Ocean Grove.

Wanda was born in 1948 and raised on a farm in rural Victoria in an Irish-Australian, Catholic family. As an adult, she became a nurse and then a psychologist. She and her husband had the first of three children in 1978 and raised them in Malvern.

Wendy was born in 1941 and raised near Geelong. As an adult, she became a hairdresser. She had the first of two children in 1970 and raised her family in Ocean Grove.

## Millennial mothers

Alison was born in 1974 and raised in a German-Australian family in Ocean Grove. As an adult, she worked in administration and sales. She married and had the first of four children (twins) in 2004, raising her family in Ocean Grove.

Amanda was born in 1959 to parents who had recently migrated from England. As an adult, she worked in office management and sales. She married and had two children, the first born in 1991, raising them in Ocean Grove.

Andrea was born in 1980 (to narrator Carol) and raised in a Catholic, middle-class, Anglo-Australian family in Ocean Grove. As an adult, she became a nurse, married and raised her three children in Ocean Grove, the first born in 2010.

Ariana was born in 1979 and raised in a Welsh-Australian, middle-class family in Malvern. Her parents separated when she was seven and she was raised by her mother (narrator Sybil). As an adult, she has partnered and works in marketing. She had the first of three children in 2010, raising them in Malvern.

Avril was born in a New Zealand country town in 1976. She comes from a Māori background. Avril has lived in Australia since she was eight years old. Her partner is Scottish-born and they both work in advertising and live near Fitzroy. They had their first child in 2013.

Caitlyn was born in 1962 and raised in an Irish-Australian, Catholic family in suburban Melbourne. As an adult, she married and moved to Ocean Grove in 1980. She had her first of three children in 1990.

Connie was born in 1971 and grew up in Greece and Melbourne to Greek-Australian parents. As an adult, she became a teacher. She had her only child in 2014 as a single mother by choice (donor conceived). They live near Malvern.

Emiliya was born in 1988 in Bulgaria and raised in Adelaide and Canberra. As an adult, she married and worked as a public servant. She had her first child in 2020.

Helen was born in England in 1978 and spent most of her childhood in the United States. As an adult, she has worked in the arts industry. She moved to Australia as an adult, married and had the first of two children in 2013, living in Fitzroy.

Heather was born in 1981 in Sydney and raised by adoptive parents in regional New South Wales. As an adult, she has worked in the arts industry, married her same-sex partner and had the first of four children in 2012. She is raising her children in Melbourne.

Justine was born in 1964 in Sydney and raised in a Presbyterian, Anglo-Australian family. As an adult, she married and had the first of two children in 1996, raising them in Malvern.

Katerina was born in the United States in 1981 and grew up in Ecuador and the US. She is a member of the Baha'i faith. Katerina has worked in public policy throughout her adult life. She met an Australian man and moved to Australia in 2007, before they married and had their first child in 2013, in Fitzroy.

Katherine was born in 1965 in regional Western Australia to Dutch-Australian parents. She was raised in Western Australia, Tasmania and Victoria. As an adult, she married, worked as a journalist and had the first of two children in 1993, raising them in Fitzroy.

Kira was born in 1981 in regional Victoria. She was raised by a single mother after her abusive father left the family. As an adult she married her same-sex partner and has worked as a professional writer. She had twins in 2015 and raised them in Ocean Grove.

Kristen was born in 1976 in London and grew up in the UK, US and Australia. As an adult, she married and worked in publishing. She had the first of three children in 2009, living in suburban Melbourne.

Lily was born in regional Victoria in 1980 and raised in an Anglo-Australian family in a country town. As an adult, she became a teacher and married. She had the first of two children in 2012 and raised her children in Ocean Grove.

Lucy was born in 1970 in Sweden and grew up in Sweden and Australia. As an adult, she married and became a store owner.

She had the first of two children in 1997 and raised them in Ocean Grove.

Michelle was born in 1979 in Mozambique to Dutch parents (narrator Mary). She moved to Australia when she was two years old. She works as an operations manager, lives in Fitzroy and had her first of two children in 2013.

Molly was born in Melbourne in 1977 into an Anglo-Australian, middle-class family. She grew up in Australia, Germany and the United Kingdom. As an adult, she married and had her only child in 2013 in Fitzroy. She works in the not-for-profit sector.

Petronela was born in 1981 in Poland and raised in a middle-class, Catholic family. She moved to Australia at the age of eight. As an adult, she became a researcher and consultant and had the first of two children in 2017 while living with her partner in Fitzroy.

Rowena was born in 1975 in Perth. Her parents were both doctors and she also became a doctor. Rowena first became a mother to a stepchild when she married. She had the first of her two biological children in 2010 and raised them in Malvern.

Sarah was born in 1983 and grew up in rural Victoria. She moved to Melbourne as an adult and worked as a nurse before marrying and becoming a mother. Sarah had her first child in 2013 while living in Fitzroy and subsequently moved to a regional town near Ocean Grove when her second child was born.

Somi was born in 1983 in Cairns and grew up primarily in Townsville. She has a Torres Strait Islander background. As an adult, she partnered and had the first of two children in 2013. She works as an academic.

Sophia was born in 1960 in Ghana. As her father was a diplomat, she spent much of her childhood living in different countries. As an adult, she worked as a careers counsellor and married. She had the first of two children in 1997 and raised them in Fitzroy.

Tessa was born in 1970 into an Anglo-Australian family in regional Victoria. As an adult, she became a social worker. She and her partner had their only child in 2013, who was born twelve weeks premature and raised in Ocean Grove.

Veronica was born in 1978 in Switzerland. She met an Australian partner and later moved to Australia. She had her first of two children in 2007 living in an inner-urban neighbourhood adjacent to Fitzroy. She works as a researcher.

# Bibliography

Abrams, Lynn. 'Heroes of Their Own Life Stories: Narrating the Female Self in the Feminist Age'. *Cultural and Social History* 16, no. 2 (2019): 205–24.

Abrams, Lynn. 'Liberating the Female Self: Epiphanies, Conflict and Coherence in the Life Stories of Post-War British Women'. *Social History* 39, no. 1 (2014): 14–35.

Anderson, Kathryn, and Dana C. Jack. 'Learning to Listen: Interview Techniques and Analyses'. In *Women's Words: The Feminist Practice of Oral History*, edited by Sherna Berger Gluck and Daphne Patai, 11–26. London: Routledge, 1991.

Arnup, Katherine. *Education for Motherhood: Advice for Mothers in Twentieth-Century Canada*. Toronto: University of Toronto Press, 1994.

Balsam, Rosemary H. 'The Mother within the Mother'. *Psychoanalytic Quarterly* LXIX (2000): 465–92.

Baraitser, Lisa. *Maternal Encounters: The Ethics of Interruption*. London and New York: Routledge, 2009.

Barnard, Jill, and Karen Twigg. *Nursing Mums: A History of the Australian Breastfeeding Association 1964–2014*. Malvern, Vic.: Australian Breastfeeding Association, 2014.

Barrett Meyering, Isobelle. 'Liberating Children: The Australian Women's Liberation Movement and Children's Rights in the 1970s'. *Lilith: A Feminist History Journal* 19 (2013): 60–74.

Barrett Meyering, Isobelle. '"There Must Be a Better Way": Motherhood and the Dilemmas of Feminist Lifestyle Change'. *Outskirts* 28 (2013): 1–15.

Basden Arnold, Lorin, and BettyAnn Martin, eds. *Taking the Village Online: Mothers, Motherhood, and Social Media*. Bradford, Ontario: Demeter Press, 2016.

Beauvoir, Simone de. *The Second Sex*. New York: Alfred A. Knopf, 1953.

BenEzer, Gadi. 'Trauma Signals in Life Stories'. In *Trauma and Life Stories: International Perspectives*, edited by Kim Lacy Rogers, Selma Leydesdorff and Graham Dawson, 29–44. London and New York: Routledge, 1999.

Bornat, Joanna, and Hanna Diamond. 'Women's History and Oral History: Developments and Debates'. *Women's History Review* 16, no. 1 (2007): 19–39.

Brannen, Julia, Peter Moss and Ann Mooney. *Working and Caring over the Twentieth Century: Change and Continuity in Four Generation Families*. Basingstoke: Palgrave Macmillan, 2004.

Brennan, Deborah. 'Babies, Budgets, and Birthrates: Work/Family Policy in Australia 1996–2006'. *Social Politics: International Studies in Gender, State and Society* 14, no. 1 (2007): 32.

Brennan, Deborah. *The Politics of Australian Child Care: From Philanthropy to Feminism*. Cambridge; Melbourne; New York: Cambridge University Press, 1994.

Brown, Stephanie, Judith Lumley, Rhonda Small and Jill Astbury. *Missing Voices: The Experience of Motherhood*. Melbourne: Oxford University Press, 1994.

Bruijn, Melissa, and Debby Gould. *How to Heal a Bad Birth: Making Sense, Making Peace and Moving On*. Kenmore, Queensland: Birthtalk, 2016.

Bueskens, Petra. 'From Containing to Creating: Maternal Subjectivity'. In *Dangerous Ideas about Mothers*, edited by Camilla Nelson and Rachel Robertson, 197–210. Crawley, WA: University of Western Australia Publishing, 2018.

Bueskens, Petra. 'Introduction'. In *Mothering & Psychoanalysis: Clinical, Sociological and Feminist Perspectives*, edited by Petra Bueskens, 1–72. Bradford, Canada: Demeter Press, 2014.

Bueskens, Petra. *Modern Motherhood and Women's Dual Identities: Rewriting the Sexual Contract*. London and New York: Routledge, 2018.

Bueskens, Petra, and Carla Pascoe Leahy. 'Defining Maternal Studies in Australia: The Birth of a Field'. In *Australian Mothering: Historical and Sociological Perspectives*, edited by Carla Pascoe Leahy and Petra Bueskens, 21–65. London: Palgrave Macmillan, 2020.

Campo, Monica, and Kerreen Reiger. 'Maternalism to Consumerism and beyond? Mothers and the Politics of Care in Childbirth'. In *Australian Mothering: Historical and Sociological Perspectives*, edited by Carla Pascoe Leahy and Petra Bueskens, 257–78. Cham, Switzerland: Palgrave Macmillan, 2019.

Campo, Natasha. *From Superwomen to Domestic Goddesses: The Rise and Fall of Feminism*. Bern: Peter Lang, 2009.

Cannold, Leslie. *What, No Baby? Why Women Are Losing the Freedom to Mother and How They Can Get It Back*. Fremantle: Fremantle Press, 2005.

Cave, Mark, and Stephen M. Sloan, eds. *Listening on the Edge: Oral History in the Aftermath of a Crisis*. Oxford: Oxford University Press, 2014.

Chadwick, Rachelle. *Bodies That Birth: Vitalizing Birth Politics*. London and New York: Routledge, 2018.

Chodorow, Nancy. *The Reproduction of Mothering: Psychoanalysis and the Sociology of Gender*. Berkeley: University of California Press, 1978.

Coontz, Stephanie. *The Way We Never Were: American Families and the Nostalgia Trap*. New York: Basic Books, 1992.

Craig, Lyn. *Contemporary Motherhood: The Impact of Children on Adult Time*. London and New York: Routledge, 2007.

Crouch, Mira, and Lenore Manderson. *New Motherhood: Cultural and Personal Transitions in the 1980s*. Yverdon, Switzerland; Camberwell, Vic.: Gordon and Breach, 1983.

Curthoys, Anne, and John Docker. *Is History Fiction?* Randwick NSW: University of NSW Press, 2009.

Das, Veena. *Life and Words: Violence and the Descent into the Ordinary*. Berkeley: University of California Press, 2007.

Davin, Anna. Imperialism and Motherhood. *History Workshop Journal* 5 (1978): 9–65.

Davis, Angela. *Modern Motherhood: Women and Family in England, 1945–2000*. Manchester: Manchester University Press, 2012.

Deacon, Desley. 'Taylorism in the Home: The Medical Profession, the Infant Welfare Movement and the Deskilling of Women'. *Journal of Sociology* 21, no. 2 (1985): 161–73.

Dixson, Miriam. *The Real Matilda: Woman and Identity in Australia 1788 to 1975*. Ringwood, Vic.: Penguin, 1976.

Fass, Paula S. *The End of American Childhood: A History of Parenting from Life on the Frontier to the Managed Child*. Princeton, NJ: Princeton University Press, 2016.

Felman, Shoshana, and Dori Laub. *Testimony: Crises of Witnessing in Literature, Psychoanalysis, and History*. New York: Routledge, 1992.

Firestone, Shulamith. *The Dialectic of Sex: The Case for Feminist Revolution*. New York: Morrow, 1970.

Fox, Haylee, Emily Callander, Daniel Lindsay and Stephanie Topp. 'Evidence of Overuse? Patterns of Obstetric Interventions during Labour and Birth among Australian Mothers'. *BMC Pregnancy and Childbirth* 19, no. 1 (2019): 226. https://doi.org/10.1186/s12884-019-2369-5.

Frank, Arthur W. *The Wounded Storyteller: Body, Illness, and Ethics*. Chicago: University of Chicago Press, 1995.

Friedan, Betty. *The Feminine Mystique*. New York: W.W. Norton, 1963.

Friedman, May, and Shana L. Calixte, eds. *Mothering and Blogging: The Radical Act of the Mommyblog*. Bradford, Ontario: Demeter Press, 2009.

Game, Ann, and Rosemary Pringle. 'Sexuality and the Suburban Dream'. *Australian and New Zealand Journal of Sociology* 15, no. 2 (1979): 4–15.

Golden, Janet. *Message in a Bottle: The Making of Fetal Alcohol Syndrome*. Cambridge, MA: Harvard University Press, 2006.

Goodwin, Susan, and Kate Huppatz, eds. *The Good Mother: Contemporary Motherhoods in Australia*. Sydney: Sydney University Press, 2010.

Grant, Julia. *Raising Baby by the Book: The Education of American Mothers*. New Haven, CT: Yale University Press, 1998.

Green, Anna. 'Individual Remembering and "Collective Memory": Theoretical Presuppositions and Contemporary Debates'. *Oral History* 32, no. 2 (2004): 35–44.

Grimshaw, Patricia. 'Mothers and Waged Work Following Equal Opportunity Legislation in Australia, 1986–2006'. In *Australian Mothering: Historical and Sociological Perspectives*, edited by Carla Pascoe Leahy and Petra Bueskens, 359–80. London: Palgrave Macmillan, 2020.

Hardyment, Christina. *Dream Babies: Childcare Advice from John Locke to Gina Ford*. London: Frances Lincoln, 2007.

Harper, Jan, and Lyn Richards. *Mothers and Working Mothers*. 2nd ed. Ringwood, Vic.: Penguin, 1986.

Hays, Sharon. *The Cultural Contradictions of Motherhood*. New Haven: Yale University Press, 1996.

Hendrick, Harry. *Narcissistic Parenting in an Insecure World: A History of Parenting Culture 1920 to Present*. Bristol: Policy Press, 2016.

Herman, Judith L. *Trauma and Recovery: The Aftermath of Violence – From Domestic Abuse to Political Terror*. New York: Basic Books, 2015.

Hill Collins, Patricia. 'The Meaning of Motherhood in Black Culture and Black Mother–Daughter Relationships'. In *Double Stitch: Black Women Write About Mothers and Daughters*, edited by Patricia Bell-Scott, 41–60. Boston: Beacon Press, 1991.

Hoffmann, Heidi, Rebecca E. Olson, Francisco Perales and Janeen Baxter. 'New Mothers and Social Support: A Mixed-Method Study of Young Mothers in Australia'. *Journal of Sociology* 57, no. 4 (2021): 950–68.

Hollway, Wendy. *Knowing Mothers: Researching Maternal Identity Change*. London: Palgrave Macmillan, 2015.

Holmes, Katie. 'Does It Matter If She Cried? Recording Emotion and the Australian Generations Oral History Project'. *Oral History Review* 44, no. 1 (2017): 56–76.
hooks, bell. *Feminist Theory: From Margin to Center*. New York and London: Routledge, 2015.
Hrdy, Sarah Blaffer. *Mother Nature: A History of Mothers, Infants, and Natural Selection*. New York: Pantheon Books, 1999.
Hrdy, Sarah Blaffer. *Mothers and Others: The Evolutionary Origins of Mutual Understanding*. Cambridge, Mass.: Belknap Press of Harvard University Press, 2009.
Jennings, Rebecca. '"The Most Radical, Most Exciting and Most Challenging Role of My Life": Lesbian Motherhood in Australia 1945–1990'. In *Australian Mothering: Historical and Sociological Perspectives*, edited by Carla Pascoe Leahy and Petra Bueskens, 179–200. London: Palgrave Macmillan, 2020.
Johnston-Ataata, Kate. 'Reflecting on the Past: The Role of Biographical, Familial and Social Memory in New Mothers' Interpretations of Emotional Experiences of Early Parenthood'. In *Australian Mothering: Historical and Sociological Perspectives*, edited by Carla Pascoe Leahy and Petra Bueskens, 297–316. Cham, Switzerland: Palgrave Macmillan, 2019.
Kedgley, Sue. *Mum's the Word: The Untold Story of Motherhood in New Zealand*. Auckland: Random House, 1996.
Kevin, Catherine. 'Great Expectations: Episodes in a Political History of Pregnancy in Australia since 1945'. In *Feminism and the Body: Interdisciplinary Perspectives*, edited by Catherine Kevin, 49–69. Newcastle upon Tyne: Cambridge Scholars Publishing, 2009.
Kevin, Catherine. 'Maternal Responsibility and Traceable Loss: Medicine and Miscarriage in Twentieth-Century Australia'. *Women's History Review* 26, no. 6 (2017): 840–56.
Kevin, Catherine. 'Maternity and Freedom: Australian Feminist Encounters with the Reproductive Body'. *Australian Feminist Studies* 20, no. 46 (2005): 3–15.
Kingston, Beverley. *My Wife, My Daughter, and Poor Mary Ann: Women and Work in Australia*. Melbourne: Nelson, 1975.
Klein, Marian van der, Rebecca Jo Plant, Nichole Sanders and Lori R. Weintrob, eds. *Maternalism Reconsidered: Motherhood, Welfare and Social Policy in the Twentieth Century*. New York and Oxford: Berghahn Books, 2012.
Knott, Sarah. *Mother: An Unconventional History*. London: Penguin, 2020.
Knott, Sarah. 'Theorizing and Historicizing Mothering's Many Labours'. *Past and Present* Supplement 15 (2020): 1–26.

Kokanović, Renata, Paula A. Michaels and Kate Johnston-Ataata, eds. *Paths to Parenthood: Emotions on the Journey through Pregnancy, Childbirth, and Early Parenting*. New York and London: Palgrave Macmillan, 2018.

Koven, Seth, and Sonya Michel, eds. *Mothers of a New World: Maternalist Politics and the Origins of Welfare States*. New York and London: Routledge, 1993.

Lake, Marilyn. 'State Socialism for Australian Mothers: Andrew Fisher's Radical Maternalism in Its International and Local Contexts'. *Labour History: A Journal of Labour and Social History* 102 (2012): 55–70.

Langer, Lawrence L. *Holocaust Testimonies: The Ruins of Memory*. New Haven: Yale University Press, 1991.

Layne, Linda L. '"He Was a Real Baby with Real Things": A Material Culture Analysis of Personhood, Parenthood and Pregnancy Loss'. *Journal of Material Culture* 5, no. 3 (2000): 321–45.

Layne, Linda L. *Motherhood Lost: A Feminist Account of Pregnancy Loss in America*. New York: Routledge, 2003.

Lerner, Gerda. *The Creation of Patriarchy*. New York: Oxford University Press, 1986.

Leydesdorff, Selma, Graham Dawson, Natasha Burchardt and T.G. Ashplant. 'Introduction: Trauma and Life Stories'. In *Trauma and Life Stories: International Perspectives*, edited by Kim Lacy Rogers, Selma Leydesdorff and Graham Dawson, 1–26. London and New York: Routledge, 1999.

Lorde, Audre. *Sister Outsider: Essays and Speeches. The Crossing Press Feminist Series*. Trumansburg, NY: Crossing Press, 1984.

Manne, Anne. *Motherhood: How Should We Care for Our Children?* Crows Nest, NSW: Allen & Unwin, 2005.

Mariotti, Paola, ed. *The Maternal Lineage: Identification, Desire and Transgenerational Issues*. London and New York: Routledge, 2012.

Marneffe, Daphne de. *Maternal Desire: On Children, Love, and the Inner Life*. New York: Little, Brown and Company, 2004.

Martin, Emily. *The Woman in the Body: A Cultural Analysis of Reproduction*. Boston: Beacon Press, 1987.

Maushart, Susan. *The Mask of Motherhood: How Becoming a Mother Changes Everything and Why We Pretend That It Doesn't*. New York: Penguin, 2000.

McCalman, Janet. *Sex and Suffering: Women's Health and a Women's Hospital*. Melbourne: Melbourne University Press, 1998.

McCalman, Janet. *Struggletown: Public and Private Life in Richmond 1900–1965*. Carlton, Vic.: Melbourne University Press, 1984.

Mein Smith, Philippa. *Mothers and King Baby: Infant Survival and Welfare in an Imperial World 1880–1950*. Basingstoke: Macmillan, 1997.

Michaels, Paula A. *Lamaze: An International History*. Oxford: Oxford University Press, 2014.

Michaels, Paula A., Elizabeth Sutton and Nicole Highet. 'Violence and Trauma in Australian Birth'. In *Australian Mothering: Historical and Sociological Perspectives*, edited by Carla Pascoe Leahy and Petra Bueskens, 239–55. Cham, Switzerland: Palgrave, 2019.

Miller, Tina. *Making Sense of Motherhood: A Narrative Approach*. Cambridge: Cambridge University Press, 2005.

Millett, Kate. *Sexual Politics*. New York: Doubleday, 1970.

Murphy, John. 'Breadwinning: Accounts of Work and Family Life in the 1950s'. *Labour & Industry* 12, no. 3 (2002): 59–75.

Murphy, John. 'Work in a Time of Plenty: Narratives of Men's Work in Post-War Australia'. *Labour History: A Journal of Labour and Social History* 88 (2005): 215–31.

Murphy, John, and Belinda Probert. '"Anything for the House": Recollections of Post-War Suburban Dreaming'. *Australian Historical Studies* 36, no. 124 (2004): 274–93.

Murphy, John, and Belinda Probert. 'Never Done: The Working Mothers of the 1950s'. In *Double Shift: Working Mothers and Social Change in Australia*, edited by Patricia Grimshaw, John Murphy and Belinda Probert, 133–52. Beaconsfield, Vic.: Melbourne Publishing Group/ Circa, 2005.

Nash, Meredith. *Making 'Postmodern' Mothers: Pregnant Embodiment, Baby Bumps and Body Image*. Basingstoke: Palgrave Macmillan, 2012.

Nathanson, Jessica, and Laura Camille Tuley, eds. *Mother Knows Best: Talking Back to the 'Experts'*. Bradford, Ontario: Demeter Press, 2009.

Oakley, Ann. *From Here to Maternity*. Harmondsworth: Penguin, 1981.

Oakley, Ann. *Housewife*. Middlesex, England: Penguin, 1974.

Parker, Rozsika. *Torn in Two: The Experience of Maternal Ambivalence*. 2nd ed. London: Virago, 2005.

Pascoe, Carla. 'A "Discreet Dance": Technologies of Menstrual Management in Australian Public Toilets during the Twentieth Century'. *Women's History Review* 24, no. 2 (2015): 234–51.

Pascoe, Carla. 'City as Space, City as Place: Sources and the Urban Historian'. *History Australia* 7, no. 2 (2010): 30.1–30.18.

Pascoe, Carla. 'Home Is Where Mother Is: Ideals and Realities in Australian Family Houses of the 1950s'. *Journal of Australian Studies* 41, no. 2 (2017): 184–206.

Pascoe, Carla. 'Mum's the Word: Advice to Australian Mothers since 1945'. *Journal of Family Studies* 21, no. 3 (2015): 218–34.

Pascoe, Carla. *Spaces Imagined, Places Remembered: Childhood in 1950s Australia*. Newcastle upon Tyne: Cambridge Scholars Publishing, 2011.

Pascoe, Carla. 'The Bleeding Obvious: Menstrual Ideologies and Technologies in Australia, 1940–1970'. *Lilith: A Feminist History Journal* 20 (2014): 76–92.

Pascoe Leahy, Carla. 'From the Little Wife to the Supermom? Maternographies of Feminism and Mothering in Australia since 1945'. *Feminist Studies* 45, no. 1 (2019): 100–28.

Pascoe Leahy, Carla. 'Maternal Heritage: Remembering Mothering and Motherhood through Material Culture'. *International Journal of Heritage Studies* 27, no. 10 (2021): 991–1010.

Pascoe Leahy, Carla. 'Public Histories and Private Struggles: The Place of Janet McCalman's Struggletown in Australian Historiography'. *History Australia* 16, no. 4 (2019): 656–73.

Pascoe Leahy, Carla. 'Selection and Sampling Methodologies in Oral Histories of Mothering, Parenting and Family'. *Oral History* 47, no. 1 (2019): 105–16.

Pascoe Leahy, Carla. 'The Mother Within: Intergenerational Influences upon Australian Matrescence since 1945'. *Past and Present* Supplement 15 (2020): 263–94.

Pascoe Leahy, Carla, and Petra Bueskens. 'Contextualising Australian Mothering and Motherhood'. In *Australian Mothering: Historical and Sociological Perspectives*, edited by Carla Pascoe Leahy and Petra Bueskens, 3–20. London: Palgrave Macmillan, 2020.

Payne, Anne Maree. *Stolen Motherhood: Aboriginal Mothers and Child Removal in the Stolen Generations Era*. Lanham, Maryland: Lexington Books, 2021.

Plant, Rebecca Jo. *Mom: The Transformation of Motherhood in Modern America*. Chicago: University of Chicago Press, 2010.

Probert, Belinda. '"Grateful Slaves" or "Self-Made Women": A Matter of Choice or Policy?' *Australian Feminist Studies* 17, no. 37 (2002): 7–17.

Raphael, Dana. 'Matresence, Becoming a Mother, a "New/Old" Rite de Passage'. In *Being Female: Reproduction, Power and Change*, edited by Dana Raphael, 65–72. Paris: Mouton, 1975.

Raphael-Leff, Joan. *Pregnancy – The Inside Story*. London: Sheldon Press, 1993.

Reid Boyd, Elizabeth, and Gayle Letherby, eds. *Stay-at-Home Mothers: Dialogues and Debates*. Bradford, Ontario: Demeter Press, 2014.

Reiger, Kerreen. 'Mothering Deskilled? Australian Childrearing and the "Experts"'. *Community Health Studies* 10, no. 1 (1986): 39–46.

Reiger, Kerreen. *Our Bodies, Our Babies: The Forgotten Women's Movement*. Carlton South, Vic.: Melbourne University Press, 2001.

Reiger, Kerreen. '"Sort of Part of the Women's Movement. But Different": Mothers' Organisations and Australian Feminism'. *Women's Studies International Forum* 22, no. 6 (1999): 585–95.

Rich, Adrienne. *Of Woman Born: Motherhood as Experience and Institution*. New York: Norton, 1976.

Rubin, Gayle S. 'Thinking Sex: Notes for a Radical Theory of the Politics of Sexuality'. In *Pleasure and Danger: Exploring Female Sexuality*, edited by Carole S. Vance, 267–93. London: Pandora, 1992.

Ruddick, Sara. *Maternal Thinking: Toward a Politics of Peace*. Boston: Beacon Press, 1989.

Scarry, Elaine. *The Body in Pain: The Making and Unmaking of the World*. New York: Oxford University Press, 1985.

Scott, Joan W. 'Gender: A Useful Category of Historical Analysis'. *American Historical Review* 91, no. 5 (1986): 1053–75.

Scott, Joan W. 'The Evidence of Experience'. *Critical Inquiry* 17, no. 4 (1991): 773–97.

Selby, Wendy. '"Raising an Interrogatory Eyebrow": Women's Responses to the Infant Welfare Movement in Queensland, 1918–1939'. In *On the Edge: Women's Experiences of Queensland*, edited by Gail Reekie, 80–96. St. Lucia, Qld: University of Queensland Press, 1994.

Simkin, Penny. 'Just Another Day in a Woman's Life? Women's Long-Term Perceptions of Their First Birth Experience'. *Birth* 18, no. 4 (1991): 203–10.

Snitow, Ann. 'Feminism and Motherhood: An American Reading'. *Feminist Review* 40 (1992): 32–51.

Stephens, Julie. *Confronting Postmaternal Thinking: Feminism, Memory and Care*. New York: Columbia University Press, 2011.

Stephens, Julie. 'Our Remembered Selves: Oral History and Feminist Memory'. *Oral History* 38, no. 1 (2010): 81–90.

Stern, Daniel, and Nadia Bruschweiler-Stern. *The Birth of a Mother: How Motherhood Changes You Forever*. London: Bloomsbury, 1998.

Stern, Daniel N. *The Motherhood Constellation: A Unified View of Parent–Infant Psychotherapy*. New York: Basic Books, 1995.

Stone, Alison. *Feminism, Psychoanalysis, and Maternal Subjectivity*. New York and London: Routledge, 2012.

Summerfield, Penny. 'Culture and Composure: Creating Narratives of the Gendered Self in Oral History Interviews'. *Cultural and Social History* 1, no. 1 (2004): 65–93.

Summers, Anne. *Damned Whores and God's Police: The Colonization of Women in Australia*. Ringwood, Vic.: Allen Lane, 1975.

Thomas, Trudelle. 'Becoming a Mother: Matrescence as Spiritual Formation'. *Religious Education* 96, no. 1 (2001): 88–105.

Thomson, Alistair. 'Australian Generations? Memory, Oral History and Generational Identity in Postwar Australia'. *Australian Historical Studies* 47, no. 1 (2016): 41–57.

Thomson, Alistair. 'Indexing and Interpreting Emotion: Joy and Shame in Oral History'. *Oral History Australia Journal* 41 (2019): 1–11.

Thomson, Alistair. *Moving Stories: An Intimate History of Four Women across Two Countries*. Sydney: UNSW Press, 2011.

Thomson, Alistair. 'New Wave Fathers? Oral Histories with Australian Fathers from the 1970s to the 1990s'. In *Australian Mothering: Historical and Sociological Perspectives*, edited by Carla Pascoe Leahy and Petra Bueskens, 219–35. Cham, Switzerland: Palgrave Macmillan, 2019.

Thomson, Rachel. 'Generational Research: Between Historical and Sociological Imaginations'. *International Journal of Social Research Methodology* 17, no. 2 (2014): 147–56.

Thomson, Rachel, Mary Jane Kehily, Lucy Hadfield and Sue Sharpe. *Making Modern Mothers*. Bristol: Policy Press, 2011.

Thorley, Virginia. 'Assumptions and Advice: Mothers and Queensland Well-Baby Clinics. A Review'. *Breastfeeding Review* 22, no. 1 (2014): 23–30.

Thorley, Virginia. 'Australian Mothers' Decisions on Infant Feeding: An Historical Analysis of Public Health Advice, Marketing, and Other Factors Influencing Their Choices, 1900–2000'. PhD, Brisbane: University of Queensland, 2007.

Thorley, Virginia. 'Feeding Their Babies: Infant Feeding Advice Received by Queensland Mothers in the Postwar Period, 1945–1965'. MA, Brisbane: University of Queensland, 2000.

Thorley, Virginia. 'Middle-Class Mothers as Activists for Change: The Australian Breastfeeding Association'. In *The 21st Century Motherhood Movement: Mothers Speak out on Why We Need to Change the World and How to Do It*, edited by Andrea O'Reilly, 219–32. Toronto: Demeter Press, 2011.

Walker, Alice. *In Search of Our Mothers' Gardens: Womanist Prose*. xviii, 397. New York: Harcourt Brace Jovanovich, 1984.

Wearing, Betsy. *The Ideology of Motherhood: A Study of Sydney Suburban Mothers*. Sydney: Allen & Unwin, 1984.

Worth, Eve, and Laura Paterson. '"How Is She Going to Manage with the Children?" Organizational Labour, Working and Mothering in Britain, c. 1960–1990'. *Past and Present* Supplement 15 (2020): 318–43.

# Index

Aboriginal peoples 5–6, 21, 106, 156
abortion 6
Abrams, Lynn 25–6
abuse 224
adoption 6–7, 119, 156, 229–30
advertising for research participants 24
advice and advice literature 2, 30, 62, 66–7, 127–43, 163, 177, 243–54
age at which women first have children 5, 31, 126
age-related competence 11
alcohol 58
alloparenting 164
American Psychiatric Association 90
Anderson, Kathryn 25
antenatal care and antenatal clinics 5–6, 57, 65–7, 92
Anthropocene era 32, 250–1
anthropology 31, 217
anticipation of birth 51–5
assisted reproductive technology (ART) 8, 71–2, 152–3, 173, 239
Astbury, Jill 90
attachment theory 134

Australia 4–9, 12, 15, 20–2, 29–31, 54–62, 79–81, 90–4, 97–100, 103–10, 127, 136, 165, 168, 171, 184, 203, 243, 250–3
autonomy 65–6, 108, 232, 239

'baby blues' 88
baby boom 93
'baby bumps' 58–9, 67–8
Baby Bunting (store) 68–9
baby health centres 127
Balsam, Rosemary 18
Baraitser, Lisa 18, 28, 68, 125, 242
Barker, Robin 136–7
Beauvoir, Simone de 14
BenEzer, Gadi 84
*Better Homes Baby Book* 98
Bevan-Brown, Maurice 133–4
birth 77–93, 110
    preparation for 77–82, 97–101, 105, 109
    retrospective dissatisfaction about 104–5
    where, how and with whom 79
birth announcements 83–4
birth control 6, 61–2, 71
Birth for Humankind (BfHK) organisation 105–6

birth rates 105
birthing centres 100
Birthing on Country models 106
black humour 52
Black Summer 22
Blaffer Hrdy, Sarah 164
bonding 30, 116, 119, 147, 149, 154
bottle-feeding 130–3
Bowlby, John 13, 127, 133–4
Brannen, Julia 26
'breadwinner' role 174, 195, 205–6, 212
breastfeeding 3, 14, 30, 107, 116, 122–6, 130–2, 136, 152, 164–5, 226
Brown, Stephanie 90
Bueskens, Petra 17
Bury, Michael 220
bushfires 22, 250

caesarean sections 106–8
Canada 4, 127
capitalism 183
care 2–5, 11–17, 21, 78, 124–6, 148, 158, 167, 173–4, 183, 194, 198
   association with women 184, 186, 249–50
career progression 70–1, 208, 212, 240, 251
Chadwick, Rachelle 79
child development 1, 13, 134
childbirth as a natural process 93, 97
childcare
   ambivalence about 199
   corporate models of 203
   government support for 193, 198
   negativity of 205

childlessness 10, 16–17, 32, 71, 175–6
childrearing 4–5, 127, 133–7, 166–7, 170, 174, 235, 249–50
   communal 164
   manuals of 13
   new aspects of 149
   fashions in 143
Chodorow, Nancy 15
Cilento, Phyllis 97
class differences 203
climate change 250
clothing for maternity 58–60, 64, 67–8
cognitive regression 228
commercialisation 29, 46, 59, 69
commodification of pregnancy 3
communications technologies 177
community support 149, 153, 164, 173, 179
conception 43
confidence 139
continuity 117–18
control of situations 44, 66, 83, 109, 203, 236, 250
corporal punishment 11
corporeality 121–3, 225–7
couple relationships 149–50
COVID-19 pandemic 22, 26, 250
Crabb, Annabel 183
cravings 55
Crouch, Mira 105
cultural context and cultural scripts 27, 41, 61, 71–2, 235, 238–41, 249–52
cultural understandings 159, 165, 168, 193

Davin, Anna 13
Davis, Adelle 63
Davis, Angela 22

# Index

Dempsey, Rhea 105–6
depression, perinatal 90, 127, 159, 162, 227, 230–3, 243–4, 251
deskilling 127
*Diagnostic and Statistical Manual* 90
Dick-Read, Grantly 96
discrimination 65, 69
 in the workplace 184
discrimination legislation 212
diversity of research participants 24
divorce 8, 198
Dixson, Miriam 13
dreams 46

education 62, 66, 81, 83, 98, 105, 109–10
early years of 5
embodiment 121–2, 125
emotional expressiveness 168
emotional honesty 238–9
emotional labour 12
emotional transition 3
emotions xiii, 4, 20, 41, 50–1, 63, 95, 119–20, 229–33, 252
employers, burdens on 184
employment of women 2–5, 11, 42, 167, 173–4, 178–9, 184–5
 *see also* paid work; work for women
encumberment 125
environmental degradation 250
equal pay 198
*Everywoman* 99
exhaustion 119
expertise 4–5, 30, 83, 127, 130, 133–6, 139–43, 178, 241
extended families 154

Facebook groups 177
family relationships 7, 48, 154, 157–60, 163, 200
family size 167
fashion 143
fathers, role of 2, 21, 98, 126, 151–3, 166–7, 178, 184, 194, 200, 210, 249–50
Federici, Sylvia 183
feelings 116–18, 122, 126, 129
 about work 186
 capacity for 1
 like a mother 116
 towards children 30
feminised professions 200
feminism 9, 15–19, 27, 57, 97, 183, 191, 198, 216, 231, 240
 first-wave 13
 matricentric 17
 *see also* second-wave feminism
'feminographies' 25–6
fertility and fertility rates 9, 250
films 9–10
financial incentives 203, 209, 212
Firestone, Shulamith 13–14
Fitzroy xiv–xv, 22, 131, 171, 194–5, 198, 204
flexible work 205, 209
folk wisdom 173
formula feeding 130–1
Frank, Arthur 84
Freud and Freudianism 13, 133
Friedan, Betty 6, 14, 168
friends 42, 160, 175–6
future-gazing 250

gender 16–17, 166, 212
gendered division of labour 197
general practice (GP) doctors 66
generational shift 229, 238–43

'generational time' 26–9, 57–73, 92–109, 126–42, 165–78, 193–212, 227–37, 249
genetics 151
gentrification 22
gestation 42–7, 56, 66, 73, 125–6
government policy 243
grandparents and grandchildren 4, 42, 154–6, 161, 208–9
Greece 175
grief 49

Hadfield, Lucy 66, 79
Hall, Tizzie 140
harm caused 127
Hays, Sharon 11
healthcare system 77
Hill Collins, Patricia 16, 164
historiography 4
History 13–14
Hollway, Wendy 18, 28, 217, 242
home, work at 183–4
home birth movement 98–101
hooks, bell 16
hours of work 12, 166
housekeeping 197
Howe Elkins, Valmai 103
Human Rights in Childbirth (HRiC) organisation 108
husbands, relationships with 153–4, 162, 167–9, 195, 197, 201, 206
hysterectomy 226

identity 3, 31, 197, 210, 217, 229, 239
in vitro fertilisation (IVF) 8, 186–7
induction 102–3
infant health centres 130–1
infant wellbeing 125–8, 133
infertility 47
instinct 128, 134, 143

intensity 217–19
intensive mothering 11, 239
interdisciplinarity 19, 28
intergenerational links 7, 154–6, 171, 175, 192
interruption 125
intersubjectivity 222–5
interviews 20, 25

Jack, Dana 25
Janov, Arthur 101

Kehily, Mary Jane 66, 79
King, Truby 92–3, 130
Knott, Sarah 79

labour, types of 183
Lamaze, Ferdinand 97
Leach, Penelope 135
learning through experience 139
Leboyer, Frédérick 97, 101–2
Lerner, Gerder 13
lesbianism 8, 71, 173
'life course time' 26
lifestyle changes 2, 56, 58
lived experience 155
*see also* maternal thinking
Llewellyn-Jones, Derek 62, 99
Lorde, Audre 16
loss through pregnancy 50–1
love xiii–xiv, 1–4, 7, 17, 116–20, 123, 126, 134, 142, 153, 167, 171, 174, 216, 219, 224, 248
Lumley, Judith 90

magazines 98
Malvern xiv, 22, 49, 53, 163, 195, 203, 209
Manderson, Lenore 105
Manne, Anne 17, 210
Marneffe, Daphne de 17–18, 117

marriage, optional 173
marriage bar for public services 60, 195
Martin, Emily 89
material culture of mothering 59, 68–9
materialisation of the self 3
maternal experiences xiii, 4, 32
maternal influences 151, 170–1, 175, 179
maternal thinking 15, 31, 124–5, 139, 189–90
'maternal time' 26–9, 42–57, 79–92, 148–65, 185–93, 217–27
maternal 'window' 126
maternality 43, 45, 48, 50, 217, 225, 239, 244, 249–53
  preparation for 55, 74
  transition to 229
maternity leave 2, 12, 201, 208
maternographies 25–31, 46–52, 73, 79–89, 92, 100, 109–10, 118–20, 126, 142, 149, 156, 184–5, 188–91, 197, 200, 203, 207, 209, 217–21, 227–32, 235, 239–43, 252–3
  definition of 26
matrescence 5, 7, 10, 18, 24–5, 28–31, 42–3, 50, 56, 74, 118–25, 148, 151, 154–60, 165–78, 189–93, 217–25, 228–38, 241–4, 248–50, 253
  preparation for 43
matrilineal influences 132, 223–4
Maushart, Sally 143
McKay, Pinky 139
medicalisation 54, 57, 61, 66, 102
  criticism of 97–8
meeting one's baby 116–19, 209

Mein Smith, Phillipa 128
Melbourne 168
memory 238
  collective 27
menstrual cycle 60
mental health and mental illness 230, 233–4, 238, 243
methodology 19, 29
Michaels, Paula A. 102
middle-class women 165, 195
migrants 95–6, 171, 194, 200
millennial mothers 23, 31, 65–73, 103–9, 126, 136–43, 172–8, 192–3, 202–12, 220, 222, 232–41, 252, 258–60
Miller, Tina 27, 83, 104–5, 202
Millett, Kate 13
mindfulness 221
miscarriages 49–51
misrecognition of work 185–6
Mooney, Ann 26
mortality 126
  perinatal 106
Moss, Peter 26
mother–child relationship 28, 48–9, 118, 125–6, 142–3, 211, 238
motherhood 1–5, 15–22, 28, 212, 223, 227, 229, 243, 248–52
  changes brought about by 2–3, 31, 117–18, 121, 124, 176, 183, 187, 192, 201, 212, 216–17, 220, 225–6, 229, 233, 240–4, 248–9, 252
  as a choice 31, 202, 239, 244, 250–1
  effect on working life 188
  expectations about 52–4
  first-time 85, 148–50, 206, 243–4
  see also primigravidae

motherhood (*continued*)
    inadequately supported and insufficiently recognised 212
    limiting and burdensome nature of 252
    postponement of 52
    preparation for 44–5, 143, 222, 230, 233, 240, 244, 252
    sacrifices of 155
    true narratives of 252
    understandings of 9
mothering 143, 203, 221, 232, 251
    of author's own children, and other people's xiv–xv
    combined with paid work 190, 240
    effect of birth experiences on 90
    experience of 9, 236
    history of 10–14, 19, 30
    learning of 128
    memories and reflections on xiv
    of mothers 147, 152–8, 161–2, 167–8, 185, 190–1, 201, 223–5
    *see also* intensive mothering
mothermorphosis 73–4, 223–4
mothers
    becoming 235
    definition of 21
    meeting their children 116–19, 209
    qualities shared by 216
mothers' groups 141–2, 147–8, 161, 176–9
mothers-in-law 159, 178
multiculturalism 6–7
'mumtrepreneur' figures 209

nappies 126
narrative patterns 84
Nash, Meredith 68
National Health Service 102
'natural' childbirth 97, 105
needs of babies 121
neoliberalism 17, 23, 166
'new motherhood' 155, 172, 178–9, 238
New Zealand 127
news media 251
nursing 201, 210
Nursing Mothers Association of Australia (NMAA) 136, 168–9

Oakley, Ann 15, 78–80, 83, 89–90, 108
observation 124–5
Ocean Grove xiv–xv, 22, 43–4, 55, 162–3, 167–9, 177–8, 203
Odent, Michel 97
*Odyssey, The* 46
'old wives tales' 54–5
Olds, Sharon 79
one-child families 10
online information 137
only children 10, 157
opportunities missed 197, 201
oral history 14, 19–20, 25–8, 92, 238–9, 251–2
O'Reilly, Andrea 17
'othermothering' 164
overwork 166

paid work
    balanced against mothering 200, 202, 206, 208
    and unpaid alternatives 183–5, 192–9, 207, 212
    *see also* employment of women; work for women
pain and pain relief 50, 84–5, 88, 102, 105
'parent', use of the term 249

parental leave 2, 5, 12, 193–4, 203, 207, 210
parenthood 149, 152
  commitment to 152–3
  interest in 169
parenting 134, 136, 143, 147, 154, 163, 171–2, 175
parents-in-law 159–60, 178
Parker, Rozsika 18
participants in research 20, 24
participation in the labour force 126, 203, 212
part-time work 2, 12, 201, 208
paternalism 103, 198
pay 251
peer group influence 135, 142
peer support 45–6, 168–9, 175–9
perinatal health regimes 5
personality of a child 116–17
physiological birth 108
playgroups 168, 179
Plooij, Frans 140–1
popular culture 9, 251–2
post-structuralism and post-modernism 16
post-traumatic stress disorder (PTSD) 90, 108
postwar mothers 23, 30–1, 58–61, 93–6, 116, 119, 127–34, 143, 165–8, 194–7, 217, 227–31, 238, 252–6
pregnancy 41–2, 45, 50–8, 62, 65, 67, 73–4, 116, 119, 226
  accidental 45
  accompanying changes 1–2
  different treatments for 55–6
  effect on the family 41–2
  effect on working life 65, 187–8
  expectations at time of 58, 67
  first experience of 42, 52, 55
  hidden history of 50
  memories of 55, 73
  preparation for 74
  supernatural aura surrounding 54
  transformative physiological effect of 41
  unannounced xiii
  unplanned 153
prejudices 212
premature babies 44, 102, 109, 178, 208
previous generations 3, 138
primigravidae 3, 9, 52, 58, 232
  risks for 41
priorities and prioritisation 204, 240
Probert, Belinda 203
professionals, medical 57–8, 62, 65–6, 87, 136
prolapse 226–7
psychology and psychological studies 5, 10, 15, 18–20, 28–31, 42, 55, 101, 125–8, 133, 217, 228–31, 238, 244
psychoprophylaxis 97
public health 5–6, 93

Queensland 129
quickening xiii

racial discrimination 5
Raphael-Leff, Joan 18
reflection 25
reform movements 29–30, 62, 65–6, 92, 96–7, 102, 109
relational objects 125
relationships
  pre-existing 178
  women's 148–9
religion 235
reproductive functions 5, 60, 62, 72

resilience 11
responsibility for a baby 116–21, 134, 231, 248
returning to work 70, 203–4, 207–12, 243
Rich, Adrienne 15
rites of passage 42, 46, 78, 217, 252
rituals 78, 217, 229
'rooming in' 101
Ruddick, Sara 15, 17, 31, 124, 139, 189–90

same-sex relationships 173
sampling 20
Schnierer, Irma 129, 133
scientific mothering 128–32, 143
Scott, Joan W. 16
second-wave feminism 5, 14–15, 17, 26, 183, 205–6, 235, 238
second-wave mothers 23, 61, 96–103, 134–6, 168–72, 198–202, 231–4, 256–8
Second World War 5, 26
self, sense of 2
self-actualisation 240, 244
self-censorship 176
self-interviews 25
self-sacrifice 235, 240
selflessness 216
separation anxiety 211
sex education 60, 62
sexual intercourse 16, 58, 60, 226
sexuality 150–1
  history of 16
Sharpe, Sue 66, 79
siblings 157, 167
Simkin, Penny 90
single mothers 154, 236
  by choice 173
single parent's benefit 8, 198

sleep and sleeplessness 133, 140
Small, Rhonda 90
smoking 58
'snowballing' 24
social attitudes 202, 205
social media 68, 84, 251
social policies 251
sperm donation 173
Spock, Benjamin 13, 133–4
stay-at-home mothers 11–12, 134
Stephens, Julie 17
Stern, Daniel 18, 44–5, 48, 154, 249
stillbirths 49
Stone, Alison 18, 26–7
stretch marks 47, 226
suffering 46–7
Summerfield, Penny 27
Summers, Anne 13
Sundin, Juju 105
support for mothers 30–1, 143, 240–4, 250
  from those around them 148, 161–5
  need for 179
support persons 87, 94, 105, 109–10
surrogacy, commercial or altruistic 9
Sweden 210

tax-benefit system 174, 203
technological developments 65, 71
  *see also* assisted reproductive technology
Thomas, Trudelle 56
Thomson, Alistair 230–1
Thomson, Rachel 18, 22, 66, 79
time, meanings of 26–7
'time present' 26
tiredness 116
trans men 9

transgender parents 21
transition 252
transitional stages 55–7

United Kingdom 4, 62, 60, 127
urbanisation and suburbanisation 6

vaginal birth 103–4
Vanderijt, Hetty 140–1
Victoria (state) 22, 130–1, 136, 160
'village' concept 164, 240
vulnerability 17, 83, 117–21
   sense of 40

Wages for Housework
   campaign 183
Walker, Alice 16
Waring, Marilyn 183
Warner, Marina 123

weight gain 131
welfare state 5
White Australia policy 5
Winnicott, D.W. 13
women of colour 16
women's liberation 13–16, 23, 62, 168–9, 183, 191, 198, 201–2, 229, 231, 239
women's movements 5–6
work for women 14–17, 31, 60, 184–6, 191–3, 240
   attitudes to 203
   colleagues 42
   definition of 191–3
   *see also* paid work;
   employment of women
working-class women 194
Wright, Dorothy 231

Young, Iris Marion 41

EU authorised representative for GPSR:
Easy Access System Europe, Mustamäe tee 50,
10621 Tallinn, Estonia
gpsr.requests@easproject.com

www.ingramcontent.com/pod-product-compliance
Lightning Source LLC
Chambersburg PA
CBHW051604230426
43668CB00013B/1970